JUSTICE AND JUDGMENT
AMONG THE TIV

JUSTICE AND JUDGMENT AMONG THE TIV

PAUL BOHANNAN

'The mistake of judging the men of other periods
by the morality of our own day has its parallel in
the mistake of supposing that every wheel and
bolt in the modern social machine had its counterpart in more rudimentary societies.'

SIR HENRY MAINE

WAVELAND
PRESS, INC.
Prospect Heights, Illinois

For information about this book, write or call:

Waveland Press, Inc.
P.O. Box 400
Prospect Heights, Illinois 60070
(708) 634-0081

Previously published in 1957, 1968.
1989 reissued with changes by Waveland Press, Inc.
Preface, 1989: Copyright © 1989 by Paul Bohannan

ISBN 0-88133-459-6

Printed in the United States of America

7 6 5 4 3 2

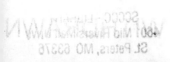

PREFACE, 1989

REREADING *Justice and Judgment* after more than 20 years, I feel impelled to say four things: (1) something about how notes and monographs age, (2) something about folk systems and "emics," (3) something about the interlinking of ethnographic theory and anthropological theory, the latter of which used to be called comparison, and (4) something about context and premises.

How Notes and Monographs Age

During the last years of his life, Radcliffe-Brown was depressed because he failed to understand that his contributions to anthropology had been monumental and successful. He could not grasp that he was an historical figure rather than a current leader, that the discipline had absorbed and gone beyond his studies. When we tried to tell him that new problems were a sign that he had won his battles, he failed to understand what we were driving at. Similarly, Mel Herkosvits, though somewhat younger, had difficulty in his last days with the notion that his ideas were much more a part of the history of his subject than they were part of its current concerns. Indeed, I am convinced that he perished not just from a heart attack but also from his dominating notion that he was, himself, the last vestige of what he stood for.

Every work of social science either passes into the history of its discipline or into oblivion. Having watched both R-B and the Mel struggle with the position of their work on the history of anthropology, not fully realizing the extent to which they had made significant segments of that history, I long ago resolved not to, as it were, play in my own theses. Therefore, *Justice and Judgment* either stands or it doesn't. I am delighted that it is getting this new lease on life, but there is no way of knowing what way the discipline may yet go to make it survive or perish.

The definition of legal anthropology has changed since the 1950s, away from a narrow concern with the manner in which disputes are settled toward a wider concern with social order of which law is only one part. Of course, that idea is at least as old as Ehrlich[1] and it underlays Malinowski's

---

[1] Ehrlich, Eugen, *Grundlagung der Sociologie des Rechts*. Berlin: Dunkler & Humblot, 1913.

short book on law.[2] As near as I can tell, it was Philip Gulliver who first
began to resuscitate that idea in the 1960s and 1970s, but he did it in a
context of ethnography rather than a more general context. The best
statement of it that I know is in a magnificently simple one by Carol
Greenhouse: "Legal anthropology is the cross-cultural study of social
ordering." Her equally simple elaboration is that its purpose is "to find
the connectedness between what courts do and what people think." The
stated aim of her own ethnography is to find out "how one group thinks
about order in its universe." [3] I note that she comes down thoroughly on
the side of ethnographic theory, and I frankly envy the simplicity of the
conceptualization and the combination of clarity and urgency with which
she writes.

Because of this kind of change, *Justice and Judgment* is part of the
history of the sub-discipline of legal anthropology. For that reason, not
a word of the original has been changed. The type face remains, with
at least two typos of which I am aware. The only thing that I have updated
is those footnotes that cite material that had not been published when
the second impression was printed in 1969.

Only one thing ages faster than the human body: field notes.
Ethnographic field notes remain valuable, but only as primary sources
for an historical period. Contributions to ideas that emerged after the
notes were taken can seldom be wrung from them. As one is further and
further removed from the field, one's field notes become less *aides
memoirs* and more and more just data. A Greek philosopher said we could
never step in the same river twice. Trying to recapture one's field
experience thirty years afterward makes one terribly aware that you can't
even step in the same stream of consciousness twice.

In the 1950s, I was interested in translation. Writing an ethnography
is, whatever else it is, a bold attempt to translate the ideas and idiom
of one culture into the language of another. I was not aware, when I wrote,
that I was much concerned with linguistics. I was just trying to translate
Tiv ideas about dispute settlement into language that would both
communicate what I had learned from the Tiv and allow readers to
highlight and isolate their own cultural ideas so that these things would
not interfere with their comprehending the Tiv ideas. As I reread the book

[2] Malinowski, Bronislaw, *Crime and Custom in Savage Society.* Originally published 1926;
reprinted 1972 by Littlefield, Adams and Co., Totowa, New Jersey.

[3] Greenhouse, Carol J., *Praying for Justice: Faith, Order, and Community in an American
Town.* Ithaca and London: Cornell University Press, 1986, pp. 27-28.

now, I am strongly reminded that I had studied Louis Hjelmslev's *Prologomena to a Theory of Language* just before one of my trips to Tivland. It was from him I learned you must never allow the same word to mean different things in two idea systems if you want to communicate clearly. About the same time, I learned from William Empson's *Structure of Complex Words* that you must never assign a technical term a narrower meaning than the same term has in the common language, and that when a word has several meanings we have to examine carefully the way we confuse swinging from one to another of those meanings with reasoning.

I think that the insistence on translation has been successful. I was convinced in 1957, and I still am, that filling Tiv data into a model of Western jurisprudence is squeezing parakeets into pigeonholes and not a way to go about ethnography. These ideas are, I believe, now pretty well accepted by the entire discipline. My problem about how to do the ethnography of law has been won, at least until the next paradigm change.

Folk Systems and Emics

To do what I set out to do, I created what today would be called a model of the Tiv way of looking at disputing and dispute settlements. I used the case method first because I admired the method as it had been used by Llewellyn and Hoebel in *The Cheyenne Way*, and I had been taught it by Max Gluckman. Moreover, the Tiv drove me to the case method. My self-assigned task was to discover as much as I could about what they were interested in. They put a lot of their time and effort into cases.

To explain in English what I understood Tiv to tell me in Tiv, I made the distinction between folk theories and analytical theories. I insisted that "law" is a folk system of the Western world and perhaps of some others but not an adequate analytical system for either ethnography or comparison. The analytical system, I now add, could take two forms: on the one hand it involves the implicit comparison of the folk systems of the subject culture and the ethnographer's culture. On the other hand was a more extensive comparison that involved more than those two folk systems in order to discover general principles.

About the same time, the emic-etic distinction became the accepted way of saying something similar. I find those two bits of neologistic jargon oversimplifying. Emic means only that the ethnographer takes the people's point of view. It says nothing about the complex systematization of folk thought on both sides of the translation barrier. Recent New Guinea scholarship, for example, has been understanding and explaining immensely complex folk systems. To call them "emic" is, to me, simply anemic. Folk system may not be the right term either, but ethnographic theory is far enough along these days that we better give some new consideration to our terms.

I find even more difficulty with the etic, which is too often used as a way of riding a preconception to the point of silencing opponents by stopping further analysis dead or else drowning all subtlety in statistics (statistics is a good thing if you know what you are counting; it has never yet told anybody what to count, which is one major point of ethnography). I am convinced that many etic studies put into their premises many of the items that ought to be in their hypotheses.

Comparison and Models

My interest in comparison came to the fore in response to the reviews of this book. As I pointed out in the 1969 Preface, Max Gluckman told me that my Tiv models were solipsistic. A lot of scrutiny on the part of many people has taken place since then. Today, Marilyn Strathern[4] has taken to their logical conclusion both Gluckman's point and the position I then upheld. She seems to say, but far more subtly than this: solipsism be damned, comparison can't be done but never mind, this is the way to do ethnography. She thus seems to have settled for ethnographic theory. Mary Douglas in her review of Strathern's book[5] disagreed with that conclusion—that is, Douglas is not willing to give up anthropological theory in exchange for even the finest ethnographic theory on which to base it. She has taken a traditional way out, saying (as I read her) that if you define yourself into a box you can indeed do comparison within the box. Of course you can. But ending up in a box may be as bad as ending up in a solipsism. When I was still seeking the box that Douglas defended, I published, in the Letters column of *Science*, a first approximation of how a model of comparison among legal systems might be devised. In a Wenner-Gren conference at Burg Wartenstein in 1966, the issue came up again. In my contribution to the papers of that conference,[6] I republished the same chart; it is given here as Chart 1.

[4] Strathern, Marilyn, *The Gender of the Gift: Problems with Women and Problems with Society in Melanesia*. Berkeley: University of California Press, 1988.

[5] Douglas, Mary, "A Gentle Deconstruction," *London Review of Books*, 4 May 1989.

[6] Bohannan, Paul, "Ethnography and Comparison in Legal Anthropology" in Laura Nader, editor, *Law in Culture and Society*. Chicago: Aldine Publishing Company, 1969.

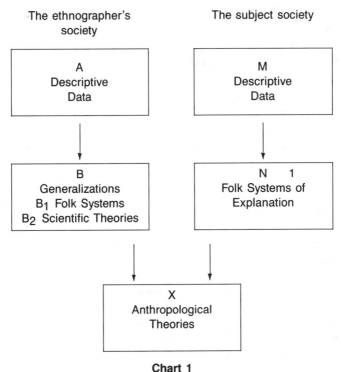

The ethnographer's society

The subject society

A
Descriptive
Data

M
Descriptive
Data

B
Generalizations
B₁ Folk Systems
B₂ Scientific Theories

N   1
Folk Systems of
Explanation

X
Anthropological
Theories

Chart 1
The Basis of Comparative Anthropological Theory
(From Bohannan 1959?)

I give it here again because I think it is a good way to check out analytical systems. However, it seems simplistic and redolent of the time when we confused anthropological theory (as contrasted with ethnographic theory) with comparison. The chart gives no guide as to what problems we could attack and perhaps solve if we were successful in getting models into Box X. This is another way of asking just what problems comparative studies are meant to solve. To sum up: what do you compare and what do we expect to get out of the comparison?

Chart 1 leaves out too many things.

Today I am convinced that comparison is the wrong word for what people were trying to do. Anthropologists have spent well over a hundred years worrying about comparison. Tylor did the first comparison that

I know; Boas condemned it. A lot of attempts have been made since. Although some insights have resulted, it nevertheless seems to me that there has been astonishingly little to show for that century of concern. There are several ways in which comparison has been done, and several things that have been compared:

(1) You can compare culture traits or clusters or patterns of culture traits.[7] Such a comparison is what the Human Relations Area Files were originally established to serve. It has provided some important correlations, but the fundamental problem of establishing statistically comparable units, the necessity to code ethnographic subtleties and insights into obscurity, and the limitations in the concept of culture trait continue to haunt it.

(2) You can compare the premises that underlie systems of thought. That is what Hoebel did,[8] calling them postulates. Outlining a specific set of such premises is also what *Justice and Judgment* tried to do when it was first published in 1957. It is what Greenhouse[9] has done, almost without cases which she specifically eschews for the good reason that her people eschew them. It is what Nader[10] has done brilliantly in her analysis of the forms, causes, and history of the search for harmony among the Zapotec. Hoebel's claim was that the task of legal anthropology, which he called comparative jurisprudence at the time, is "to seek out the jural postulates of different law systems and to determine how they find expression in the juridical institutions of the societies under consideration."[11] He also said that such premises are used in the kind of thinking that, in our society, would be called legal thinking; that may not be true because in many cases those premises are unconscious to the people from whose activities anthropologists have derived them.

(3) You can compare social structures. This has never been an important method in legal anthropology, but it is what Fortes and Evans-Pritchard

---

[7] Murdock, G.P., *Social Structure*. New York: Macmillan, 1949, to cite one highly successful example for many.

[8] Hoebel, E. Adamson, *The Law of Primitive Man: A Study in Comparative Legal Dynamics*. Cambridge, MA: Harvard University Press, 1954, especially pages 13-17.

[9] Greenhouse, Carol J., *Praying for Justice: Faith, Order, and Community in an American Town*. Ithaca and London: Cornell University Press, 1986.

[10] Nader, Laura, *Harmony Ideology and the Construction of Law: Justice and Control in a Zapotec Mountain Village*. Stanford: Stanford University Press, 1990.

[11] Hoebel, *op. cit.*, p. 16.

were doing in *African Political Systems* and it influenced us all.[12]
(4) You can compare social processes. Processes are patterns or series
of events and activities that repeatedly follow one another in a fairly
precise order. They tell you how to achieve specific ends if you start
with such-and-such a situation. The processual charts of this book
are attempts to delineate social processes. Anthropology was busy,
in the late 1950s, discovering such processes on the basis of the then-
neglected work of Van Gennep.[13]

One necessity for investigating social processes is to turn culture
from a noun into a verb; Leslie White suggested that long ago, but
his "culturing" has remained an oddity. We are necessarily concerned
with cycles of events, trajectories of events, and with what personalities, choices, political currents, and ecological conditions do to repeating cycles or to trajectories.[14] That idea is beginning to catch on,[15]
but is still too closely tied to the process of evolution which is only
one of many processes.

(5) You can compare models. Both (3) and (4) above lead to models, the
one to a structure of social groups and the second a structure of social
processes. *African Political Systems* discussed a structural model of a
lineage system, among other models. *Justice and Judgment* discussed
a processual model of a jural institution in one society.

There is quite another way to devise and use models that Collier[16] has
discussed in instructive detail: models of ideal types that are based on
extensive consideration of ethnographic models, but are not themselves
models that exactly represent any specific society. Rather, they explain
much about many different societies, but not all about any one society. The
ideal type goes back at least to Weber, but Collier uses it in an instructive
way. After noting that "it is impossible simultaneously to analyze particular societies and build ideal-typic models of social systems"[17] she

[12] Colson, Elizabeth, *Tradition and Contract: The Problem of Order*. Chicago: Aldine
Publishing Co., 1974, makes some enlightening comments on this point.

[13] Turner, Victor W., *Schism and Continuity in an African Society: A Study of Ndembu
Village Life*. Manchester: Manchester University Press, 1957.

[14] Bohannan, Paul, "Some Models for Planning the Future," *Journal of Social and
Biological Structures*, 1983.

[15] Thompson, Michael, *Rubbish Theory*. London: Oxford University Press, 1979.

[16] Collier, Jane Fishburne, *Marriage and Inequality in Classless Societies*. Stanford:
Stanford University Press, 1988.

[17] Collier, *op. cit.*, p. xii.

builds models that are not contradicted by any ethnographic sources (exceptions can be explained; contradictions cannot). Such models are the result of comparison, but the comparison is in the method, not the designated result. Her models comprehend major segments of the culture: "the systematic connections between relations of privilege and obligation, the organization of economic activities, kinship and family forms, household composition, manifestations of discord, procedures for managing conflict, powers available to leaders, folk models of social structure, concepts of personhood and gender, rituals, and ideas of ultimate order."[18] That seems to me to be pretty comprehensive.

Collier built three models. All three illuminate societies in which labor is divided primarily by sex and age. In such societies, she finds, "marriage organizes the distribution of privileges and obligations between the sexes and generations." She therefore names them after the form of acquiring a bride in the societies represented by each, although she started the research which led to her monograph by looking at modes of dispute settlement. Her method will need more examples and it must go through the processes of re-trial and criticism, but it looks fruitful so far.

Context and Premises

Two problems now appear. Anthropology is, whatever else it is, the science of context. The moment we go beyond a single ethnography, we have lost the context in which the models were relevant. But we have never established a context in which comparison is sensible. Earlier anthropologists were looking for universal generalizations that could be seen, Radcliffe-Brown fashion, as general laws of society. Many anthropologists seem to have given up that search not merely as futile but as wrong-headed. That leaves comparison without a context.

Moreover, the premises that legal anthropologists have dealt with in their ethnographic work are convincing, but we have generally not stated our premises for comparison.

Context and premises are basic issues in anthropology.

Thus, I would no longer ask how we compare ethnographic models, but rather how we create context when those ethnographic models are placed in some new kind of juxtaposition, and what premises we assume when we do it.

Here is a beginning of a list of premises for an anthropological theory of law rather than an ethnographic theory of a particular set of jural institutions:

18 Collier, *op. cit.*, p. 1.

1. Conflict exists in animal life, including human life.
2. Society is a tool for animal survival.
3. To exist successfully, society requires order: a way of either eliminating, denying, avoiding, living with, or managing conflict.
3a. No way of eliminating conflict has been found. There is a sizable literature on utopias, all of which seem to be based on the model of harmony, and few of which go into the fact that harmony imposes deep responsibilities for internalizing conflict.
3b. Denial of conflict is the simplest mechanism of defense.[19] It is often found in neuroses, but is not an adequate social mechanism for dealing with conflict.
3c. Conflict can be avoided. It is done by retreating, and perhaps by making a virtue of the retreat: of constantly creating a situation in which conflict is denied. This idea may be stated positively: it is the search for harmony, and condemning litigation and instilling and practicing the actions and attitudes that are culturally said to lead to harmony.
3d. Conflict can be lived with.[20] There are cultural devices for allowing the conflict, but controlling its range.
3e. Conflict can be managed by a mechanism like the law.

Thus, as I now see it, the folk system is relevant in the context of ethnography, and its premises are the premises of the subject people. That much I understood when this book was first written. Its price is solipsism.

The analytical system falls into the context of social science and its premises are the premises of social science, including but not limited to anthropology. Its price is a definitional box.

But those two systems are no longer enough. They leave out planning. Neither of these two is adequate to create scenarios or to give advice to anyone planning social action. We thus need a third system for explaining the way people think about things when they want to change them. The third system must draw on both the folk systems of the people concerned and on the analytic systems of social science. The word plan means a way of making or doing something that has been worked out beforehand; a scheme of action. It implies that we do not have to learn

[19] Freud, Anna, *The Ego and the Mechanisms of Defense*. New York: International Universities Press, 1936.

[20] Merry, Sally Engel, *Urban Danger: Life in a Neighborhood of Strangers*. Philadelphia: Temple University Press, 1981.

everything by experience. We had no experience in going to the moon. I have not yet completed such a model for any topic; when I do, it will not be on the subject of Tiv jural institutions.

We thus have:

(1) the folk model—this is what I was talking about in this book and what Strathern was talking about in *The Gender of the Gift*. The question that underlies the folk system is, "What can I do to explain a people's ideas of order?" The context is ethnographic.

(2) the analytic model—this is either the kind of ideal-typic model that Jane Collier was talking about in *Marriage and Equality in Classless Societies*, or else quantitative models or some other fundamentally comparative device. The question that underlies the analytical system is, "How do I establish a set of generalizations that allows me to look at the insights of many societies at one time?" The context is social science.

(3) the planning model—this is a kind of model not of cause but rather of event chains, about which I started thinking while I was creating the processual models of this book. It tells us what we have to do as individuals, as groups, and as a society to make changes we claim to want to make—how to get from here to there. The question that underlies the planning system is, "How do I have to see these people's culture and the principles of social science in order to introduce change or new practices?" The context is something like that of the SETI people who are planning in great detail what they will do if E.T. ever answers.[21] It is the realm of policy.

Three Rivers, California
June, 1989.

---

[21] Eberhart, Jonathan, "Listening for E.T." in *Science News*, Vol. 135, No. 19, May 13, 1989, pg. 296-298.

PREFACE, 1967

IN considering a reprint of this book, I reread it for the first time since the original page proofs were dealt with in 1956. It was then early October, 1966, just ten years later, and *The New York Times* was carrying reports about the slaughter of Ibo in Northern Nigeria. No coincidence could have driven home more dramatically that this book is over ten years old, that the events it reports are over fifteen years old, that it deals with a political and social system now gone, and that ethnographers cannot go back again. I have also reread the reviews and criticisms of this book, most of which were largely cogent and even generous. However, there was one consistent criticism that I thought and still think was uncomprehending (but because so many people read it that way, the shortcoming must be mine) and one other flaw that I have found that had passed unnoticed, or at least largely unnoted.

The Problem of Comparison

The critics, almost without exception, claimed that the material in the book is presented in such a way as to make comparison impossible. Hoebel,[1] Gluckman,[2] Ayoub,[3] Nader[4] and some others have claimed that the book is not only itself not comparative, but that it does not allow other scholars to use the material in comparative problems. Gluckman even claimed that I was so slavish a reporter of Tiv culture that I had achieved what he called 'cultural solipsism'—a left-handed compliment, which he did not intend as such. Even I, under the influence of these criticisms but without having reread the book, have noted that a comparative chapter

---

[1] E. Adamson Hoebel, 'Three Studies in African Law', *Stanford Law Review*, Vol. 13, No. 2, pp. 418–42, 1961.

[2] Max Gluckman, *Politics, Law and Ritual in Tribal Society*, Chicago: Aldine Publishing Company, 1964. *The Ideas of Barotse Jurisprudence*, New Haven and London: Yale University Press, 1965. *The Judicial Process among the Barotse of Northern Rhodesia*, 2nd edition, Manchester: University of Manchester Press, 1967.

[3] Victor Ayoub, 'Review: The Judicial Process in Two African Tribes', in Morris Janowitz, ed., *Community Political Systems*, New York: The Free Press of Glencoe, pp. 237–50, 1961.

[4] Laura Nader, 'The Anthropological Study of Law'. *American Anthropologist* Special Publication, Vol. 67, No. 6, Pt. 2, pp. 3–32, 1965.

should have been appended.[1] Today, with an opportunity to add
that chapter, I have changed my mind: I not only think it unnecessary, but I am certain that it would detract from the purpose of
the book.

I have discussed the problem of comparison in legal anthropology in a review of Gluckman's *Ideas of Barotse Jurisprudence* that
was originally prepared for the *American Anthropologist*; because
of space limitations resulting from a financial crisis in 1967, the
editors could not publish so long a review. I thereupon published
the original review in Kroeber Anthropological Papers[2] and wrote
a 200 word summary for the *Anthropologist*. I have, moreover,
answered at some length the charges and complaints that Gluckman and others have made about this book, in an essay to be published in a forthcoming volume, edited by Laura Nader,[3] of the
proceedings of a Wenner-Gren Conference at Burg Wartenstein in
the summer of 1966. In those places I have again set out my ideas
about the problems of translation, have defended the folk system,
and have essayed initially a typology of comparative methods.

After considerable thought, I have decided not to repeat or recast any of this material for the present second edition of this book.
It is my firm opinion that both the criticisms and the defence are
of a transient nature and that to include this discussion would add
nothing to understanding the Tiv institutions. Moreover, both the
original criticism (especially that of Gluckman) and my response
verges on polemic—and I know no book in which polemic does not
age more quickly than factual and interpretative substance, and
I do know some (like Malinowski's book on law[4]) that are made
almost unreadable by polemic that has long since ceased to be
relevant. In short, I am much more interested that Tiv institutions
be understood in their own terms than that any theoretical or
methodological predelictions of mine be defended.

Here I will note only two points: (1) my insistence that Tiv
ethnography be seen in its own terms has been read to mean that
I said that Tiv ethnography was unique. I find that I said nothing

---

[1] Paul Bohannan, 'The Differing Realms of the Law'. *American Anthropologist* Special Publication, Vol. 67, No. 6, Pt. 2, pp. 33–42, 1965.
[2] Paul Bohannan, 'Review' of Max Gluckman, *The Ideas in Barotse Jurisprudence*. *Kroeber Anthropological Society Papers*, No. 36, Spring, 1967.
[3] Laura Nader, . : . forthcoming.
[4] Bronislaw Malinowski, *Crime and Custom in Savage Society*, London:
Routledge and Kegan Paul, 1926.

so absurd as that. Whether or not the culture traits that I have reported for the Tiv are unique to them is not important for purposes of this book. What *is* important is that they are valued and understood by Tiv as part of a system, and that to deal with culture traits in any other terms before dealing with the system and their place in it, is to misunderstand and misconstrue the ethnographic scene. (2) My insistence on clarification between what is ethnographic fact and what is analytical frame of reference has been interpreted as hostility to or ignorance of jurisprudence. I want only to make it clear that the hostility is to using jurisprudence (or anything else) as a *deus ex machina* to deliver us from the difficulties either of ethnographic reporting or careful comparison.

It seems clear and obvious that I am not here saying that comparison is unimportant or impossible. Rather, I would note that, from the earliest anthropological times, there have been two schools of thought on the subject. One can be summed up by the early writing of Tylor on traits and clustering[1] and the other by an early article of Boas on the need for comparative categories to arise from ethnographic investigations.[2] The descendants of Tylor have turned to computers; those of Boas have turned to semantics. The two need each other desperately, but they begin from different premises. The Tylorians first define and then classify and correlate; the Boasians first inquire and then subdivide and look for pattern. I essayed the problem of cross-cultural comparison in a piece in the 'Letters' column of *Science* as early as 1958.[3] There I outlined, in rough form, the way these two types of comparison can be brought together. The material was repeated, a little extended, in *Social Anthropology*.[4]

Again, I choose not to repeat this material here—both because I have already published it in two places, and, perhaps more important, because I am still *in media res*. I intend to deal with the subject of comparison at some length in a cross-cultural study of divorce that I have been working on since 1963, and which will,

[1] Sir Edward B. Tylor, 'On a Method of Investigating the Development of Institutions; applied to the Laws of Marriage and Descent', *Journal of the Royal Anthropological Institute*, Vol. 18, pp. 245–69, 1888.
[2] Franz Boas, 'The Limitations of the Comparative Method of Anthropology', *Science*, New Series, Vol. IV, No. 103, Dec. 18, 1896, pp. 901–908.
[3] Paul Bohannan, 'Anthropological Theories', *Science*, Vol. 129, No. 3345, Feb. 6, 1959, pp. 292–94.
[4] Paul Bohannan, *Social Anthropology*, New York: Holt, Rinehart and Winston, 1963.

with luck and tenacity, lead to a monograph on the subject of intersocietal comparison of that set of institutions. That monograph, as it is now projected, will contain a discussion on what different authors have called 'comparative', with the successes and shortcomings of each of several methods.

The Problem of Law and Society

In the process of rereading this book, I have become very much aware of another flaw that none of the published criticisms has explored, although it was mentioned in a recent note by Monga.[1] I am uncomfortable about the chapters on the marriage *jir*. After having made the point that what is important in legal anthropology is the institution of judgment and compromise, and that what can be compared among societies are the 'legal institutions' and certainly not the substantive law, I went ahead and talked about the substantive law of marriage, divorce and bridewealth and did not associate that particular law with the rest of the Tiv institutions of marriage and family. In an article published in Nader's *Ethnography of Law*,[2] another and more general version of which appears in the *Encyclopaedia of the Social Sciences*, I have stated my views on what I have called 'reinstitutionalization'—the process in which some particular usages within an institution are recast so that they can be used as a basis for conflict resolution by legal institutions. I have worried the subject about for several months now, and have come to the conclusion that I had better admit that I cannot at the present time do the job I think should be done in this regard—primarily because my analysis of Tiv family and marriage institutions is not finished. At the moment I can go no farther—but I do think that the relationship between the legal institutions and the other institutions of society is one of the frontiers on which legal anthropology should concentrate its next attacks.

Acknowledgements

In addition to my continuing gratitude to the people who originally helped me with this book, I want now to add that association

[1] Veena Monga, 'On Bohannan and the Law', *American Anthropologist*, Vol. 69, No. 2, pp. 227–8.

[2] Laura Nader, 'The Anthropological Study of Law', *American Anthropologist* Special Publication, Vol. 67, No. 6, Part 2, pp. 3–32, 1965.

with John Coons and with Julius Stone has been most stimulating and rewarding, that Laura Nader has, delightfully, badgered me to continue working in this field which I would otherwise have abandoned long since, and that Herma Hill Kay has always been a most valued critic and source of cogent information. Discussions at Burg Wartenstein in 1966 with many anthropologists interested in legal problems, and throughout the years with my colleagues at Northwestern University, both in anthropology and in other fields, have been stimulating and rewarding.

PAUL BOHANNAN

Northwestern University
August 1967

PREFACE, 1956

SHOULD this book fall into the hands of lawyers, I hope they will realize that it is a book of social anthropology, not a book of law. As will be obvious to them, I am not trained in the law. I do not apologize for this fact, but merely state that I am aware that my knowledge of law and my reading in it are extremely limited. Lawyers, in attempting a task like mine, would be under a similar handicap: indeed, I believe it a greater handicap. They would not have the discipline of social anthropology, which ought to imply systematic definition of the cultural blinkers of one's own society, upbringing, and prejudices so that one can see the ideas and prejudices of other people when one looks for them. Lawyers (except comparative jurists) seem not to be bothered with this problem; they proceed within the view permitted by the blinkers of their own society. Indeed, they help to make them. Their job is organizing and conceptualizing social action of given sorts within our own society. The anthropologist's job is studying the conceptualizations of social action in alien societies.

Therefore, the province of the lawyer and that of the social anthropologist are once for all different. They overlap, primarily in their words, sometimes in their subject matter. Findings in one can often illuminate the other. Their disciplines for understanding that subject matter and their canons for dealing with it remain distinct.

I repeat, this is a book of social anthropology, the subject matter of which may possibly interest lawyers. I request that it be judged by the canons of social anthropology, not by the canons of jurisprudence.

My wife and I used no interpreters among the Tiv until we had been with them for almost a year. By that time we spoke Tiv quite fluently and understood it well. About that time, my new steward, Orihiwe Takema, gradually became my 'scribe' (*malu*) and within a few months I recognized the fact and hired another steward. Orihiwe grew up in close proximity with missionaries, who taught him to read and write and made him Christian. He learned some English, though it is not the policy of this sect to teach much English. Orihiwe was with me the rest of my time in Tivland. He wrote text, and helped me to translate it. Many days he accompanied me on my round of calls; many other days he did not, but went off to work on his own. One of Orihiwe's favourite tasks was recording cases. We often attended courts together.

During my second tour in Tivland, I hired Iyorkôsu Ageva as a second clerk. Iyorkôsu knew no English at all. He wrote much more slowly than Orihiwe, but he was not a Christian, had learnt what writing he had from a 'clan school' and was, for a man of his age, unusually cognizant of lore and also of the problems of Tiv religion and witchcraft.

When I first went to Tivland in 1949, I was invited by chiefs and elders to attend court sessions. I soon gave them up. I knew their importance, and knew that they formed a late stage in field-work, when my knowledge of language and culture was fuller. Most of my case material, then, comes from my third tour in Tivland, in 1952-3. My own knowledge of the language was such at that time that I could understand most court cases easily as they proceeded. I was never able to understand all of them easily or probably any of them fully, for the Tiv language—like all African languages—is highly allusive and its perfect understanding demands not only a thorough knowledge of its idiom and of its myths and stock metaphors, but also of the incidents which have occurred in the specific neighbourhood in the last forty or fifty years. Needless to say, an anthropologist cannot learn all the incident which provides the basis for fresh metaphor and illustration.

Our method of working was that Orihiwe and Iyorkôsu took their notes and then did reconstructions in narrative form. Both the notes and the reconstructions were worked over, and I usually but not always made translations. In the *jir* itself, I took down as much direct quotation as the effort of following the cases allowed me to do. I took this part of my notes entirely in Tiv. The 'continuity' I wrote in English, usually in shorthand.

I also made it a practice to follow up interesting cases by discussing them with Chenge, the *Tyo-or* of MbaDuku. My huts were in Chenge's compound. He was my next-door neighbour for a total of some eighteen months. We spent many evenings talking together. He knew what I was doing, and was anxious that I should get it right. Finally, I discussed with the principals involved as many cases as it was practicable or seemly to do.

I often took one of my scribes with me when I talked to the principals.

Tiv are not a people amongst whom it is possible to exhume a case a few months or years—or even a few weeks—after it has occurred: the judges have forgotten the details, each of the principal litigants has again warped the evidence to his own viewpoint and, worst of all, the entire action has been thoroughly assimilated to the 'ought' notions of Tiv culture. These notions may be of great value, but must be studied in connexion with actual social action. Therefore, it became an absolute necessity that my work be done by the 'case method'.

By other techniques, such as sound recording, it would have been possible to get fuller transcriptions of the cases. I am not sure that it would be desirable, for I have found, in trying to use it, that gadgetry so absorbs the attention of the field worker that it is very easy for him to forget that he must gear his life to the people he is studying, not to his gadgets. He is introducing a false note into the flow of social life much more strident than his own mere presence: he soon begins to 'produce' and 'direct' the social action and the actors to comply with the limitations of his gadgets. The only sensible gadget for doing anthropological field research is the human understanding and a notebook. Anthropology provides an artistic impression of the original, not a photographic one. I am not a camera.

I would like to thank the Social Science Research Council and the Wenner-Gren Foundation for the grants which made possible the 26 months' field research on which this study is based. I am also indebted to the Colonial Social Science Research Council and the Government of Nigeria for travel grants.

Several colleagues and friends have read and criticized the manuscript: among anthropologists, Professor E. E. Evans-Pritchard and Dr. J. H. M. Beattie read and discussed the full book. Captain R. M. Downes read the book and made valuable criticisms from his extensive knowledge of the Tiv. I want particularly to acknowledge Professor I. Schapera's detailed care and assistance. Sir Carleton Allen and Dr. T. Oluwale Elias read the manuscript and made invaluable criticisms; if I have misused legal concepts, it is my fault, not theirs. I would like to thank all of them, and all those of my colleagues and students with

B

whom I have discussed parts of the book. My thanks are also due to the International African Institute for undertaking the publication of this study, and particularly to Mrs. B. E. Wyatt for her painstaking editorial work. My wife, Dr. Laura Bohannan, shared the field-work and criticized the book in all its stages.

PAUL BOHANNAN

Oxford

17 August 1956

CONTENTS

REGISTER OF CASES

PLATES

CHAPTER I

THE PEOPLE AND THE PROBLEM

THE Tiv are a semi-Bantu tribe of subsistence farmers living on both sides of the Benue River in northern Nigeria, some 150 miles from its confluence with the Niger. In 1952 they numbered about 800,000.[1]

To understand the social relations of the Tiv, the cultural idiom in which they are conducted, and the terms in which both are imaged and valued, we need to know something about one concept that is fundamental. That concept is *tar*. A *tar* is a territory occupied by a lineage segment (*ipaven*).[2] Tiv organize themselves into what is called, in anthropological English, a lineage system. They formulate this organization in terms of genealogies running back patrilineally seventeen or eighteen generations from themselves to 'Tiv', the original ancestor of them all.[3] Each of the ancestors in the genealogies who is postulated to have lived more than four or five generations ago lends his name to the social group of his agnatic descendants. These social groups, who call themselves by the plural form of their agnatic ancestor's name, form the basis of communities. The smallest lineages to form local groups inhabit areas of about 1,200 acres or so, and contain from 150 to as many as 1,500 people. This area, within which 83 per cent. of the resident males are agnatic members of the associated lineage, is called the *tar*. The *tar* has the same name as the agnatic lineage which inhabits it. All the homesteads and farms within this area—and they are spread fairly evenly over the ground—are the homes of agnatic members of the lineage, or of kinsmen or 'guests' to whom they have given temporary cultivation and building rights.

In such a situation, Tiv refer to the lineage (*nôngo*) which is associated with a *tar* as a 'segment' (*ipaven*). The term 'segment'

---

[1] For a preliminary report on Tiv ethnography, see Laura and Paul Bohannan, *The Tiv of Central Nigeria*, International African Institute, 1953.

[2] Some of the material about *tar* in the next few pages was originally published in a different form in *The Southwestern Journal of Anthropology*, 1955.

[3] Sections of the genealogy are printed and discussed in Laura Bohannan, 'A Genealogical Charter', *Africa*, Vol. XXII, No. 4, October 1952.

is applied to a social group; the word *tar* is applied to the area occupied by that social group.

Two minimal *utar* which adjoin, and whose associated lineage segments are descended from a common ancestor, form a larger, inclusive segment and a larger, inclusive *tar*, both named after the common ancestor. At this new, higher level of the lineage system the same statement can be made: two adjacent larger *utar*, whose associated segments are descended from a common ancestor, are taken together to form a still larger segment and a still larger *tar*. The largest *tar* which Tiv see, in this particular set of images, is 'Tivland'—*Tar Tiv*.[1]

Thus, the first meaning of *tar*—and I believe it can be said to be the 'basic meaning'—is the notion of a territory associated with and defined by a social group, in this case a lineage that Tiv will consent to call an *ipaven*, or segment. We might say that the system of *utar* is a view of geography, for Tiv have no place names (other than those for streams and hills) except the names of their *utar*. The *tar* is the country, the land of the Tiv; it contains many smaller *utar* which are defined by the lineages into which Tiv divide themselves and in terms of which they see some of the most significant of their relationships with one another.

Tiv have a commonly used expression, 'to spoil the *tar*'. When I asked what this phrase meant, the immediate reply was always, 'A man who goes around looking for a quarrel spoils the *tar*', and some—especially in the area which had recently experienced war—would add, 'A war spoils the *tar* more than anything else.' One elder compared peace-making with 'repairing the *tar*', and said that the real meaning of the phrase is to sit and listen quietly and dispassionately to all sides of a dispute, then to give a just decision. Repairing *tar* is a matter of arbitration. Repairing *tar* is government.

But the phrase also has a second meaning, the investigation of which takes us immediately into the difficult idiom of ambiguity and metaphor in which Tiv discuss religion and witchcraft. This second meaning is to be found in the secret language of the *mbatsav*. *Mbatsav* are thought to form an organization of the elders of the community, in their combined roles of 'witches' and mystical protectors of the community. In their nocturnal meetings

[1] A fuller discussion of these points is found in Paul Bohannan, 'The Migration and Expansion of the Tiv', *Africa*, Vol. XXIV, No. 1, January 1954.

—and also in communicating with one another in daylight—they are said to use a special 'language'. This 'language' is in fact a series of noun substitutions which varies from one part of the country to another. *Tar* is one of the everyday words that are given a special symbolic meaning in the language of the *mbatsav*. Akiga says and Captain Abraham also notes,[1] and my southern informants agree, that *tar* refers to the magical instrument which Tiv call an owl pipe (*imborivungu*). Another magical apparatus sometimes called *tar* is the one that Tiv call the 'father's head' (*ityough ki ter*). My own informants in eastern Tivland (Ukum) told me this, and Captain Downes tells me that he has heard the word *tar* so used in Turan.

To 'repair *tar*', then, sometimes means to perform a ceremony for the owl pipe or the skull. The use of 'repair' in this context is not unusual, for performance of almost any rite associated with fetishes is referred to by this word. Akiga says that the ceremony for repairing the individually owned owl pipe requires the sacrifice of a mere mouse, but the owl pipe of a patrilineal descent group—repairing *tar*—requires the life and blood of a person.

In the same way, 'to repair *tar*' may sometimes mean performing a ceremony involving killing a chicken for purposes of activating a force thought to be inherent in a properly consecrated 'father's head'. As with the owl pipe, this is thought to involve the sacrifice of a human life in some way or other. Usually the actual mechanism is a mystery, and its being a mystery is part of its value. Any death which occurs in the community can be—but may not always be—attributed to the *mbatsav*. They need human lives to carry out their work of repairing *tar*, which involves the prosperity of the social group. All reports agree that 'repairing *tar*' (owl pipe or father's head) is connected with the fertility of farms and crops and women, with hunting, and with health.

My first task in illuminating the idea *tar*, was to illustrate extensively the distinction between *tar* and the idea of 'earth' or 'soil' (*nya*) and at the same time to write an account which I hoped would be comparable to other studies of land usage and settlement patterns.[2] The next step was obviously to discuss in detail the distinction which Tiv make between the two types of 'repairing

---

[1] *Akiga's Story*. London: International African Inst., 1939. R. C. Abraham, *The Tiv People*, London, 1940.

[2] Paul Bohannan, *Tiv Farm and Settlement*. H.M.S.O., 1954.

tar'. The present book deals with that aspect of 'repairing *tar'* which centres around arbitration and government. It is concerned, that is, with the jural institutions embraced in the Tiv concept of *jir* meaning 'court, case, moot'. A later study is planned on the other sense of 'repairing *tar'*, which centres in the concept *tsav*, talent or witchcraft substance. It will strive to be, as well as the explanation of Tiv ideas, a contribution to the anthropological literature on witchcraft, magic, and religion.

The problem which faces any ethnographer writing about 'law' is twofold. First, he must report accurately the ideas and institutions of the people he has studied, in a language (English) in which most of the words and concepts of social control have been pre-empted by jurists and given precise and technical meanings. That is the translation problem. Secondly, he must report his material in such a way as to illuminate the work of his predecessors and his colleagues. Seeing his work and the ideas of his people in relation to a body of knowledge already in existence might be called the theoretical or comparative problem.

'Law' is a rich and ambiguous word, with wide ramifications in ordinary speech. It has also been adopted and given even more widely ramifying technical meanings by two separate disciplines. The first is the discipline of lawyers. To lawyers the law is the core of that highly refined system of ideas and practices of which the legal institutions of our own society consist. To ethnological or comparative jurists, on the other hand, 'law' is any system of jural institutions which controls, wholly or in part, the 'force' inherent in any 'politically organized society'.

The method by which I attempt to avoid inaccuracies of translation as well as confusion between sociological theory and our own folk theory of social control is, I believe, a simple one. Events that occur within a social field (however defined) can only be perceived in company of an interpretation. Obviously, the human beings who participate in social events interpret them: they create meaningful systems out of the social relationships in which they are involved. Such a system I am going to call a 'folk system' of interpretation, by analogy with 'folk etymology'.

There is also a second sort of system: that which sociologists and social anthropologists create by more or less scientific methods. This system may be called an analytical system. It is determined by the anthropologist *qua* anthropologist to explain the material which he has gathered *qua* ethnographer. But it is very important that he should also give the folk system which, if he is a good ethnographer, he *learned* (as opposed to created) during the course of his research. For example, a certain field of Nuer social relationships is explained by Nuer in terms of an agnatic genealogy. That is the folk system. The same field is explained, in English, by Professor Evans-Pritchard, as a lineage system based on the principle of segmental opposition. That is an analytical system.[1]

The folk system is, surely, the core of anthropological studies. We start with social relationships expressed in particular cultural terms. When we try to understand this 'process', we find that the people who live in the system, and thereby create it, have systematized it themselves. Their systems may be inadequate for purposes of our analyses—indeed, it would be a sad reflection on social anthropology if they were not. But folk systems are *never* right or wrong. They 'exist'. They are. And the key to the folk system—almost the only key—is the language in which it is stated.

A folk system is a systematization of ethnographic fact for purposes of action. It might well have been called an 'action system', had that term not already been given too many definitions. An analytical system, on the other hand, is a systematization of ethnographic fact (including the folk system) for purposes of analysis.

'Law', in the lawyer's sense, is a systematization of ethnographic fact for purposes of social action. It is thus, in the present terminology, the 'folk system' of the English-speaking countries for dealing with their own institutions and ideas of social control. The 'law' of comparative jurists is an analytical system. It concerns principles and idioms for understanding social control of the 'law' type wherever found. The use of the same vocabulary for these two distinct purposes, however necessary, is confusing.

The anthropologist's chief danger is that he will change one of the folk systems of his own society into an analytical system, and try to give it wider application than its merit and usefulness allow.

I have tried, in this book, to translate the Tiv folk system of jural control. In order to do so, I have had to compare it and contrast it with our own—that is, with lawyer's—'law'. But I have

[1] E. E. Evans-Pritchard, *The Nuer*, Oxford, 1940.

tried *not* to 'explain' it *in terms of* our own system of 'law', which would do violence to the Tiv ideas and folk systems. I have, at the same time, tried to elicit from the data an analytical system which makes it more easily understood in generalized sociological terms.

CHAPTER II

THE GRADE-D COURT

I. THE DUAL MANDATE

THERE are today two folk systems operative in Tivland. There is that scheme of looking at social institutions which characterizes the tribal Africans and which includes their views not merely of 'indigenous institutions' but also of European inspired and dominated institutions. There is also the scheme of looking at things which characterizes a colonial administration and is shared more or less fully by other local Europeans; it includes views not merely of governmental and mission institutions, but also of other African institutions into which the Europeans do not enter directly. The two systems are seldom congruous.

Therefore it is not surprising that administrative officers and other Europeans living in Tivland refer to those bodies officially termed 'Grade-D courts' as 'native courts', while the Tiv refer to them as 'government courts'.

The exact jurisdiction of these 'native courts' is laid down in the Statutes of Nigeria. 'Native courts', at the time this study was made, were divided into four grades. Grade-A native courts wield 'full judicial powers' (save that death sentences must be reviewed by the Governor). At the other extreme, Grade-D courts are limited to civil claims not exceeding £25 and criminal cases involving a maximum of 3 months' imprisonment or £10 fine.

Ultimate political authority in Tivland rests with the British Administration; that administration's idea of court systems is a social fact. But Tiv do not see the courts from the same point of view as their administrators. Tiv call 'native courts' *jir*. They also apply the word *jir* to other institutions and tribunals which the Europeans do not term 'native courts'. These latter we shall call 'moots' in this book. The distinction between courts and moots is necessary because of the presence of two folk systems. Today the distinction is recognized in both folk systems. When Tiv distinguish between the two types of tribunal, they call courts '*jir* of the D.O.' or '*jir* of the N.A.' (Native Authority) and moots '*jir* at home' (*jir sa ya*) or '*jir* of the lineage' (*jir ityô*). The first part of this book deals with courts, and the second part with moots or '*jir* at home'. A *jir* is not only a tribunal, it is also a case. I discovered early in writing this book that attempts to translate *jir* into either of these two English words raised certain difficulties of meaning. In English we can say, 'The case before the court'; Tiv would have to say 'the *jir* before the *jir*'. They do not; they say only 'the *jir*', and it means a tribunal in action hearing a case.

In order to retain the essential ambiguity of the Tiv concept, I am retaining the Tiv word *jir*. I realize that this throws a burden on the reader, in that he must call up a new and, at first, unnatural meaning and image. But only the effort of calling it up will eventually lead to its clarification as a concept rather than a welter of parts fitting into familiar pigeon-holes. I cannot translate *jir* by one English word; to translate it with several is to dissipate its force and truth.

II. PERSONNEL AND ORGANIZATION OF A GRADE-D COURT IN TIVLAND

There are, today, fifty-four administrative districts in Tivland. Each has a Grade-D court, called a 'clan court' in the *Nigeria Gazette*. To explain the internal division of Tivland into administrative units we must go into the history of the British penetration, because the present-day organization has historical, not sociological, causes.

We have seen that Tiv organize themselves on the basis of a segmentary lineage system, and that there is no 'head' of any lineage. The largest social unit in Tivland which has an indigenous head, with constituted authority of the sort we think of as accruing to headmen, is the compound. The compound is a group of huts of close kinsmen, built close together around an oval open space. It contains from 7 to 170 people.[1]

The British entered Tivland from the east. At the time, about 1907, the Tiv had adopted from the Jukun what was among the latter a conception of divine kingship. Among the Tiv, who took over most of the trappings and paid the Jukun large amounts for the symbols and the ceremonies, it fitted immediately into the system of prestige (*shagba*).

[1] There may be a very few which are larger, and some which are smaller. In Paul Bohannan, *Tiv Farm and Settlement*, 1954, compounds are discussed fully.

The new British Administration was accustomed to the Jukun trappings, and understood their meaning in Jukun society more or less clearly because many of its officers were familiar with Frazer's theories of divine kingship then in vogue. Not unnaturally, they assumed that the same meanings held in Tivland and that the Tiv, like the Jukun, were divided into a series of small divine kingdoms; that each man occupying the position which they called 'drum chief' (a translation from Tiv, not Jukun) was the same sort of official as his Jukun counterpart, a priest with at least nominal secular authority, and that he was the centre of community life.

As a result of this misunderstanding, a large lineage area called Ukum, in eastern Tivland bounding the Jukun, was recognized as an administrative district 'under' a drum chief. It is in the nature of a lineage system that once one unit has been picked out, equivalent units in adjoining areas readily emerge. Throughout the rest of eastern and most of central and southern Tivland, drum chiefs were found to 'represent' other lineages, and it was assumed that they had at least as much authority as Jukun divine chiefs.

Once they had 'determined the administrative unit', the early administrators sought the 'responsible' officials within it. It did not occur to them—at that time it had not occurred to anybody— that there might not be responsible officials. Indeed, the notion of 'responsibility' is a difficult and refined Western concept, even though its analogues are to be found in some other societies. To Westerners a lack of responsible persons implies anarchy. Since anarchy did not exist in Tivland, they assumed that there must be responsible persons. The 'drum chiefs' were accordingly assumed to be these responsible persons. But in other areas, particularly in the west and north which are furthest removed from Jukun influence, there were no 'drum chiefs', though men of influence were in evidence. The same series of assumptions prevailed, and their positions were understood as involving 'authority'.

With the passage of time, most 'drum chiefs' proved to be what the administrative files of the period call 'broken reeds'. The Administration once again sought for men of responsibility and authority—for the so-called 'native' positions or offices which they could be said to occupy.

The Tiv, who do not think of political organization in terms of a paradigm of authority, but rather in terms of paradigms of juxtaposed lineages (*ipaven*), had many words and phrases for describing

c

persons in terms of the prestige system. They kept offering these descriptive terms, which administrative officers kept understanding as titles for offices. The misunderstanding was complete. Today each administrative district has an official called *tyo-or* who is recognized and paid a salary by the Government. He is often referred to as the 'clan-head'.[1] Needless to say, Tiv do not even now recognize him as 'head' of anything. The derivation of the term *tyo-or* is obscure, but folk etymology derives it from 'man of the *ityô*', *ityô* being any agnatic lineage seen from the standpoint of its members. The word does not, so far as I am aware, occur in the early literature on the Tiv or in the early administrative files. It could well be a label invented by Tiv in order to provide the term which the Administration sought for one of its reorganizations. I shall translate it as 'chief', though the English word carries connotations of authority not present in the Tiv word.

There are other officials within the district who are of importance to the *jir*. Since Tiv say that no person whatever should ever act autocratically or alone, and since Government believes that a chief should act only with a council to keep check on him, they have agreed upon the appointment of lesser officials. Those within the district are selected in such a way that they 'represent' the segments of the lineage associated with that *tar* known as the 'district'. There are usually four (but there may be three or as many as eight) of them (including the chief), thus:

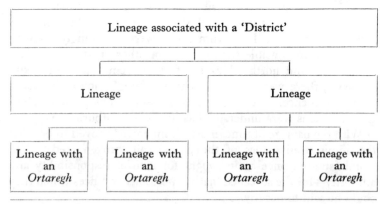

---

[1] The administrative use of the word 'clan' does not follow anthropological usage, nor does it translate any Tiv word. The same is true of the administrative use of the word 'sept' for lineages which include several 'clans', and 'kindred' for lineages smaller than 'clans'.

Each of these officials, including the chief, holds the title *ortaregh*. This term unequivocally means 'man of the *tar*': *tar*, remember, is the spatial or district aspect of the lineage segment.

The word *ortaregh* occurs in Tiv administrative files from very early times—long before it was used to describe an official position. In the early days it seems to have meant 'the important people of the countryside'. Almost anyone who 'repaired the *tar*', either by acting as arbitrator or by performing ceremonies, merited the descriptive term 'man of the *tar*'. It was not an office in a hierarchy of offices until the late 1930's.

The term *ortaregh* and its plural *mbatarev* are today in general use as terms of reference. In address, both chief and *mbatarev* are called '*tor*',[1] which Tiv use to describe all 'chiefs'—not only those appointed over them by the Government, but also the divine priests of the Jukun and the Queen of England. Tiv use the vocative *tor* for the same purposes as they use kinship terms—to remind a person that he occupies a position in which he has obligations to them. In other contexts the given name is generally used.

One duty of an *ortaregh*, as a civil servant, is that he attends court and acts as a judge. In this capacity he is usually called *or-jir*, man of the *jir* (plural *mbajiriv*), which can be adequately translated 'judge'.

It is, in Tivland, the chief and the other *mbatarev* of a district who officially constitute a Grade-D court. Tiv say that they are the most important persons in the *jir*. The anthropologist can add that at least it is they who sit on chairs. Tiv make several types of chairs of their own and have taken to the deck-chair with great fervour. Each *ortaregh* brings his own chair—usually a light deck-chair carried by one of his junior sons, a lad of twelve years or so who, during the meeting, sits close by, fills his father's pipe, runs small errands and is generally useful. Sons usually vie with one another for the privilege of carrying their fathers' chairs, because not only does it mean that they are singled out, but many of them also see it as an opportunity to 'learn the things of Tiv' and prepare themselves for similar positions. All Tiv agree that sons of *mbatarev* have a greater knowledge of 'the things of Tiv' than have other Tiv youngsters.

Although they are not officially part of the Grade-D court, the

[1] Genetic relationship between the words *tor* and *tyo-or* is doubtful.

tax-collectors usually sit with the *jir* and some of them make significant contributions to its working. Tax-collectors are appointed from smaller lineages than *mbatarev*. There are usually two, three, or four such lineages contained within that lineage which is characterized by an *ortaregh*. A tax-collector is called 'man of the tribute' (*or kpandegh*). His work, although paid, is considered by many to be thankless and unpleasant. However, it has the advantage of being a stepping-stone towards the position of *ortaregh*, for it makes one known to administrative officers, whose concurrence is necessary in the appointment of *mbatarev*. Some tax-collectors are elders with real knowledge of Tiv custom; others are young men whose only qualification is that they can collect tax. Many tax-collectors are called *tor* by their 'constituents' and others, especially if the latter want something from them.

Tax-collectors, when they attend the *jir*, usually sit on low stools or on sheep-skins which are, like the chairs of the *mbatarev*, usually carried by a child. When the *jir* is meeting, they sit near the *mbatarev* of their respective lineages, so that all the representatives of any single lineage form a block.

The other officials who must be present at a *jir* of this sort are the scribe (*malu*) who acts as court clerk, one or more of the Native Administration policemen (called *dandoka* or *dogari*, both Hausa terms) and a messenger (*mesinja*) or two.

Attached to each chief is a scribe whose duty it is to write notes and letters for him, to act as his amanuensis generally, and to keep the court records. The scribe issues receipts for all money collected in court fees or in fines, and keeps a summary of each case and a record of the number of cases heard during the month.

Akiga has described in detail the early days of the scribes and their rise to power.[1] Today, since the reorganizations of the 1930's, their power is somewhat curtailed, but—as educated, or at least literate, persons—they are often consulted as specialists on administrator's notions; therefore they still wield considerable influence. It is my opinion that the corruption with which Akiga and others[2] have charged them has been largely corrected. Most scribes receive presents—but few, I think, take them for services rendered.

---

[1] *Akiga's Story*, pp. 394–6.

[2] See T. O. Elias, *Groundwork of Nigerian Law*. Capt. Downes considers Akiga's account exaggerated, even for the days when he wrote.

The Native Authority policemen not only arrest people and maintain order, but also summon litigants and witnesses; moreover they sometimes act as prosecutors in criminal cases, particularly of those wrongdoers whom they have themselves arrested. They are armed only with night sticks, and their authority depends largely on their own personalities and on those of their superiors, the chief and *mbatarev*.

Messengers carry messages from one chief or *jir* to another, and from the chiefs to the administrative officers, but they may also summon people to court when cases are called by outsiders (people within the same N.A. court jurisdiction usually summon one another). Yet there are seldom sufficient messengers and policemen to get all the witnesses and principals to the *jir* at the same time until the third or fourth attempt. Often the more junior tax-collectors or the sons of the *mbatarev* are pressed into service. Some chiefs also have private messengers—men who are neither paid nor recognized by the Government, but who attach themselves directly to a chief and run his errands in return for their board, lodging, and occasional presents.

Although there are no other court officials, many private citizens attend sessions of the *jir*, for Tiv are a litigious people and enjoy listening to and participating in *jir*. Young persons usually stand or sit outside the court circle (one of the most difficult tasks which a *jir* performs is to keep them all seated so that they do not shut out the breeze). Elders usually sit closer in, often among the judges. Any Tiv has a right to be heard in any *jir* held in his own lineage area, but he will not be suffered gladly unless what he has to say is brief and to the point. Seldom, in fact, do persons other than the *mbatarev*, tax-collectors, policemen and messengers, and those persons directly concerned in a *jir*, take any active part in it.

Since Native Authority courts are organized more or less on a British model, the notion of appeal has been introduced into Tivland. The appeal from the Grade-D or 'clan' court, is to the Grade-C or 'sept' court. Comparatively few cases are actually appealed, however.

Above the Grade-C court (composed of the total membership of its component Grade-D courts) is the Tribal Council, *Jir Tamen*, which meets twice a year, either in Gboko or in Katsina Ala, in order to consider legislation, either initiated by it or, more commonly, put before it by administrative officers. It also hears some cases. *Jir Tamen* is a Grade-B court, but few *jir* are deemed serious enough to be heard by it, and few appeals from Grade-C courts are made to it.

The possibility of appeal from the Grade-D 'clan' courts to the Grade-C 'sept' courts is frequently used as a threat on the part of the judges against recalcitrant litigants.

III. MBADUKU JIR

The Grade-D court in which I did most of my work was that of the MbaDuku district, a distinct area in southern Tivland occupied by some 10,000 people. Most of its male residents consider themselves to be the agnatic descendants of a single ancestor, Aduku, who is some nine or ten steps removed in the genealogies. The rest are sisters' sons or more distant kinsmen who reckon their connexion through at least one female link. There are also a few strangers—no more than 2 per cent.—living in MbaDuku as guests of age mates or friends.

Although we need not go into the position of MbaDuku in the lineage system, and in the genealogies comprising the folk system, its internal organization is relevant. MbaDuku subdivides into lineages morphologically precisely like itself:

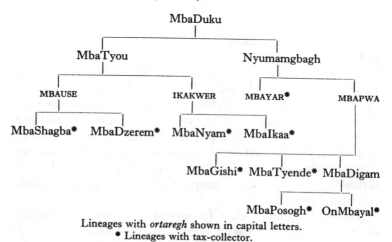

Lineages with *ortaregh* shown in capital letters.
* Lineages with tax-collector.

In the indigenous scheme, there are no 'heads' of any of these lineages.

MbaDuku is also an administrative district. It has a chief recognized by Government as the representative of all MbaDuku, and a *jir*, gazetted as a Grade-D court, which meets in the chief's compound.

During the time of my field-work the chief of MbaDuku was Chenge, son of Kyagba. The situation was rather unusual, for Kyagba himself was still alive (he died late in 1951), but he had been called by the Administration to be chief of Jecira, a lineage (officially termed 'sept') which included some twelve lineages the size of MbaDuku. He was moved to Vande Ikya, a more central location, and Chenge was selected to act as chief of MbaDuku in his absence. After Kyagba's death, Chenge became chief of Mba-Duku in his own right and another son was made chief of Jecira.

Chenge was, when I knew him, a man of about sixty. He had, as a youth, been a government messenger when southern Tivland was still part of the Eastern Provinces of Nigeria, and in early manhood had spent several years working at blacksmithing. He was considered by the Administration to be a little better than the average in carrying out his duties as chief.

Chenge, besides being chief of MbaDuku, was also the *ortaregh* of Ikakwer lineage. There were, in addition, three other *mbatarev*, representing the other MbaDuku lineages of the same order as Ikakwer: Gbegba of MbaUse, Huwa of MbaYar, and Ikpokpo (and later some others) of MbaPwa.

At one time, while Kyagba was under governmental disapprobation, Gbegba was chief of MbaDuku. The people of MbaDuku (including many of MbaUse) protested loudly in the late 1930's, and Kyagba was restored. Gbegba is the eldest of the four *mbatarev* and, with Chenge, the most experienced. Together they represent MbaTyou, the lineage which includes them both. They often say that they are both MbaTyou and use this as a legitimate charter for opportunist co-operation. Just as often, when such co-operation is not convenient, one reminds the other that they are respectively Ikakwer and MbaUse—an equally valid use of the same charter.

The *ortaregh* from MbaYar was a young man of thirty-five or so named Huwa. When I began my study in MbaDuku, Huwa was acting for his old and invalid father, Jijingi, who had been a respected elder, judge, and man of the *tar* for many years. After Jijingi's death, the people of MbaYar, the other *mbatarev* of

MbaDuku, and the district officer readily decided that Huwa, because of experience and character, should occupy his position in fact as well as in deed.

When this study began, the fourth *ortaregh*, from MbaPwa, was Ikpokpo. He was, however, removed from office in 1950 as a result of his activities in connexion with the Tiv–Udam border affray, and had not yet been definitely replaced at the end of 1952 when I finally left MbaDuku. At that time there were two favoured candidates, Apaa and Tyukwa, both of whom sat in court, though neither took a very active part in the proceedings.

These four men formed the focus of the '*jir* circle' (*ahwa jir*). Tiv often use the expression 'enter into the *jir* circle' to denote appearance before the *jir*.

Each *ortaregh* was surrounded by his tax-collectors, eight in all. The lineages characterized by tax-collectors are indicated in the diagram, p. 14. The two tax-collectors of MbaNyam and MbaIkaa, lineages which together form Ikakwer, usually sat near Chenge. The three men formed a sort of block representing Ikakwer. The tax-collectors from MbaShagba and MbaDzerem sat near Gbegba, with whom they formed the block representing MbaUse. In describing seating in a *jir*, MbaDuku people say that all the representatives of MbaUse and Ikakwer sat adjoining one another, thus forming the representation from MbaTyou. Actually, they may do so and they may not. They will always do so on formal occasions, but otherwise, since there is comparatively little jealousy and rivalry within the group, they usually sit wherever convenient; for example late-comers, be they tax-collectors or *mbatarev*, may sit at one or other end of the arc rather than push into a formally correct position.

MbaDuku *jir* owns a lock-box, which is kept in the hut of Chenge's favourite wife with the rest of his property. It also owns a table and a chair, which are kept by the scribe in his reception hut. During my first period in MbaDuku, the scribe was Igbana; later (during the period when the major portion of this study was carried out), Akpwe Suye held the office. They lived in compounds a few hundred yards outside Chenge's, and both were always friendly and helpful. Scribes, being literate and keeping records, are obviously useful friends for an ethnographer. My understanding of Tiv notions of their own jural process owes much to them, particularly Akpwe.

The chief, the other *mbatarev*, the tax-collectors, the scribe, together with two policemen and two messengers made up the personnel of the MbaDuku Grade-D court.

It is Government's view that every Grade-D court should meet at least once a month, preferably for several succeeding days, to settle as many as possible of the cases before it. Actually, even the best seldom meet quite so often. MbaDuku court, which, at the time I studied it, was considered to be a little above average without being a model, met for three to six days about every six weeks.

MbaDuku *jir* met in Chenge's compound; the various officials sat in a sort of semi-circle outside under the trees. Some *jir* have built special shelters in which their meetings can be held, but they are generally used only in inclement weather, for they are usually too dark and too warm. Chenge's compound, in 1949–50, had a circle of posts which formed the beginning of a court shelter, but they had disappeared when I returned in 1952. If inclement weather overtook the *jir* the officials removed either to Chenge's reception hut or to that of one of his wives, and the litigants and onlookers found what shelter they could with other persons of the compound or under the eaves of the houses.

The other *mbatarev* would arrive at Chenge's about ten o'clock in the morning—they had probably already supervised the work on their farms and put their compounds in order. Both Gbegba and Ikpokpo had some four miles to walk. If three of them were kept waiting by the fourth for an unusually long time, they might fine him—usually two shillings.

It is difficult to tell just when a *jir* actually begins. There have been people milling about, shouting, talking to the *mbatarev* and the tax-collectors and to one another, reciting litanies of complaints and shouting accusations. Several men and an occasional woman may have approached the two or three *mbatarev* who were the first to arrive; others sit in the circle formed by the arc of chairs and seats of the officials, asking advice about their particular complaints before paying the 2s. fee for calling a *jir*. The officials present will usually listen to enough of the complaint to determine, 'Yes, you have a valid complaint; give your 2s. to the scribe and get your paper' or else to say, 'This is a silly and preposterous argument—go home and make it up. Have your elder hear this matter.'

When all, or a major portion, of the court officials had arrived and taken their seats, the chief would go into his reception hut and bring out *swem*. *Swem* is a pot of ashes and medicines which is the symbol of right and justice and plays a large role in both religious and political life. It is also used for oath-taking. *Swem* is put down in the circle, the chief washes his hands after touching it, and the *jir* is ready to start.

At this point, the chief, or perhaps one of the *mbatarev*, begins to shout, 'Shut up! Shut up!' The cry is taken up by everyone until the entire crowd is roaring 'Shut up!' 'Silence!' Then they quieten down and the *jir* is ready to begin. Meanwhile, several people have crowded into the open circle, sitting on the ground with their heads uncovered (and their shoulders as well unless they are in European shirts) and trying to get the attention of the judges, who eventually select one of them and tell the others to move back to the outer circle.

The whole proceeding is interspersed with shouts at the on-lookers standing round about the circle to sit down so that the breeze can get through, and for everyone to shut up and be quiet. Tiv are noisy people.

The procedure for hearing the *jir* is for the accuser to tell the *mbatarev* and assembled onlookers his side of the story: it ends with a request to the *mbatarev* to see that his opponent makes reparation of some sort: i.e. gives him his wife, his money, his livestock or whatever it may be. The accuser, if he speaks well and to the point, is allowed to finish. If he wanders, or seems unable to tell a connected story, the *mbatarev* interrupt and conduct a sort of cross-examination. They then turn to the accused and say something like: 'Is that the way it was?' or 'What do you know about this matter?'—a signal for him to tell his side of the story. They are somewhat less likely to let him finish uninterrupted, though a good speaker who sticks to the point is likely to be heard to the end. His story usually agrees with the accuser's on all but the vital points and ends self-righteously, 'So why have you called me here?'

If there are disagreements over matters of fact which the investigation (*mtôv*) cannot reconcile, witnesses are called. This almost always means a postponement of the case—perhaps for a few hours, perhaps for several days, perhaps for ever. Usually, the principals rather than the *mbatarev* or their messengers are respon-sible for getting witnesses to the *jir*.

Chenge

Messengers and scribe

PLATE I

Gbegba

Huwa, Chenge and Gbegba 'investigate' a *jir*

PLATE II

Witnesses, when they arrive, are usually sworn on *swem*, the pot which the chief brought out earlier. Once a witness is sworn, judgment on perjury is between him and the supernatural forces (unless it be detected, when the court takes notice of it). Principals in a case are almost never allowed to swear (one exception will be noted), for were they allowed to do so the judgment would no longer rest solely in human hands, and the *jir* would be powerless to act.

The *mbatarev* now begin to 'examine' or 'investigate' (*tôv*) the *jir*, though they may first make a tentative suggestion as a basis for arbitration which, if accepted, will end the matter. Usually, however, the 'examination' means cross-examination. Any *ortaregh* will ask any question he thinks necessary; he continues until he has finished or until interrupted. The court is open to all, and any person may take part in 'examining' the case by asking a question or giving an opinion, but only those full of age and prestige do so without asking permission from the *mbatarev* to speak.

On the basis of the statements of the principals and the witnesses, and of their answers to questions, a decision is reached by discussion among the *mbatarev*, and perhaps a few other important men. The decision seldom overtly involves a point of law, in the sense that we think of a rule or a law. I have often heard Tiv express rules of action that might be considered laws, but seldom in a *jir*. It is true that the Government and the Native Administration have inserted into some cases what seems to Tiv an alien factor—and in the course of these cases they may refer to the 'laws' (*tindi*) of the Native Authority or of the 'Europeans'. Usually, however, the decision involves pointing out a mode of action that will be satisfactory, or least unsatisfactory, to both parties; action to which both will agree, and which will resolve the dispute. Both should concur (*lumun*) in the decision, and each must agree (*lumun*) to carry out his part of it. If such concurrence and agreement are not obtained, the case will probably be said to have been settled arbitrarily (*sa apela*). No chief or *ortaregh* who develops a reputation for such arbitrary rulings can long retain his prestige or his influence.

The purpose of most *jir* is, thus, to determine a *modus vivendi*; not to apply laws, but to decide what is right in a particular case. They usually do so without overt reference to rules or 'laws'.

CHAPTER III

A DAY IN COURT

THE best way to get an idea of how a *jir* works, of the cases it handles, and its methods of handling them, is to follow through a single day in MbaDuku *jir*, to analyse the cases, and trace out the events. I have selected the *jir* held on 3 August 1952, because, although representative, it contains rather more colourful cases than usual.

That day the *jir* got started about 10.30. It had rained the night before and the day was hot and steamy. When the chief and the *mbatarev* were settled in their chairs and had called for silence, the man who had outshouted the rest, so that his case was to be heard first, yelled, 'I call Kwentse.' When making a complaint the standard phrase is: 'I call so and so.' The *mbatarev* often ask the man who omits this simple procedure, 'Whom do you call?'

JIR NO. 1 *Gbivaa calls Kwentse to get his wife back*

Kwentse, who was called as defendant, to put it in our terms,[1] is one of the local tax-collectors. On being called, he took off his red felt fez and squatted in front of the *mbatarev*, a few feet from the man who had called him. He had to be reminded two or three times to sit on the ground instead of merely squatting. Gbivaa turned to Kwentse and said in a loud voice, 'Give me my wife.'

Kwentse was supercilious: 'I don't have her.'

Gbivaa repeated, 'Give me my wife.'

Neither was willing to explain any further, so the *mbatarev* had immediately to begin asking direct questions and to 'investigate' the case. After much probing they discovered that Gbivaa had married Kwentse's daughter several years ago. A few months before the case was called, she had run off with another man from Gav lineage, and the husband wanted either his wife or the bridewealth he had expended for her.

When the facts of the case were complete, Huwa, the youngest *ortaregh*, said that it was plain what was to be done: Kwentse must either go himself or send one of his youngsters to Gav to discover just

---

[1] Tiv do not have words for plaintiff or defendant. During the process of the case, each is called the 'partner' (*ikyar*) of the other. The distinction between plaintiff and defendant is the distinction between the subject and the object of the verb 'call' (*yila*).

what the woman, his daughter, intended to do; only then would it be possible to continue the case. Kwentse promised, with much reluctance, to send one of his sons to Gav within the next few days. This amounted to a postponement of the case. It would never be reopened unless Gbivaa again came shouting to the MbaDuku *jir*. Kwentse did not, I believe, send his son to Gav to find out his daughter's intentions.

JIR NO. 2. *Akpalu calls WanDzenge about a nanny goat*

The next *jir* to catch the attention of the *mbatarev* was that of Akpalu, a youngster who had left a nanny goat with a man named WanDzenge. It is not customary in Tivland to keep one's own livestock at home, for then it is subject to the legitimate claims of one's kinsmen. Rather, live-stock—and especially goats—are left with friends or distant kinsmen. Then one can say with truth that all the goats in one's own compound belong to someone else. This practice is called 'releasing' (*tuhwa*) your goat with the person who becomes its caretaker. As his reward he receives one kid in three. Obviously a very complicated debt structure is built up; certainly these practices are a very fertile source of litigation.

This particular dispute centred around the number of kids borne by the nanny goat. Akpalu, the owner, said that she had borne four kids, of which WanDzenge had taken two. WanDzenge said that she had borne only two, and that he had received nothing at all for keeping her. After some fifteen minutes of cross-questioning and haranguing, it was decided that WanDzenge owed the boy a small billy goat some three or four months old.

JIR NO. 3. *MbaTyuna calls her husband, seeking a divorce*

Some time before the case of Akpalu's goat had been finished, a stolid, stubborn-looking woman had sat down in the middle of the cleared circle and refused to move for anyone. She was well known to the *mbatarev*, for they had heard her case before. She said in a loud, whining voice that her husband wouldn't give her any cloth. This is the standard complaint against husbands.

Gbegba, the sharpest tongued of the *mbatarev*, asked her where she got the cloth she was wearing. She replied that she had had to sell her last chicken to buy it. Her husband then came forward and said he had given her that cloth, and two others, to induce her to return the last time she had run away to her parental home. She looked at him petulantly and said she had not seen either of the other cloths. The *mbatarev* told her that she had no grounds for divorce, that they had heard her complaint before, and had told her to go home with her husband and be a sensible woman.

She left the court circle and started alone down a path leading out of the compound. One of the *mbatarev* called to her husband and her guardian, who was also present, to catch her and take her home. They then turned to the next case.

JIR NO. 4. *Lankwagh calls Dagba, who eloped with his ward*

This case began when a man of forty or so, who had been shouting throughout the last part of the previous case, got the attention of the *mbatarev*. He said that Dagba had stolen his child, and that he wanted her returned. Dagba came forward. The *mbatarev* asked where the girl was. Dagba said that she was at his home, where a good wife should be.

He was told to bring her tomorrow, and that the *jir* between him and her guardian would be heard only if she herself was produced.

During all this time, people were bringing their 2s. court fees (*jinga jir*) to one or other of the *mbatarev*. If there is a break or a dull patch in the case that is proceeding, an *ortaregh* and some interloper will discuss a forthcoming case, or the *ortaregh* will give advice about just how the new-comer should pay his costs to the chief, who turns them over to the scribe, from whom the man gets a receipt. The case of Dagba and his wife was twice interrupted by other cases, bits of which were heard—enough to determine that there was a real *jir* and not a simple difference of opinion. The 'paper' is very important, and, though of the *mbatarev* only Huwa can read and even he only with the greatest difficulty, the paper must be in evidence to show that the *jir* has indeed been registered with the clerk, and that everything is in order.

JIR NO. 5. *A husband calls his wife's guardian to recover his bridewealth*

Next came another marriage dispute which was actually called against the woman's guardian by her husband, for repayment of his bridewealth. The wife had given repeated trouble and had finally run away once and for all. The guardian said that he had done his best but he was unable to make her stay with her husband, and just now he had no money. In such circumstances the *jir* is always much more lenient than when the fault lies with the guardian. The husband claimed that he had paid £11 bridewealth; the guardian admitted only £6. There is usually a dispute about the amount of bridewealth paid. Witnesses were requested.

It began to look bad for the guardian when he said that his witnesses had gone on a trip, and even worse when he objected to the husband's witness as being the latter's close kinsman. The *mbatarev* paid little attention to the objections, and when the husband's witness came forward from the crowd, he was asked to swear on *swem*. He did so willingly (witnesses who want to lie usually find good reason or at least good arguing points for not being required to take an oath). He said that the sum actually paid in his presence was £11 and that he had counted the money. Because he had made his statement on oath—and no doubt also because of the guardian's behaviour in objecting to him—his statement determined the amount. The *mbatarev* again tried to get the woman to go back to her husband and settle down and be a good wife, but she refused—she said she had had all that she could stand of him. The terms of repayment were made fairly lenient: the first payment was to be made in some three months when the crops were saleable. The important point was that the woman's guardian had agreed to the amount of the debt, £11.

JIR NO. 6. *Concerning custody of a child*

This *jir* never really got started. It concerned the custody of a child, and the decision was that the case must be settled by the *jir* of Mba-Kaange district, some 16 miles away, where the child was living.

JIR NO. 7. *An unsettled debt from a* jir *previously heard*

This *jir* had been heard and decided earlier; Konkuagh had paid £4. 19s. for his wife, who then refused to have anything to do with him. Her guardian said he had received only £3, which he had repaid. Thereupon the young husband, or ex-husband, produced his receipt on which the scribe had made a note at the first hearing several months before. The guardian complained loudly that a mere paper was taken as evidence against his word, that Tiv were becoming as bad as Europeans in regulating their lives by papers, and that talking a matter over would be much better than looking at a paper and making a decision out of hand. However, the paper was produced, and it showed that the guardian had repaid only £3 and still owed £1. 19s.

The guardian began to argue. Chenge got up, grasped him by the wrist, and handed him to Gbegba, who, as *ortaregh* of his lineage, should see to it that the amount was paid. Gbegba had no authority to force the old man to pay, but the fact that the latter was made publicly to admit his debt was considered the first step towards its payment. The young ex-husband did not know just when he would get the money, but he could now go to Gbegba rather than to the court to have the guardian reminded of the debt.

JIR NO. 8. *A girl is returned to her father's custody*

The next *jir* concerned the custody of a child—a young girl of about ten years. Her mother had died a year or so after she was born and she was then reared by her mother's mother. Gbegba, hearing this much of the matter, observed that there seemed to be no problem: the child's father should give the old woman a gift of ten shillings for rearing her, and the matter would be finished. The child should then accompany her father home; her filiation was not in doubt.

The grandmother, however, objected strongly. She had reared the child from infancy; the child had ruined many of her cloths by urinating on them; therefore she was entitled to £3 from the child's father for the expenses of bringing her up.

The father came into the *jir* circle and said that everyone so far had done well and had 'said well'. 10*s*., he said, was not enough, for his mother-in-law had done a good job of rearing the child, and she was right to say so. He produced 20*s*. and gave it to her.

Gbegba turned to the old woman and noted that this was very ample reward for the fact that the child had urinated on her cloth, for she was after all the child's grandmother. He then turned to the child and told her to go with her father.

The girl began to whimper. As her father came towards her, she began to scream. When persuasion failed he tried to carry her away. She screamed more loudly. Chenge walked over to them: 'Softly, softly,' he said to the father. 'Look, my child, this man is your father. He won't do anything to you. He will give you plenty of food. And besides, in a year or so you will be getting married and will go to your husband in a new compound in any case. Go with your father and don't give us all this trouble.'

I have seen Chenge make this sort of speech on several occasions. Either the youngster becomes quiet and says she will go, or she kicks and screams more loudly than before. Today's child screamed. Chenge lost his temper and told the father to get this noisy youngster out of the compound so that the *jir* could proceed. When the father tried to pick her up to carry her away, the mother's mother's classificatory sister—an old woman who is half mad, and who was angry with Chenge in any case because all her sons were in gaol for larceny—went after Chenge with a stick and had to be forcibly restrained by a policeman. Everyone, including Chenge, thought this very funny.

A scene of this sort takes place every time a girl who has been reared away from her father is sent back to him prior to her marriage. Such scenes are often considered heart-rending by Europeans, whose values seem to be thoroughly outraged, and some officials insist on reversing the decisions. They are not doing the child a service: by the time a girl is twelve she is considered, and considers herself, ready to become an adult. She is, as Tiv say, going to a compound where she will be given plenty of food and companionship. Tiv recognize that it is reasonable for these girls not to want to go to their fathers, who are comparative strangers. They do not, however, consider it repugnant to make them do so, for they know that such children are seldom subsequently as unhappy as they think they will be.

It was now about two o'clock in the afternoon. I left the *jir* for about thirty minutes for lunch (Tiv eat a snack in the morning and have their main meal about dark). After morning hours, the crowd of onlookers thins considerably. *Jir* become more diffuse and take longer to decide in the afternoon.

JIR NO. 9. *An MbaGishi man calls a 'sister's son' for exceeding the privileges of that status*

The first of the two important *jir* heard during the afternoon hinged on a decision about a man's right to take food and livestock from the people of his mother's agnatic lineage, his *igba*. This word is the reciprocal term of address between a person and all the members of that lineage. Tiv custom allows a sister's son to take certain types of property in reasonable amounts from his mother's close agnatic kinsmen without redress. If a man needs a chicken, he can go to his mother's compound, take it and walk off with it. This is called 'eating *igba*'.

In this particular case, a youth whose agnatic lineage was MbaYar, and whose mother's lineage was MbaGishi of MbaPwa, both within MbaDuku (see p. 14), went to the compound to his mother's people in MbaGishi and took five chickens. The man who called the case today was the owner of the chickens. He said that he was not closely related to the MbaYar boy, and that taking five chickens from an *igba* who isn't a close kinsman is stealing. The boy, who admitted having taken the chickens, said that he was 'eating *igba*' and certainly not stealing at all. What Europeans would consider the facts of the case were not in question. The boy had taken the five chickens. The question was: had he a right to do so?

Gbegba turned to him and asked, 'On the day that you caught those chickens, to whom did you show them?' The boy replied that he had shown them to no one. He tried to continue, but Gbegba interrupted to ask what he had done with the chickens.

The owner now broke in and said that he had taken them to sell. The accused contradicted this; he said that he hadn't sold them. Gbegba asked if he had eaten them on the spot. (Several people explained to me later that, to be perfectly correct, one must either kill and eat immediately or else sacrifice any animals taken from the *igba*.) It was obvious that the 'thief' had not eaten the chickens.

D

After considerable discussion among the four *mbatarev*, it was decided that he should return two of the chickens. He refused, saying that they were his right: the man from whom he had taken them was his *igba*.

Chenge exploded and told him that since he had talked back to the judges he must give back all five chickens or they would decide he had stolen them. The youngster said he had only one hen left, so how could he possibly return two?

Chenge, still severe, told him that was his affair—and that it was now too late to return merely two; since he had talked back to the judges he must repay three. Chenge then said to the other *mbatarev* that he thought taking two chickens from an *igba* in one day is stretching a point. To take more than that, especially without eating them immediately, is stealing.

One of the onlookers now suggested that the boy return the hen he still had, and five eggs. Other onlookers jeered at this. Finally, after much debate, all the *mbatarev* agreed that either he must return three chickens equivalent to those which he took, or pay their value in money.

Huwa suggested that 9s. was adequate payment for the three chickens. The owner said that he wanted 4s. 3d. each (a price somewhat closer to what chickens cost in the market). Chenge said that was too much; 4s. 3d. is the price of a full-grown hen, and in all probability these weren't *all* full-grown hens. However, he thought Huwa's suggestion of 9s. too little, and said he thought 10s. ought to cover it.

The owner shouted that the case was being decided 'by force': that is, sufficient consideration had not been given to arriving at a settlement in which both parties could concur. His chickens, he thought, were worth more than 10s. The scribe spoke up and told him that he was much better off with three hens or 10s. than he would have been with one hen and five eggs. Chenge said in a firm voice that the case was finished— three hens or 10s. The accused, grumbling, admitted the debt and agreed to pay it in two days' time, when the *jir* would again be in session.

JIR NO. 10. *Divorce proceedings*

The other *jir* heard on this afternoon was called by a girl of not over seventeen. She told the court that she had been married to a man whom she didn't like and who had never slept with her. Every time she tried to encourage him, she said, he couldn't stomach it [lit., his stomach prevented him]. The *mbatarev* asked the youth about it. He said that she was lying; he had slept with her, was perfectly capable of doing so, and would even do so before witnesses if there was an unused hut in the compound. Before any *ortaregh* could say a word, the girl refused loudly to have anything to do with him. The boy's father then came into the circle and sat down. He said that he had got this wife for his son. She had now insulted his child and had told lies. He suggested that the girl should go home, and he would find his son another wife from another *tar*.

Chenge leaned back in his deck-chair and commented in a pleased tone that this was a very intelligent way to conduct a *jir*. Here, he noted, was a man who wanted a settlement rather than a wrangle.

Everyone was satisfied with the arrangement. Chenge then turned to the girl and told her she could have her divorce for 2s.—the usual arrangement. She said that she didn't have 2s. Gbegba commented that this was short-sighted of her, but she said she'd get it by tomorrow and would come back then and get her divorce.

This left the settlement of the bridewealth to be made. The divorce had been granted; the debt had yet to be settled. There was, of course, a discrepancy in the amount which the husband said he had paid and that which the guardian said he had received. The *jir* was adjourned so that both parties could get their witnesses.

It was by now after four in the afternoon. Gbegba, a man of sixty, had over four miles to walk before dark. He began to get restive. At this time of day, *jir* become even more noisy and disorderly than in the morning. The scribe left, with a small boy carrying his table and chair. The onlookers and elders began to drift out of the chief's compound along the paths towards their homes.

CHAPTER IV

THE STRUCTURE OF THE *JIR*

I. INTRODUCTION

THIS chapter is concerned with what we should, if we were lawyers, call procedural law: the regularities which can be found within the *jir*. We shall, so far as possible, set forth Tiv conceptualization of the *jir* by discussing folk descriptions of it.

The concept of 'procedure', the English categorizing term for adjectival rules and laws, came very late in the development of jural and legal ideas in Britain and America. The term was first used officially, both in England and the United States, in the middle of the 19th century. As Millar notes[1] it became a categorizing term for those acts or parts of a case, each of which earlier lawyers had been content to call by a distinctive name: pleading, practice, evidence, and the like.

Tiv have no broad, generalizing concept such as 'procedure'. Except for the appearance of witnesses, different acts in a *jir* are described by verbs. I shall deal first (in section ii) with the act that we should term 'pleading', but which Tiv know as 'calling (*yila*) a *jir*'. Its scope is wider than that of pleading; it denotes everything that the principals, particularly accusers, do, from the time they decide to call the *jir* until they have finished laying their complaints before the *mbatarev*. It is the 'caller' (*or yilan jir*) and his 'partner' (*ikyar*) who perform these actions. Section iii deals with the activities of witnesses and with Tiv ideas of evidence, oaths, and ordeals. Section iv is concerned with the activities of the *mbatarev* or other arbitrating persons, who are said to 'investigate' or 'get to the bottom of' (*tôv*) the *jir*. This verb applies to all activities of the court officials except judgment. Judgment, dealt with in section v, is part of the broader Tiv idea of 'finishing' (*kure*) the *jir*. As we shall see, 'ending' a *jir* properly involves activities not only of the judges but of the principals, and sometimes of other persons too. 'Ending the *jir*' contains acts that go beyond the

[1] Robert W. Millar, 'Procedure, Legal', *Encyclopaedia of the Social Sciences*, Vol. VI, 1933.

session of the court itself, extending into other aspects of life, just as 'calling a *jir*' is an activity that overlaps the *jir* and the social acts preceding it.

These four sets of ideas, each summed up by Tiv in special terms, form a framework for investigating the various acts that occur in the course of a *jir*, and for setting forth the ideational background of what a *jir* should do.

II. CALLING A JIR

The sort of advice which we in the West have come to associate with legal counsel is, in Tivland, usually given by the persons who are going to judge one's case. We have seen already that it is common, during the sessions of Grade-D courts, for litigants to approach the *mbatarev* for advice. Many more people approach the *mbatarev* singly at their compounds or at market. Chenge attended Tsar market regularly. There was a special shelter which was considered his: he sat there, usually with a couple of wives and some men of his small lineage. He was often joined by Huwa and a few of his people, less often by Ikpokpo, and seldom by Gbegba. When Gbegba attended market, he usually set up his chair and his circle of followers on the opposite side of the market place, the side nearest his home, and made what amounted to a formal 'call' at Chenge's shelter. It is at such times that the chiefs and *mbatarev* prefer to be approached by those needing advice about disputes. Persons thus approaching them usually brought a gift of a few kola nuts or a large calabash of millet beer or, particularly to Chenge who was known to prefer it, a gourd of palm-wine. Then, over a drink (which was always shared by all the important people present), the case was discussed. Everyone present partook of the discussion as well as of the wine. Many potential court cases were settled in these discussions. Others, however, could not be settled, and people were then told to bring formal complaints before the *jir*.

Mbatarev settle many disputes in the course of being informed of situations by their people. An *ortaregh* may—in fact, should— know perfectly well that there is bad blood or a land dispute between two persons of his *tar*. However, unless one of them or a third person 'tells' him of this situation before witnesses, he does not consider himself aware of it. This idea resembles judicial ignorance, though it applies only before disputes are brought before the *jir*. Tiv consider silly any suggestion that a judge should not utilize all his knowledge, however acquired, in the actual hearing of a case.

People often rush to the compounds of elders during the course of their disputes, rather than wait for a *jir*, in order to have them settled. If an *ortaregh* is nearby, he is very commonly chosen as the arbitrator. One of the complaints Tiv make about the Grade-D courts is that they are too slow.

INSTANCE NO. 11. *Chenge interrupts a meeting to settle a marriage dispute*

One morning in September 1952, Chenge and Huwa were both attending a meeting at Uta's. Uta's daughter, a girl of Ikakwer (Chenge's lineage), had married a youth of MbaYar (Huwa's lineage). It is Tiv custom, seldom observed, that a man gives his wife's guardian a pig to be butchered and shared out among the girl's lineage. On this occasion, the custom was being observed. Uta's son-in-law had brought and offered a small shoat as his payment, and had invited Huwa, his *ortaregh*, to accompany him. Uta called all the important elders of his lineage (MbaGôr) so that they could examine the pig to see if it would do. It was declared too small, and the son-in-law was instructed to find another and larger one. Uta fed the assembly and gave them a small pot of beer.

During the two hours spent at Uta's, several interruptions were caused by people bringing disputes. The longest was made by two very excited men and a woman who burst into Uta's compound, having discovered that Chenge and Huwa were there. The bickering about the pig was interrupted while all the elders present heard the dispute. It concerned the woman, who had gone to a husband in MbaKaange. That husband had never paid bridewealth, so her guardian had recalled her and sent her to a husband in another lineage area, who did pay bridewealth. She bore this second husband a daughter; a few months later, he sickened and everyone expected his death. Whereupon the woman left his compound and returned to her first 'husband' in Mba-Kaange. The men who burst in upon the meeting were the second husband and the guardian. The husband declared that he didn't want his wife to return because she had deserted him when she thought he was dying. He merely wanted his daughter and the remainder of his bridewealth. The guardian added that he had no money with which to repay, especially as the MbaKaange man refused to pay any bridewealth at all. The assembled elders of MbaGôr all participated in the arbitration. In fact, Fiyase, the oldest man present, actually did most of it.

A lecture of high moral tone was delivered to the woman, the guardian was told to repay the bridewealth within three months, and the husband agreed to wait that time. The elders then again turned their attention to the matter of the pig that was being paid as part of the bridewealth for one of their 'daughters'.

That same afternoon, Chenge spent about three hours supervising the building of a long shelter in which field medical teams were going to carry out physical examinations and treatment of MbaDuku people as part of a yaws and anaemia campaign. During this time, he was approached by five different sets of people for advice and help in disputes. An *ortaregh*'s work is never done.

When Tiv search out their *mbatarev* or other respected elders in this way and ask for advice and arbitration, they are said to be 'calling a *jir*'. Land cases, which are plentiful, especially in the crowded southern areas, are usually decided by the *mbatarev*, but are seldom brought before the court. The *mbatarev* of Mba-Duku spent many days in the late wet and early dry seasons walking from field to field, arbitrating land disputes. During these long walks, in which there are frequent stops for rest, they are often approached by people who have other kinds of disputes to be settled as well. One such example occurred in November 1949:

INSTANCE NO. 12. Mbatarev, *while on another mission, are asked for advice*

The *mbatarev* of MbaDuku were settling land disputes between Ikakwer and MbaYar.[1] On the path they met a party going to Chenge's in search of advice. A girl and her father and her guardian were upset because they had found some medicines in the possession of the girl's husband, which they said were designed to keep her from straying while he went off to attend to his job as a road labourer. The husband said that the medicine was not made for that purpose, but was a charm which he had bought from an Ukan man. Such medicines are considered dangerous, and it was decided that a formal case should be called and that the husband should get the Ukan man to come to MbaDuku for the court session to act as his witness.

To call a *jir* has, however, a more restricted meaning in the context of Native Authority courts. There it means the payment of a two-shilling fee termed *ikojir* (though, if repaid to the 'plaintiff'

[1] One land dispute heard on this day is reported in *Tiv Farm and Settlement*, p. 56.

at the end of the hearing, it is termed *jingajir*). After a fee has been paid, the dispute is heard at the first subsequent meeting of the court at which all the principals and witnesses can be collected together. Once all are present, the precedence of one's *jir* depends, as we have seen, on one's ability to outshout (*hule*) other litigants.

Occasionally the *mbatarev* refuse to hear a particular dispute, saying it is not their affair, and adding that the *jir* must be called before some other court. Although there are many exceptions, Tiv believe that a *jir* is best called in the *tar* of the defendant. The obvious exception is found in criminal cases, especially those involving stealing, which are usually called in the area where the crime is said to have been committed: thieves are usually tried in the *tar* in which they have stolen.

It sometimes happens that the *mbatarev* of one *tar* send a messenger to those of another, asking that litigants be sent to them for participation in a *jir*. The request may or may not be honoured.

JIR NO. 13. *Refusing to send litigants to another* jir
[From a text by one of my scribes]

'The *mbatarev* Mbara sent to the *mbatarev* M baDuku saying that an MbaDuku man had married (*er*) the wife of a m an in their country, and requested that the *mbatarev* MbaDuku send the youngster and his wife to them with the policeman who brought the letter. Chief Chenge sent for all the people, and when they came, he asked the youngster, "Where did you marry this woman?" The youngster said it was in Mbara. Chenge asked, "Whose woman did you marry?" The youngster said it was his father-in-law who gave him the wife. Chenge then turned to the policeman. "Is one of those men who came with you the father-in-law of this child of mine?" and the policeman said that the girl's father had indeed come. Chenge asked the father-in-law, "Did you give this youngster of ours a wife?" The father-in-law agreed that he had done so, and said that he would return the money to the other husband in Mbara. Chenge had a note written to the *mbatarev* Mbara saying that he and the other *mbatarev* of MbaDuku would not give up the woman, because she had been properly married from the home of her father, who had undertaken to straighten out the case in Mbara.'

I have recorded several instances of this sort, as well as others in which persons calling *jir* were told to do so in the *tar* of the person they were calling. Women, particularly, seem to prefer to call their *jir* before their own *mbatarev* rather than before those of their husbands' lineages. Thus many of them call *jir* against their guardians in disputes which are actually with their husbands —the husbands are sent for and usually come.

Tiv say that a *jir* which is transferred from one *tar* to another may never be settled; they say also that it is unwise to have more than one Grade-D court involved in one's disputes, for each may try to discredit the other in the eyes of the Administration. If one gets involved in such a situation it is best to withdraw one's *jir* and have it arbitrated unofficially.

That part of calling a *jir* which most resembles the European idea of 'pleading' is the actual presentation of one's complaint or defence before the assembled *mbatarev*. If, as occasionally happens, a man is not allowed to finish his story, he says that 'the *mbatarev* cut off (*kighir*) my *jir*'. It is considered bad form for the *mbatarev* to 'cut off' a 'man who calls', unless he is particularly long-winded and inapposite. They know he will say later that he was 'cut off arbitrarily (*sa apela*)'. No *jir* wants to get a reputation for acting arbitrarily.

When the 'man who calls' and his 'partner' have both finished their pleas, the '*jir yilan*' is completed. That is to say, the initiative passes from the principals to the judges and the witnesses, whose activities form the subject matter of the next two sections.

Professor Gluckman has used the notion of 'the reasonable man' liberally in his analysis of Lozi law.[1] The Tiv have similar concepts which are useful in analysis.

A man who calls a *jir* well, presenting his story in a concise and orderly manner, is said to be a 'man who knows things' (*or u fan kwagh*). This phrase, indeed, is used of any person who is well versed in Tiv custom and belief, and who governs his external life according to the standards of propriety compatible with such custom and belief. A man who cannot tell a connected story, or who constantly makes errors in calling and pleading his cases, is a 'man who doesn't know things' (*or u fan kwagh ga*) or even— if he is particularly inept—a *bumenor*. This latter word comes from the verb *bume* (not to be confused with *bum*, to swear); 'to be unreasonable' is about as good a translation as any. A person who through ignorance, neglect or wilfulness fails to act in accordance with those customs to which Tiv attach moral value is said to *bume*. The foolish or unreasonable act is itself *ibumegh*.

[1] Max Gluckman, *The Judicial Process among the Barotse*, 1955.

Thus, a man who knows things may beat his wife, but only a *bumenor* will beat his wife until she cannot work: it is a foolish thing (*ibumegh*) to do. A man 'who knows things' may try to sleep with as many girls as possible, but only a *bumenor* commits incest, and incest is the greatest *ibumegh*. A man who knows things may (even though it is wrong) steal from distant lineages, but only a *bumenor* steals close to home.

Tiv like to be considered 'people who know things', and say that such persons have *inja* or 'character', while a *bumenor* has no character at all. This epithet becomes the more diagnostic when we realize that the word *inja*, which I have here translated as 'character', also means 'habit' and 'custom' (see section iv). We might say that *inja* is the opposite of *ibumegh*.

There is a further set of modifying phrases which, however, apply to the reasonableness of acts and not persons. An unreasonable or wrong act can be committed in three different ways: by ignorance (*sa lanegh*), by accident (*sa aikor*), or by wilful going against custom (*sa apela*). One informant added a fourth—to do a thing through 'wrong-headedness' (*sa dang*). A 'man who knows things' may commit faults by ignorance or by accident. But if a man wilfully commits an act which, according to Tiv custom, is wrong, he is either a *bumenor* or a scoundrel (*dang-or*) or both. It is in terms of all these ideas that the 'reasonableness' of a man's actions are judged by Tiv judges and laymen. The 'reasonable man'—he who knows things—is one who follows custom, who has 'character', and does not act wilfully against the norms to which Tiv subscribe.

III. OATHS AND WITNESSES

This section examines Tiv notions of witnesses (*ashieda*), oaths and swearing (*bum*), the testimony of sworn witnesses in a court, and Tiv ideas of truth.

Witnesses

The Tiv word usually translated witness is *shieda*. The word doubtless derives from the Hausa word *shaida* and ultimately from Arabic *shahada* or *shahéd*. It is used with a much more restricted field of meaning by Tiv than by Hausa. Tiv do not use it as a verb, and in fact usually do not use it at all except in connexion with court cases or with marriage payments and other monetary transactions in which each party gets witnesses to the transaction.

The indigenous Tiv expressions for witnessing derive from the verb *pase*, which means 'to explain, relate, tell'—and which also means 'to give or to release'.[1] 'A man who tells' (*or pasen*) is an expression which can be used where we might use the word witness, as a witness in a court trial. But it is also the only word for 'preacher' in mission circles, and it can mean 'orator'.

Three distinct ideas and sets of social relationships must be examined if we are to understand Tiv notions of witnesses and evidence. At least two of these concepts extend beyond the jural context. First, there is the witness to a financial transaction; if the act to which he stood witness ever comes up in a *jir*, he is bound to come and tell what he knows. He is said to be the *shieda* of the man who pays or who receives the money. In marriage, however, where this practice is very common in payments of bridewealth, the *shieda* also takes on other duties and other names. Secondly, there is the sort of witness who has no relationship whatever to either party to the *jir*, but comes into the matter on the initiative of the *mbatarev*. Thirdly, there is the sort of witness which we might call 'witness by private contract'. We shall examine these different sorts of witnesses in that order.

When a man makes a payment of bridewealth to his wife's guardian, he usually does so by handing the money to his witness (his *shieda*) who, in the presence of them all, counts it and hands it to the *shieda* of the guardian, who again counts it and hands it to the guardian himself, who very probably counts it again. It is usually sufficient for one man to act as *shieda* for both husband and guardian.

The witness in such a situation has other duties and there may be other ways of referring to him. He may be, and very often is, the 'secondary guardian', as we have called him, to the wife. He has a moral but no financial interest in the marriage, being only the witness to the financial transaction which occurs in conjunction with it. He is usually called to testify to the correct amounts paid by the husband.

Witnesses in *jir* concerning debt are also usually found to have

[1] The flavour of the word is similar (except that it is not slang) to the American slang 'to give', meaning to tell what one knows.

a prior relationship to the persons whom they represent, because Tiv have witnesses to most financial transactions. Such a relationship is not so close as the relationship between witnesses and principals in marriage. I discovered this custom of witnessing financial matters very early in my field-work. When I paid Chenge for building my compound within his own, he insisted that I have a witness and that he should have one as well, and that the payment should be made in the presence of both together. I asked my cook to act on my behalf, which he did; the chief asked Fiyase, one of the senior elders of MbaGôr, his own minimal segment. In this case, the chief was redistributing the money among those who had contributed work to my huts, and he hoped to avoid accusations of not having distributed it all. Although it was never suggested that he did not distribute all that was presented before witnesses, I learned much later that there had been considerable speculation about the amount I had given him when there were no witnesses present. Needless to say, there had been no extra payment.

Once the relationship between a man and his witness has been established, it is incumbent upon the witness to go before a court, if he is called, and state whatever he 'knows' about the transactions to which he was witness. Witnesses who go before a Grade-D court are usually required to take an oath, and the judges usually accept their word, once they have been sworn, as correct. It is also usual, I think, that before a *jir* the principal and the witness agree between themselves on the amount to be sworn by the witness. The principal is never sworn, and is therefore not pledged to be 'correct' as the witness is.

JIR NO. 14. *Anongo calls Iyorkyaha and accuses his witness of lying*

Anongo had married Iyorkyaha's ward and, when the marriage broke up, said he had paid £12 bridewealth. When Iyorkyaha said the sum was not correct, the *mbatarev* called for witnesses. Anongo's witness was sworn on the decorative tongs (*gbegba*), having been instructed how to swear by one of the *mbatarev*. His oath ran: 'This is a fetish. If I swear wrongly (*sa apela*), the fetish will seize me.' He then stated that the bridewealth amounted to £7 and one hen.

Anongo immediately challenged this statement and accused his witness of lying. The witness replied that if there was more than £7 in this case, it did not go through his hands; he was swearing, not to the whole amount, but to the amount which he had himself handled, and he repeated several times, 'I will say nothing save what I know.'

The judges told the guardian to repay £7 and a hen to Anongo. Anongo insisted that the correct sum was £12, that the witness had lied, and that therefore he did not intend to surrender his 'paper' to have a lie written on it.

The *mbatarev* threatened to appeal to Grade-C court. Anongo shouted that he intended to call a *jir* against his witness for lying, but a record was made of his debt of £7.

The relationship which exists between a man and his witness, more particularly when that witness is also the person with whom the guardian lodged (*sughul*) his ward, is precise and definite and can be stated by Tiv in terms of rights and duties. Breach of these duties is itself basis for action before the *jir*.

JIR NO. 15. *Umem (husband) calls Hindan (his 'witness')*
Failure of witness to comply with norms of his role

Several years ago Umem married and Hindan acted as his witness. After a year or two the wife left Umem. Hindan collected the money for return of bridewealth from the guardian, but did not hand it all to Umem. He kept for himself ('ate') £1. 5s. After several years of fruitless efforts to collect it, Umem called a *jir* in the court against Hindan. When the *mbatarev* asked Hindan about it, he denied that he had ever collected any money which he had not handed immediately to Umem. Whereupon the *mbatarev* called for witnesses. Umem replied that there were no witnesses—this man had been his witness, and one does not have witnesses of witnesses. The wife's guardian was dead and there were no witnesses. But, he added, 'I will be my own witness.'

Chenge told him that would not be necessary just yet, and turned again to Hindan. 'Hindan must be his own witness. He must swear on *swem* and tell us the entire matter of the payments in this marriage.' Hindan refused to swear on *swem*, and insisted that this would make the affair too important. Within a moment it became apparent to all that he was lying—his reluctance, indeed his fear, of swearing could have no other interpretation. The court became noisier and noisier as bystanders began shouting that it looked as if Hindan were lying. Finally, one of the judges yelled for silence and, eventually getting it, declared, 'If you do not swear on *swem*, this *jir* will catch you.' Hindan insisted that this was not the way good judges would handle the matter and again tried to tell them that, since he was Umem's witness in this transaction, he would not have cheated him, thus swearing was unnecessary. Without letting him finish the judges told him that he had until the next day to bring £1. 5s. to give to Umem, else they would put him in gaol.

The significant points on the swearing of the principals to a *jir* will be considered below. Here we are interested in the relationship between a man and his witness: the relationship with the secondary guardian (*orsughul*) should be such as to make further witnesses unnecessary. Therefore when one of the persons to the relationship defaults, the defaulter can be sued, not merely for the matter of the debt (which would, normally, require witnesses), but for default of his obligations in the relationship (which by its nature does not require witnesses).

In marked contrast is the second type of witness. This witness is in no way associated with either of the principals, and as a result is often not sworn.

JIR NO. 16. *A woman gives impartial evidence in a dispute about a bicycle*

A Tiv youngster was hiring out, at market, a bicycle which belonged to a Bamenda, but which had been given him for this purpose. One of the persons hiring it paid a penny and, instead of riding it round the market-place a few times as the penny entitled him to do, went away with it. When the youngster looked for the bicycle, he could not find it. Thereupon he went to the market officials, who turned the matter over to the *mbatarev.*

At the time the *jir* was heard the bicycle had not yet been returned, but a man had been arrested because the youngster identified him as the culprit. This man steadfastly refused to admit that he had ever seen the youngster before, or that he had ridden a bicycle at all on that particular day. Whereupon the chief and the other *mbatarev* asked the assembled audience if they had seen the man on a bicycle. A young man living near the market said that he had seen the man ride a bicycle along the path past his compound, and that the man had stopped for a few moments and talked with the wife of his 'brother', who lived in the same compound as himself. The *mbatarev* thereupon asked him to bring his brother's wife to give evidence.

The woman came next day. She sat on the ground with the accused, and was asked if she had ever seen him. She said that she had indeed, for this was the man who had ridden past her cassava patch on a bicycle and asked directions from her. Someone in the audience shouted a suggestion that she should be made to swear. It was taken up by others. When the *mbatarev* restored quiet, the woman said she did not want to swear, because she feared *swem* and because she had no motive for lying. It was none of her business—she knew neither the man's name nor his lineage; she did not know either the Tiv youngster or the Bamenda man who was owner of the bicycle. The *mbatarev* considered an oath unnecessary. They listened to her evidence, thanked her and she left.

Here, unlike the cases in which the witness has a manifold relationship with one or other of the principals, an oath was not required. Furthermore, this woman came reluctantly into a matter not her affair. It is a serious breach of manners in Tivland to interfere in the business of anyone with whom you are not acquainted. The *jir* often has trouble in getting witnesses of this sort, even though the number of people who have seen an act is legion.

The *mbatarev* occasionally use 'expert witnesses', especially when it is necessary to assess the amount of damage done to fields by livestock. So far as I am aware, such witnesses are always selected either because they have no obligations to either party to the dispute, or because they are officials.

There is one other sort of witness—principal relationship: that in which the witness makes a sort of 'contract' with the principal.[1] Here is a text written by one of my two clerks when I asked simply for a text on 'witnesses':

'If something of yours disappears and another man sees it, he will say "Come, give me some money and I'll tell you who took it." So, if you have any money, you give it to him, and he will say, "It was so-and-so who took it." If, for example, I had lost something and was looking for it, and it was Gbatoho[2] who took it, and Shima saw Gbatoho with the thing, Shima would come to me and say, "Iyorkôsu, give me money, and I shall tell you who stole your goat." I asked Shima, "How much must I give you?" and Shima would say, "Give me one pound." So, when I have taken the pound and given it to Shima[3] he will say, "Iyorkôsu, it was Gbatoho who stole your goat." So I go to make Gbatoho give me my goat, and when I get there Gbatoho will say that he caught no goat of mine. So I'll go call a *jir* against Gbatoho with the *mbatarev* of his country in order to recover my goat. The *mbatarev* will ask Gbatoho, "Did you catch a goat of Iyorkôsu?" Gbatoho will deny that he did anything of the sort, and the *mbatarev* will tell him to bring witnesses.

'Hereupon, I call Shima, who will come into the court circle, and the *mbatarev* will tell Shima to make the ritual movements and swear

---

[1] See Cases No. 54 and No. 59 for examples.

[2] The original names were members of my household. When Iyorkôsu invented stories he always set them amongst ourselves, carefully rotating the wrongdoer.

[3] Needless to say, had such a bargain been arrived at, it would have taken hours of dickering.

on *swem*, then act as witness in the matter of Iyorkôsu's goat, which he says Gbatoho stole. Shima will make the ritual movements to the effect that if he did not see Gbatoho steal Iyorkôsu's goat, *swem* will afflict him. After finishing the ritual movements, Shima will take the *swem* pot and touch it to his feet, his knees, his belly, and his head. Then he will place it again on the ground. Thereupon he will indicate to the *mbatarev* how he had seen Gbatoho with my goat. When the *mbatarev* have heard him out, they will begin to investigate (*tôv*) the *jir*. Then, when the *jir* catches Gbatoho, they will tell me to put a value on my goat, and I will say that Gbatoho must give me £2. I will also say that I gave my witness £1 to tell me and that Gbatoho must pay that. The *mbatarev* will then ask Shima, "How much did Iyorkôsu give you to act as his witness?" Shima will reply, "He gave me one pound." The *mbatarev* will tell Gbatoho that he must also pay this pound. This is the way the matter of giving witnesses money is done.'

The meaning of this text is not that Tiv sell themselves as witnesses, but rather that they seek to establish a relationship with the man to whom their testimony is advantageous so that they will not be charged with interfering in affairs not their own. A defendant can understand a man's giving evidence against him if he is a kinsman or in some other way related to the plaintiff. He can also understand it if he has been paid. But if he does so without any relationship and without *quid pro quo* (itself a relationship, of course) he is then guilty of an act of aggression.[1] Unless the witness is forced by the necessities of a relationship, such as being secondary marriage guardian or being in receipt of money (or unless he is forced by the *mbatarev* to act as witness, as happened with the woman who saw the man on the stolen bicycle) Tiv say that giving evidence is 'spoiling the *tar*'.

This text also indicates something else: Iyorkôsu, who wrote it, never once considered that Gbatoho, whom he supposed in his example to have stolen the goat, would have admitted doing so, unless he could construe the action as a retribution for some wrong done to him. Indeed, his supposition was right. The principals of a *jir* are expected to 'lie' about the situations under consideration, and certainly to tell only that portion of the story which does most credit to themselves and most discredit to their adversaries. We shall examine these ideas below when we investigate Tiv notions of truth, and the relationship between truth and evidence. Here it is sufficient to say that witnesses are usually

[1] See discussion of *iwuhe* below, pp. 140 ff.

expected to tell what we would consider to be the 'truth' of the matter—that is, the more or less verifiable facts of an event. Tiv swear witnesses to tell the truth; they do not—save in exceptional circumstances like Umem's *jir* against Hindan (No. 15)—swear the principals to any litigation, for this would take the matter out of the hands of human judges.

Oaths

Tiv do not have, so far as I am aware, a noun which means 'oath'. They express this notion with the verb *bum* which means 'to swear'. The word does indeed form two verbal nouns, but both refer to the act of swearing rather than to the oath itself. The verb 'to swear' can be either transitive or intransitive. When it takes an object, this object is the name of the fetish on which the oath is taken.

I shall first describe the act of swearing on *swem*, and then mention briefly some of the other fetishes used for purposes of oath-taking.

Swem is the most important of the forces which Tiv see manifest in the emblems and fetishes of their religion. Although *swem* may exist independently of any emblems, if it be represented by emblems the most common is a small cooking pot filled with ashes, camwood and two sorts of leaves.[1] Once made up, or 'dressed' (*wuha*), this pot is kept by the *swem*-holder. Today most government chiefs are *swem*-holders; if they are not, they get a *swem* from someone who is. It is brought out from his reception hut by the chief for each session of the court. He places it in the middle of the court circle. Although litigants are careful not to touch it, they otherwise ignore it except when witnesses are sworn.

The act of swearing consists of picking up the pot (in the case of women, touching it may suffice) and, usually under instruction from one of the *mbatarev*, repeating some such statement as: 'This is *swem*; if I swear falsely (*sa apela*), *swem* will catch me.' The clearest and most precise oath on *swem* recorded in my notes runs: 'This is *swem*, is it not? Whether anyone else has spoken indiscriminately I do not know. But whatever I indicate is precise. Whatever I know, I shall indicate straight.'[2]

---

[1] *Ayande* (Marantochloa flexuosa) and *ikula i nomsu*.

[2] *Ka swem ne ga. Or gen ôr wuewue m fa ga, kpa kwagh u m tese la, ka kwagh vough. Kwagh u m fe la, m tese vough.*

E

The pot is then made to touch the feet, the belly, and the head. Sometimes the knees are included. It is then replaced on the ground and the *jir* goes on. It is said that if the witness has taken such an oath and then testifies falsely, his feet and belly will swell, his head will ache, and he will die. Most Tiv refuse to assign a time limit within which *swem* must work but, when pressed, say that it usually works within three or four months. In the most specific instance I have, it required several years:

INSTANCE NO. 17. *Gbe's first wife's guardian swore falsely on* swem

Gbe married a woman from Mbara and paid an initial sum of £4 bridewealth; he also made gifts to her father, mother, guardian, and elders. After she had lived with him for a few months, she left him and returned to her natal home. Gbe went to Mbara to fetch her back but, when he arrived, he found that she had 'gone to another husband', so he asked for his bridewealth to be returned. The woman's guardian said he had received no bridewealth. Thereupon Gbe went to the *mbatarev* of Mbara and called a *jir* against the guardian for the return of the bridewealth. His own witness, however, had left Tivland to get work, and the guardian's witness took a false oath, swearing on *swem*. After taking the oath, he said that Gbe had paid no bridewealth at all, but only made miscellaneous gifts to the woman's kinsmen, and these were deemed not returnable. Several years later, during the time I was living in the same compound as Gbe, a messenger arrived from Mbara to tell him that the witness was very ill, that he had admitted taking a false oath on *swem* during the course of this *jir*, and that, having made the admission, *swem* was repaired for him.[1] Gbe could, if he liked, reopen the case and would be given his £4 bridewealth. He set off within a few days to do so. He got his money without going before the *jir*.

Swem is, in Radcliffe-Brown's classification, a supernatural sanction. Tiv believe that it works automatically on the breach of specific norms.

There are also specific jural penalties for lying. The clearest case in my records of a secular penalty being imposed to reinforce the supernatural penalty is found in a *jir* similar to *Jir* No. 5 already examined (p. 22), in which the amount of bridewealth to be repaid was in dispute:

[1] To repair is to counteract by ritual. I was the only one of those who heard this story interested in the subsequent recovery or death of the perjurer. I was never able to discover his fate, and had no chance to inquire in Mbara.

JIR NO. 18. *Asev (husband's father) calls Agba (guardian)*
Witness takes a false oath in a bridewealth dispute

When Asev's son's wife left him, there was a dispute with her guardian, Agba, about the amount of bridewealth which had been paid and how much was returnable. The husband, when asked by the *mbatarev*, stated that £12 was returnable. However, his father interrupted and said that the correct amount was £18, adding that his son had not been aware of all the payments which had been made (a reasonable situation, for a man's first wife should always be provided by his father). The wife's guardian said that he had received only £5. 18s. of returnable bridewealth. The judges asked, 'Where did you lodge this woman?' They replied that the secondary guardian was a man named Batur. The *mbatarev* adjourned the hearing until Batur could be fetched.

When he came, the *mbatarev* began to hear his evidence before requiring him to take an oath on *swem*. It very soon became evident that his story was long and involved, and they asked him to take the oath. He did so without hesitation. Then one of the judges asked him, 'The day that Asev gave Agba the money, how much did he give him?' Batur replied, £17. The *mbatarev* asked for an itemization of the amounts which made up the £17. As Batur struggled to make his amounts total £17, murmurs began to be heard that he was obviously lying. The *mbatarev* took things in hand; Chenge announced that he knew Batur was lying, and that 'Batur has spoiled our *swem!*' He said it seemed to him that £12, the amount originally stated by the husband, was probably correct, as it fell approximately half-way between the two claims. The other judges concurred that the guardian should return £12 to the husband's father, and the *jir* be settled. The *jir* was again adjourned. Three days later the guardian arrived with a substantial part of the payment. After the judges themselves had seen £7 handed over, and a note had been made to that effect in the records of the court clerk, they turned to the matter of Batur's false evidence.

Chenge asked him sternly, 'Batur, why have you sworn on our *swem* falsely (*sa apela*)—why have you spoiled our *swem* in this way?'

Batur answered that he had not done so, and that his original testimony of £17 was correct. He then intimated that the judges had made a forced (*sa apela*) decision.

Chenge, becoming heated, immediately said that he should be fined £2 because 'he has greatly spoiled our *swem*, and now he is trying to spoil our *jir*'.

Batur still denied that he had taken a false oath. All the *mbatarev*, in different ways, advised him to admit his wrong and have *swem* repaired, for if he did not, his feet and belly would swell up and he would die. Batur still refused to agree that he had sworn falsely. Chenge, at the end of his patience, told him bluntly, 'Batur, if *swem* doesn't pay attention and seize you for this, I shall seize you myself! *Swem* may catch you tomorrow—I do not know, for that is not my affair. But I shall catch you today for spoiling our *jir*. That *is* my affair. Do you agree to the £2 fine or must we put you in gaol?'

Batur agreed to pay the fine, and was handed over to a policeman until the £2 was brought by his kinsmen.

This case happened only a few months before I left this part of Tivland, and I do not know whether Batur was ever 'caught' by *swem*, or whether he admitted that he had been lying and had *swem* 'repaired' for him.

It is sometimes very difficult for the judges to make the witness swear an oath, but it is usually assumed that if he tries too hard to avoid taking an oath, he intends to lie. A good example of stubbornness on both sides is to be found in:

JIR NO. 19. *Nguhar (husband) calls Tarkighir (adulterer)*
A woman tries to bear false witness

Tarkighir, accused of committing adultery with the wife of Nguhar and giving her 6*d*. for the privilege, denied having done so, and told a story that she had sent him for another man to commit adultery with her. The wife denied that either Tarkighir or any other man had had intercourse with her, or that she had sent Tarkighir for anyone. However, one of her 'co-wives' (the wife of some member of her husband's compound) had been in Tarkighir's compound with her at the time when the adultery was alleged to have occurred. The *mbatarev* sent for this co-wife, whose name was Girgi, to act as witness in the *jir*.

Girgi was a small, compact, stubborn woman who began to talk the moment she sat down before the *mbatarev* in the court circle. She talked very rapidly but had barely got beyond the point of saying that she and her co-wife were hoeing farms and Tarkighir came by, when Chenge stopped her and told her she must swear on *swem*. Scarcely pausing for breath, she told him she would tell him the truth without swearing on *swem*, and that she shouldn't swear because she was a woman. She launched back into her story; Chenge again interrupted and instructed her to take the *swem* pot in her hands and make the ritual motions of swearing. She said that she didn't want to swear— that *swem* was a thing of men, and that women shouldn't touch it. When Chenge assured her that women often swore on *swem*, she told him she was pregnant (almost surely a lie). He told her that this had nothing whatever to do with the matter. She again said that she was telling the truth, so there was no point in swearing. For over ten minutes,

Chenge and the other *mbatarev* cajoled, threatened, bullied, teased, before she finally agreed to swear. She picked up the pot, made the ritual gestures quickly, set it down and said:

'My co-wife, Ierun, and I often go to Tarkighir's compound. It is near our farms, and we go there to rest. We sit in the reception hut and talk. On this day, Tarkighir asked Ierun to go into his hut with him. I was shocked and surprised that Ierun did so.' She looked about her and back at the ground, as if she were ashamed of what she was saying. 'I sat in the reception hut. Tarkighir was in his sleeping hut with Ierun. After they had been there a long time, I became uneasy and went and rapped on the door.'

Chenge interrupted to ask, 'Was the door shut?'

With a look that indicated that she disliked him greatly both for having made her swear (and thus to tell the truth) and for asking this particular question, she replied, 'Yes, the door had been pushed to. I rapped on the door and told my co-wife to come out and that we should go. Ierun came out, and we went to our farms. That is all I know.'

Chenge and the *mbatarev* now agreed that she had probably told the truth, that this was indeed all she knew about it and that she could go. Obviously extremely angry, she left the court circle and walked immediately out of the compound.

Here was a woman who evidently had every intention of giving false evidence in support of her co-wife, but was not prepared to do so on oath. She was not allowed to testify without swearing, for it was almost certain that any woman in her position would lie in order to preserve the relationship between herself and her co-wife, as well as that between her co-wife and their husband. When I discussed this case with Chenge on the following evening, he said that Girgi had to be made to take the oath, for had she told what she did otherwise than under oath, she would have been 'spoiling the compound' (*vihi ya*).

All the cases thus far cited involved swearing on *swem*, and indeed most oaths taken in Native Authority courts during the time of my field-work were on *swem*. However, cases from the 1930's recorded in the administrative files show that most Tiv were then sworn on 'stone and steel'. The Tiv fire-making device, consisting of a piece of flint and a small piece of bent iron, is associated (as is lightning) with the *akombo iwa*, which is, again, associated with blacksmiths. The *akombo iwa* is one of the most complex elements in Tiv religion, and its transgression includes such appalling fates as impotence, constant backache, and other ailments, though it can seldom cause death. When it does, it is death by lightning. The *akombo iwa* is, it seems to me, the fetish most closely related to God, *Aondo*; the prehistoric celt, called God's axe, is its symbol.

I have never seen Tiv sworn on 'stone and steel', but one does often see them sworn on the *akombo iwa*. The stone and steel as the emblems of the *iwa* have been replaced by either the stone celt or a pair of tongs. Many elders wear as an ornament a sort of decorative tongs with beads. These tongs, resembling black-smith's tongs, are considered an adequate representation of the *akombo iwa* for the administration of oaths. They are not often used when *swem* is present, but the MbaDuku *mbatarev* often swore witnesses on tongs when they were away from Chenge's compound and hence away from his *swem* emblems (see *Jir* No. 14).

The only other common fetish emblem used for oaths is the palm-branch, an emblem of the *akombo igbe*, which causes—or, more precisely, *is*—dysentery and other blood symptoms. It is rarely used in court.

It is evident, in discussing oaths with Tiv, that they see all oath-taking in accordance with the same set of ideas as they see ordeals. Taking an oath on the *akombo iwa* or the *akombo igbe* is 'touching' (*bende*) this fetish. If you lie on oath, you have 'pierced' (*pev*) the fetish. Both words are used when one has fallen foul of a fetish—the notion of 'touching' is usually passive, indicating no blame attaching to the victim, while the notion of 'piercing' usually does assume such blame, more or less strongly, and hence might be translated as 'transgression' of an *akombo*.

The relationship—indeed, the identity—of oaths and ordeals is, however, best seen when considering *swem*. In explaining the nature of oaths on *swem*, Tiv draw the investigator's attention to what we would call, in English, the ordeal by sasswood. They say, in effect, that the principle of *swem* and the principle of sasswood are the same, but that sasswood works very much more quickly. Sasswood is occasionally today administered to chickens, in a manner reminiscent of, but very different from, that described by Professor Evans-Pritchard for the Azande.[1] That oracle is in the hands of men who also perform divination by other means. Formerly sasswood is said to have been administered (under the direction of moots and of age-sets) to two disputants in cases of

---

[1] E. E. Evans-Pritchard, *Witchcraft, Oracles and Magic among the Azande.* Oxford, 1937.

witchcraft if the accuser demanded it. In demanding it, however, he was aware that he must drink the sasswood first. Sasswood is a strychnine poison and if a man died from drinking it his guilt was proved and his punishment accomplished. If he vomited it and recovered, his innocence was established.

I have on several occasions been told by elders, particularly in Iharev but not only there, that although *swem* and sasswood work in the same way, *swem* is so much slower and less sure that there has been no effective means of controlling witches since the sasswood ordeal was outlawed. I have discovered only one case in which sasswood was administered to human beings in recent years. This was an instance some time in the 1940's when a man, who thought himself wrongly judged by the appeal court (Grade C) of Jecira lineage in Vande Ikya, rushed into the court circle and drank off a large calabash of sasswood, which he had prepared himself. He immediately vomited it, thereby proving his innocence to himself and his kinsmen and neighbours. The Assistant District Officer present sentenced him to six months for attempted suicide.

Oaths are in the nature of minor ordeals. Their purpose is not, however, to judge guilt or innocence but only to act as penalty if norms associated with that oath are breached. Oaths are administered to witnesses because the witnesses' only concern in the dispute is with what we would call the truth.

Oaths are not, however, administered to the principal litigants. The oath-ordeal would judge principals not merely on the possible breach of norm of truth-telling, but also on the breach of norm before the *jir*. Were an oath of this sort to be administered to the principals of the case, the purpose of the *jir* would no longer exist. The dispute would be removed from the social to the supernatural plane, and the penalty would be supernatural instead of one administered and controlled by human beings.

Truth

We must, finally, consider just what it is for which Tiv *mbatarev* are searching when they call or admit witnesses, and what criteria they use for truth. It is notable that in Western judicial systems the 'truth' means the verifiable 'facts' of what took place. Western jurists have a single standard of 'truth'—verifiability—and they have provided themselves with an elaborate mechanism for determining it. They demand the same standards of 'truth' from all persons who appear before a court, be they witnesses, expert witnesses, or principal litigants. They have created complex systems of procedure which are known as 'rules of evidence' in order to elicit and judge this verifiable 'truth' in the course of court action.

As one discusses witnesses and what we should call 'evidence' with Tiv, one comes to realize that they do not have a single criterion for truth. They do not require the same standards of 'truth' from principals in a *jir* as they do from witnesses. The common word usually translated 'lies' (*yie*) has, actually, two antonyms in Tiv instead of the single one which the English word 'lie' or 'falsehood' has. When one begins to use the word, and more particularly when it is used to one, the meaning becomes very uncertain. The earliest entry in my notebooks about this word occurs some three months after my arrival in Tivland. I had learnt the word *yie* in connexion with land cases. On this day, however, I noted that, after a short talk with a stranger, I had given the standard parting phrase 'Go well' (*dza dedo*), and he had replied 'That is no *yie*.' I noted that I must have misunderstood him. The next entry, a few days later, recalls an incident in which people asked me for tobacco—I usually carried small amounts to give away. I replied that it was finished, but that I would have some next time I came to their compound. They were pleased and answered, 'That's no *yie*.' It began to be evident that *yie* didn't mean merely 'lies' extended to 'broken promises', though it does mean both.

Again a few days later, I recorded that on the way to market I stopped at the compound of an elder to rest. In typical Tiv fashion, he asked me where I was going. I told him. He replied, 'That's no *yie*', obviously meaning that it was a good thing for me to be going to market. I began to understand this word *yie*. A few months later, after the first Tiv–Udam war, I was again asked one day where I was going. I replied that I was cycling to Obodu to deliver to the District Officer there a message which I had received from officials in Tivland. When I had finished the explanation—I knew the inquirer well—he answered, 'That's no *yie*', and it meant 'What you are doing will bring no harm to anyone, and is not a thing to be disapproved of.'

Yie can be the object of two verbs: *er*, which means 'to do or to make', and *kaa* which means 'to tell or to say'. Many Tiv say that there is no difference between doing *yie* and telling *yie*, but others have carefully set forth the difference for me. To 'tell' a *yie* is to say something or make a remark which disturbs the even flow of social relationships—it makes no difference whether the remark is 'true' or 'false', in the sense that we use these words in English, *unless* it be to someone's detriment, in which case it is judged worse to tell a false *yie* than a true one. On the other hand, 'doing *yie*' is acting in bad taste, usually to the detriment of someone. If a man tells his wife a bit of scandal in strict confidence and she repeats it, she is 'doing *yie*', even though the statement may be true, as we think of the word 'true'. To 'tell *yie*' indicates that the *yie* is in the thing told. To 'do *yie*' is to indicate that the *yie* is in the act of telling.

In *Jir* No. 19 above, the *mbatarev* had to make Girgi take an oath before she gave evidence concerning the adultery of her co-wife. Had they not done so, she would have 'told *yie*', that is, given the *mbatarev* false information about the actions and movements of her co-wife. Had she told what we would consider the truth about her co-wife's actions, thereby creating difficulties for her co-wife, she would have been 'doing *yie*'. Under oath, Girgi did not either tell *yie* or do *yie*: but it was the oath which saved her from the necessity of one or the other.

In my effort to learn the word *yie* and its correct use, I recorded one statement which amused me at the time: 'A *yie* is not a thing of truth' (*mimi*). This statement does not mean merely 'A lie is not the truth', which is what dictionary definitions would give, but rather 'To do a *yie* is not right.' The difficulty is now in the word *mimi*, one of the two antonyms of *yie*. *Mimi* means 'right'; it contains some of the same ambiguity as the English word 'right', in that it means both the morally good thing and the socially correct thing, a distinction which is not easy to make in the Tiv language. What it does not necessarily imply, though it may do so, is the factually correct thing. If this aspect of 'right' is to be emphasized, the correct word is *vough*, which means 'straight or precise'. In hut-building a door placed in just the right spot is *vough*. In farm mounding, a truly straight row is *vough*. In recounting a story or an event, to give the precise facts is to 'speak *vough*'.

In considering the evidence presented to the *jir*, one must always keep in mind the similarities and distinctions between the two words *mimi* and *vough*. We must also realize that each speaker also weights these words from his own point of view. Therefore, an accuser in a Tiv court action may 'speak *mimi*', but this does not mean that we can, translating, say that he is telling the truth. He is, rather, telling that version of the story which does least damage to social relationships from his own point of view. He might, at a later date, even admit that he did not 'speak *vough*'. The accused in his turn will 'speak *mimi*', but *mimi* is not the same thing from his point of view as it is from that of the accuser. Therefore, the two stories are both *mimi* to the teller and *yie* to his opponent. This merely means that, because of the concatenation of social relationships found in any social action, the criteria of *mimi* may differ according to the standpoint of each actor.

Tiv judges do not expect principal litigants to speak *vough*, but only to speak *mimi*. For principals, the two may be opposed.

It is generally conceded, however, that for a witness to speak *vough* is *ipso facto* to speak *mimi*. From the standpoint of the witness, the 'right' thing to do is to smooth over social relationships, and hence to report what actually occurred so that the judges will have a way of knowing what the rights of the matter are. Tiv compare this to divination—a diviner can ask any questions he likes of his clients; if the clients do not do *mimi* by speaking *vough*, the apparatus will be misinformed and hence cannot give a correct (*vough*) answer. However, it seems to me that no Tiv would blame a witness for telling what we should consider to be untruths, if by so doing the criterion of *mimi* were maintained, and the judgment could still be wholeheartedly concurred in by both principals.

There is one other truth-concept current among Tiv which should be investigated here, though it plays a relatively minor role in jural action. This is the matter of acting with one heart (*shima i môm*) and with two hearts (*asema a har*). The phrase, 'with two hearts', is more often descriptive of specific relationships. As one informant put it, in a text I recorded myself:

'If a man likes you with two hearts, he is not truly your friend. He can kill you or give another person money to kill you with medicine. But if a man likes you with one heart, he really likes you. He cannot speak ill of you or gossip about you. And if another man starts to gossip about you with him, he will stick up for you.

'There are also stories of two hearts and those of one heart. A story [the same word means conversation] of two hearts is when somebody does not speak precisely (*vough*). If a man asks you something and you don't want to tell him correctly, he will say, "What is this? I ask you something, but you don't want to tell me with one heart. Why do you tell me things with two hearts?" '

The expression 'with one heart' can also be used as an emphatic, where it means 'wholehearted'. All meat is sweet, say Tiv, but pork is sweet 'with one heart'. A man can be wholeheartedly a bad lot.

'Truth' in Tivland is an elusive matter because smooth social relationships are deemed of higher cultural value than mere precision of fact. We must not judge Tiv litigants or witnesses by our standards. They are not liars, as they are sometimes called: their truth has other referents than has European truth.

IV. INVESTIGATING THE JIR

In the preceding sections we have examined the actions of the principal litigants and of the witnesses during the course of a *jir*. This section concerns the activities of the *mbatarev* as judges. The actions of the judges are directed towards examining or investigating (*tôv*) the *jir*. To 'investigate' a *jir* involves listening, asking questions, discussing with other *mbatarev* and elders, making suggestions for settlement. After the *jir* has been 'investigated' it is 'ended', which will form the subject of the next section.

To 'investigate' or *tôv* a *jir* is to establish both the facts and the interpretation of the facts. *Jir* No. 20 illustrates the judges' methods for eliciting facts. In *Jir* No. 21 the 'facts', as we understand the term, are not in question, but only their correct interpretation is in doubt.

JIR NO. 20. *The judges seek the facts of filiation*

This *jir* began when MbaVelen's husband, an Mbara man, told the *mbatarev* that his wife had been in MbaDuku for a long time and he would like her sent back to him. She and her brother Bukwagh came into the court circle. Bukwagh said that he could not let his sister go until her husband paid him something towards bridewealth, as he had received nothing whatever. The husband replied that he had paid more than £6, though not to Bukwagh. Chenge asked Bukwagh which of his kinsmen had received the money; Bukwagh answered that he knew of

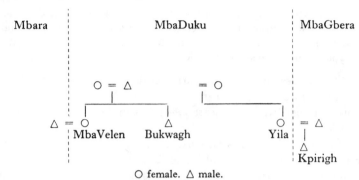

Mbara   MbaDuku   MbaGbera

O female. △ male.

none. The husband then stated that he had paid it not to anyone in MbaDuku, but to an MbaGbera man.

Gbegba immediately asked Bukwagh, 'Is this woman a child of MbaGbera or a child of MbaDuku?' Bukwagh answered that she was a child of MbaDuku, and gave enough of her genealogy and lineage position to satisfy them. Gbegba then turned to the husband and asked, 'If this woman is a child of MbaDuku, why is it that you paid bridewealth to a man of MbaGbera?' The husband replied he had been under the impression that she was an MbaGbera girl.

The *mbatarev* now adjourned the *jir* and sent for Kpirigh, the MbaGbera man. He arrived a few days later with the messenger. The *mbatarev* re-opened the *jir* and asked him how it was that he had accepted bridewealth for an MbaDuku girl. He replied that she was his sister (*wango*). They asked for a more precise description of the relationship, and were told that she was his maternal half-sister. 'In that case,' said Gbegba, 'she may be your "sister" but she is not your agnate, and you cannot accept bridewealth for her.'

Bukwagh intervened and said that MbaVelen was not Kpirigh's sister, she was his own sister, by the same mother and father. Gbegba asked how Kpirigh fitted in. 'Kpirigh is an MbaGbera man. The daughter of our father [i.e. my half-sister] married an MbaGbera man and bore him Kpirigh.' The *mbatarev* asked Kpirigh if his mother was MbaDuku. He replied that she was. 'Who is her father?' 'The same man who was father to Bukwagh.' There was no close kinsman older than Bukwagh. Chenge said that in view of this situation, Kpirigh's mother must be sent for to tell them how MbaVelen got into an *ingôl*-group in MbaGbera.

Again the *jir* was adjourned. A few days later Kpirigh's mother appeared. She said that she was a half-sister, and MbaVelen a full sister, of Bukwagh. When their father died some time after her marriage, Bukwagh and his younger siblings were left almost alone, and were very poor. She had taken MbaVelen, then two years old, and raised her as her own daughter. About two years ago, however, Kpirigh had taken the girl as his ward. She had complained at the time that MbaVelen must return to MbaDuku to be married from there, but Kpirigh and his father had overruled her, and the girl was married to this Mbara man.

MbaVelen had been with the Mbara husband for over a year, and had had a miscarriage and was ill for several months afterwards. He went to a diviner, who told him that there was some trouble over a marriage ward. He thereupon went to Kpirigh in MbaGbera and said that something was wrong. Yila (Kpirigh's mother) then told him that the wife was MbaDuku, and that that was the trouble. When he suggested that she be taken to MbaDuku to have the therapeutic ceremonies performed, Kpirigh and his father again overruled them. They said that they would themselves perform the ceremonies. He brought her to MbaGbera, but instead of carrying out their promise, they gave her to another husband.

The *mbatarev* asked Kpirigh if this was true. He said, yes. Gbegba informed him that he had done a very bad thing—refusing to let his 'sister' return to her agnatic lineage, and accepting two bridewealths for her. Kpirigh said nothing.

Yila continued that soon after MbaVelen had been sent to a second husband, she ran away from him, because she did not feel any better, and went to Bukwagh's compound in MbaDuku where she had been ever since. Asked what she wanted to do, MbaVelen said that she wanted to return to her Mbara husband. The *mbatarev* thereupon told the husband that he must pay bridewealth to Bukwagh, who was obviously the girl's true guardian, and in order to get back what he had paid Kpirigh, he must go to the latter's compound with his witnesses. If Kpirigh refused to pay, he must call a *jir* before the *mbatarev* of MbaGbera, to whom, if necessary, the *mbatarev* of MbaDuku would send a letter stating what had been done. The husband consented to pay a small bridewealth to Bukwagh and to bring sacrificial animals for the rites for repairing the fetishes necessary for his wife's health. He further agreed to pay more when he got a refund from Kpirigh. MbaVelen was left in Chenge's charge (though she was living at home) until her husband had gone to Mbara and returned with the money.

The task before the *mbatarev* in this case was to determine what had actually happened—how MbaVelen's agnation had come into dispute, and the correctness of the claims and counter-claims of the litigants. In doing so, they cross-examined the principals and called witnesses; they also discussed the matter amongst themselves. All these factors together constituted the 'investigation' of

the *jir*. In other *jir*, however, the facts seem to be undisputed, and it is the intentions of the parties to the various relationships that must be determined in order to make a correct interpretation of the facts.

JIR NO. 21. *Determining the intentions of litigants*

Ngohambe married (*er*) the ward of Ngiehi. Shortly afterwards she left him and married (*vaa*)[1] another man. Thereupon, Ngohambe went to Ngiehi to reclaim his money, but Ngiehi said he had nothing. Ngohambe therefore called a *jir* before the *mbatarev*. When they had heard him, they turned to Ngiehi and asked, 'Is that correct? Do you have this man's money?'

Ngiehi replied that he had indeed been given some money by Ngohambe, but had not returned it because there was no need to do so. The *mbatarev* asked, 'How much money has he given you?' Ngiehi replied that he had received £2. 12s.

'Oh,' said Gbegba. 'This man did not marry (*er*) a wife, but only took her as a recognized mistress (*kpa a kpa kwase*).'[2]

Ngiehi said, 'That is right. When a man pays a woman's guardian and her parents for his mistress, he doesn't expect to get his money back when she marries.'

Ngohambe, however, broke in and said, 'This was not a matter of a mistress, but of a married wife. The £2. 12s. is what I have paid him to marry a wife, and he must give it back to me.'

Chenge asked, 'Ngiehi, who is your witness to this affair?'

Ngiehi named Sortumbe.

Chenge turned to Ngohambe. 'Who is your witness?' he asked. Ngohambe named another man.

'In this case,' Chenge said, 'Ngiehi will return the £2. 12s. plus 2s. costs to Ngohambe, for you do not have witnesses to an arrangement for a mistress, but only for a marriage in which a man takes a wife.'

Ngiehi returned the entire amount three or four days later, in the presence of the court elders.

In this *jir* the 'facts', at least insofar as they pertained to the actual amount of bridewealth payment, were not in doubt. Since the amount was small, there was some dispute as to exactly what

---

[1] Both these words mean marry, and both may be used of any legal union, and of many others besides. *Er* means primarily to acquire rights in a woman and its reciprocal is, 'to go to a husband (*za nom*)'. *Vaa* means conjugal sexual intercourse and the emphasis is on the sexual aspect of marriage; there is another word entirely for sexual intercourse outside marriage.

[2] See Laura and Paul Bohannan, *The Tiv of Central Nigeria*, p. 75, for details.

arrangements had been made between the principals, and the *mbatarev* were seeking for a correct interpretation of the facts.

The next question to be asked is this: once the *mbatarev* know the facts of the individual *jir*, what are their standards or criteria for pronouncing judgment or making suggestions for settlement? European courts determine the facts and then determine what laws, customs, and precedents are involved. This brings our analysis to the heart of the difficult question of whether or not Tiv 'have' law.

The word used by English-speaking Tiv to translate the English word 'law' is *tindi*. However, the contextual range of *tindi* is very different from that of 'law'. To 'make a law' is *wa tindi*. *Wa* is a very difficult verb, but we might explain it chiefly by the English word 'acquire' and note that in Tiv it can often take a dative as well as an accusative object. When plants *wa* (or acquire) they bear fruit; a pregnant woman acquires a belly (*wa iyav*), and her husband may say that he acquired her a belly (*wa un iyav*).

Wa tindi is the Tiv way of discussing what we should call legislation. *Wa un tindi* means 'to place an injunction on him'. When a law is made, it is felt to be something that is acquired. There are two ways in which a *tindi* can be acquired today: one is direct from the European administrators, and the other is through the Native Authority, the tribal council or 'big *jir*' which must vote on all Native Authority regulations. In the administrator's way of looking at the Native Authority regulations, they are then part of 'native law and custom'. The whole idea of legislation is, however, of European origin.

When a law is repealed or cancelled, the term used is *sagh tindi*, to 'untie' (as of a knot) or 'release' (as of tied animals) the law. To transgress a law is literally to fall on it (*gba sha tindi*), though it seems to me that the English word transgress contains a little too much of the notion of purpose. One can 'touch' or 'fall foul' of the law just as one can of a fetish.

The two most common characteristics of *tindi* which Tiv cite when they explain the idea are: (1) a *tindi* is a matter which affects everyone, not just individuals or a particular group or category of people,[1] and (2) a *tindi* is permanent.

A fetish may have a *tindi*; these are not axioms on moral be-

---

[1] One is reminded of Austin's distinctions between laws and 'occasional or particular commands'. *Lectures on Jurisprudence*, 3rd ed., 1869, p. 95.

haviour, but rather on the ritual behaviour of repairing the fetish. For example, it is a *tindi* of the *akombo igbe* that the ceremonies must be carried out with the left hand. It is also a *tindi* of the *akombo megh* that the emblems made in connexion with its ceremony must be kept by the beneficiary of the ceremony. The *akombo megh* is transgressed if someone commits adultery with the wife or close kinswoman of the master of the fetish. But to commit adultery under this circumstance is not to 'fall on the *tindi*' of the fetish, but to pierce (*pev*) the fetish. You can pierce the fetish either by committing adultery or by disregarding one of its *tindi*. But the act of committing adultery is *not* in itself transgression of the *tindi*. In the same way, there are many *atindi* associated with the *akombo swende*, and 'falling on' any one of them may be sufficient to make one fall foul of that fetish; another way of falling foul of it is to kill a man. However, it is not a *tindi* of the *swende* that thou shalt not kill. In explaining this to me, one elder said that the injunction against killing was a *tindi* of the *tar*, not of the fetish. I never heard, so far as I know, the phrase '*tindi* of the *tar*' in any other circumstance—at least, I did not record it.

When Tiv talked to me about *atindi*, they tended to emphasize the prohibiting aspect rather than the regulating aspect. The Tiv language is extraordinarily rich in words for prohibition. For example, the word which means a minor individual prohibition, such as a parent's injunction to a child, is *acin*. *Ihange* is another such word, but emphasizes the giving of the order rather than the order itself. The only one of these words which concerns us here is *mtswer*. *Mtswer* differs from *tindi* in that it may affect only one person or a limited number of people, and it may be of somewhat shorter duration. Fetishes can have *mtswer* as well as *atindi*. Thus, when Ende had sore eyes and one of the fetishes which he had repaired for him was the *anigbe i dzwanya*, I discovered that it was a *tindi* of this particular fetish that the medicine had to be gathered and cooked by the man who was to benefit by it. However, there was also an *mtswer*, placed on it by this particular medicine man, that Ende must not speak while he was stirring the medicine or had the stirring spoon in his hand. Therefore, although I was allowed to watch him prepare the medicine, I was warned not to speak to him until he had laid the stirring spoon on the rocks beside the hearth, after which we could speak and converse normally until he was ready to pick it up again. *Mtswer* has been translated as 'taboo' in the literature, though this translation is of doubtful value, for the Tiv word has few of the Polynesian or Victorian connotations latent in the word 'taboo'.

Tindi means law in the sense of a generally accepted rule prohibiting something or other. Yet I was constantly aware, in using the word and in speaking about *tindi*, that it did not mean the same thing as 'law'. Although this sort of intuitive knowledge of when a word is right is an adequate guide for learning and speaking a language, it is not, of course, an adequate guide for analysing the concepts of a culture. In a translation matter of this sort, one must realize that the words and concepts in one's own language, into which one is translating, must be as clear-cut as those of the exotic language from which one is translating. Tiv do not talk about divine law, using the word *tindi* or any other word. Neither have they laws of 'nature'. In the first place, there is no concept of 'nature' running by 'laws' or any other way, and—as with divine law—the notion of somebody or something which could *wa tindi* of this sort is simply not a Tiv way of looking at the world.

We are left, therefore, with the English idea of 'human law' when we set out to compare 'law' and *tindi*. The relevant definition in the *Shorter Oxford English Dictionary* is: 'A body of rules, whether formally enacted or customary, which a state or community recognizes as binding on its members or subjects.' The second definition reads, 'one of these rules'. Here is the core of the difficulty in the comparison of the Tiv and English concepts. 'One of the rules' which a community recognizes as binding on its members is as good a definition of *tindi* as it is of law.[1] A *tindi* is a rule of conduct which is recognized as binding on the members of the Tiv community.

However, the other part of this definition—the 'body of rules' —will not do for a definition of *tindi*. The idea of the 'body' of laws must be excised from the English concept 'law' when it is used to translate *tindi*. Tiv have 'laws' but do not have 'law'. To speak of a *corpus juris* among Tiv, as Professor Gluckman speaks of it among Lozi,[2] would imply reference to an analytical system, not a folk system.

In Tivland there are *atindi* or 'rules', but they have not been

---

[1] A. L. Goodhart, *English Law and Moral Law*, 1953, pp. 18–19.
[2] Max Gluckman, *The Judicial Process among the Barotse of Northern Rhodesia*, 1955, pp. 164 ff.

F

especially organized for jural purposes. Neither do Tiv recognize a body of custom. Europeans can understand the notion of random and unformalized custom somewhat more easily than they can understand a random and unformalized law, because they, like Tiv, have not with any degree of uniformity formulated or 'codified' their custom.

The Tiv word for custom is *inja*. We have referred to this word in discussing the reasonable man among Tiv. Tiv say that if another Tiv does not do what it is the *inja* of Tiv to do, he is not a wise person—he does not 'know things'. *Inja*, or custom, differs from *tindi* in that it is not a definite injunction. It is the *inja* of Tiv to be farmers; but if one does not make a farm it is not wrong, but merely foolish.

Inja also means habit, for it can often be used to refer to the customary actions of an individual. My steward once noted that it was my *inja* to brush my teeth before coffee in the morning, whereas it had been the *inja* of his former employer to drink a cup of tea before he got up, and to brush his teeth afterwards. In his statement, the word means 'habit'. When I told him that coffee in the morning was the *inja* of Americans while tea was the *inja* of the English, the word meant custom. In Tiv it is a single concept.

Inja also means 'use'—it is the *inja* of a hoe to make mounds. Finally, it means reason or meaning—the *inja* of a word or phrase or act is its explanation.

Any action performed repeatedly can be called an *inja*. If it is performed by most people, it is *inja i Tiv*—Tiv custom. If it is performed by only one person, it is a peculiarity or habit and is called *inja i Uvia*, the habit of So-and-so. There is, obviously, no organized body of *inja* except as they are organized in the course of social action.

In precisely the same way, there is no organization of *tindi* or laws. *Inja* is an attribute of a person, a group of persons, or a thing; it is the nature of each. *Tindi* is an attribute of a social situation, to be observed by people participating in that situation; it is also, thus, an attribute of the behaviour of all right-thinking and right-acting men and women. Neither has existence, as a body or individually, apart from people in social action. Neither has ever been divorced from social action. Neither has been collated into a *corpus*.

One often hears, in Tiv *jir*, the statement 'It is the custom of the Tiv to do such and such.' One much less often hears, 'The *tindi* involved is such and such', though the statement is made and has been reported in several cases earlier in this book. One very rarely hears precedents cited, though instances do appear in the preceding cases. *Inja*, *tindi*, and precedent all enter into the investigation which the *mbatarev* perform. But they do so only in an informal, unorganized way.

The final question which must be investigated in this section is that of the authority of the *mbatarev*. Most litigants look upon the *mbatarev* as arbitrators to whom they may or may not bring a *jir*, as they are inclined. It is my opinion that in the eyes of most people no *ortaregh* has any authority whatever; or, at least, no *ortaregh* or anyone else *ought* to have any authority. This does not mean that people do not yield them a great deal of power in virtue of their influence, derived from their personalities and social positions, and a great deal of power in jural matters. It means rather that Tiv are, ideologically, fierce egalitarians in the matter of authority, even while they are realists in the matter of personal power. Most *mbatarev* are respected and, to some extent, feared. The fact that the power of the British Administration lies behind them is known to all and is, I think, greatly over-estimated. The Government would probably not back up the *mbatarev* to the point that most Tiv think.

Cases of contempt of court in Tivland always arise from contumacy—the expression of personal contempt for the judges—and seldom or never from failure to carry out court orders. They centre around two actions: *hule*, to outshout, and *laha*, to behave presumptuously, beyond one's age or influence.

JIR NO. 22. *An* ortaregh *calls a case for contempt*

In a land dispute between MbaAji and MbaKov, Adev on two occasions—once in the court circle and once on the disputed ground—insulted Gbegba. Gbegba had expressed an opinion. Adev did not merely disagree civilly, which all expected him to do, but became abusive and insulting in his language. Gbegba and Chenge both called him down. A day or two later, when Adev insulted Gbegba for the second time, in the court circle, tears sprang into Gbegba's eyes. He left his seat, took out two shillings and called a *jir* against Adev because the latter had *laha* him. The *mbatarev* immediately took Gbegba's side in this matter, and Adev was fined 2s. Huwa suggested that another five shillings be added because Adev had made a lot of noise in court and had shouted them all down (*hule*). Chenge refused to consider this. Adev paid the 2s. and was very subdued for the rest of the *jir*. It was popular opinion at the time that Adev had bribed Gbegba to make the boundary in his favour, then when he did not do so, became angry with him.

Tiv have on several occasions told me that it costs money to *laha mbatarev*, but that it is sometimes worth it. The most instructive case I know in this regard, though it is not unique, is:

JIR NO. 23. *Ada calls Uta in a land dispute*
        Uta in contempt of court

Ada called a *jir* against Uta and accused him of selecting his field on his own old site. The *mbatarev* asked Uta if it was true that the land on which he had begun to farm had belonged to Ada. Uta said that he had chosen a site on almost the precise spot where his compound had formerly been located: the field, he said, was in his own kitchen gardens.

Gbegba said that he remembered this land well. If, he asked, Uta was going to claim it now, why had he let the matter drop when Kyagba (Chenge's father) had told Ada to farm there? Uta replied: 'Kyagba didn't give Ada this land, but merely requested me to let Ada use it for a crop rotation, and I agreed.' He went on to say that the only reason why he did so was that Ada had to move because all his people were dying on his old site, and there was no other place to which he could go; after all, Ada was a sister's son.[1] This statement caused considerable stir. Actually, everyone knew that Uta was right. On the other hand, the undisputed female link in Ada's attachment to MbaGôr was three generations old; Ada's ancestors had lived in MbaGôr all that time and were treated as if they were agnatic members of the local lineage. In the end, the *mbatarev* refused to agree that Uta had not relinquished all right to the site when Kyagba's original judgment had been given several years before.

Uta was a man of quick and violent temper. He was also somewhat feared by most of the local community. He stood and put his hand into his leather shoulder-bag and drew forth a handful of shillings, which he flung on to the ground before the assembled *mbatarev*. 'I have never,' he shouted, 'heard such infamous decisions as to give land to a sister's son which should belong to a child of the lineage! There is your fine. I am about to be thoroughly in contempt of court (*laha mbatarev*)!'

[1] Uta was over-simplifying. For Ada's true position, see *Tiv Farm and Settlement*, p. 11, and Chart 10, page 71 (Ada is No. 19; Uta is No. 10).

Uta was not allowed to be in contempt of court—the combined *mbatarev*, tax-collectors, and onlookers shouted him down. Chenge himself picked up the coins and returned them to him.

The part which the *mbatarev* play in the *jir*, then, is called 'investigating the *jir*'. In performing this task, they ask questions, call witnesses, and weigh evidence and causes in the light of cultural values and norms and the merits of individual cases. They can and do impose fines as penalties on persons who do not assist them in getting to the bottom of a given dispute.

V. ENDING (KURE) THE JIR

The final step in settling a *jir* is the 'ending'. Both judges and litigants have parts to play at this stage. Briefly, the *mbatarev* suggest a settlement, and the litigants must concur if the case is to be considered thoroughly successful. The *mbatarev* confer together and reach an agreed decision. The procedure, like most Tiv social actions, is informal. Younger men do not, as a rule, flatly contradict elders, but they often disagree with them. Certainly there is no special order in which the *mbatarev* speak or think they ought to speak.

The activities of the *mbatarev* in 'ending' a *jir* are generally described as 'giving' (*na*) the right (*isho*) and giving the fault (*ibo*). In every case, even though a complete compromise is reached, one party can be said to have the right on his side—to eat the *isho*—while the other eats the *ibo*. That is, he is at fault.

The two words, *ibo* (fault) and *isho* (right), are sometimes translated as 'guilt' and 'innocence', though these translations are really not very precise. Every case, if properly finished, must have one litigant in the right and the other at fault. Although men whom we should consider guilty are indeed said to 'eat the fault' in a Tiv settlement, it is not possible to reverse the translation and say that all men who 'eat the fault' are guilty of the actions with which they are charged. The nearest parallel to these words that I know in anthropological literature is a distinction made by Nuer in both a jural and a religious context, between 'right' and 'wrong' or between 'fault' and 'righteousness'.[1] Tiv also use their words in

---

[1] E. E. Evans-Pritchard, *Nuer Religion*, 1956, pp. 172 ff. P. P. Howell, *A Manual of Nuer Law*, 1954, pp. 22 ff.

a religious context. In the simplest ceremony for repairing fetishes, the critical rite, performed in a stream, is accompanied by the words 'fault descend, righteousness arise'.[1]

Sometimes when a litigant eats the *ibo*, he has been seriously at fault. Such an instance is:

JIR NO. 24. *Abaji (husband) calls Kpirigh (guardian)* Eating the fault

Abaji called a *jir* against his wife's guardian's brother who had, as he put it, taken his wife away without reason. In the course of the hearing it emerged that Kpirigh and his brother had each been given a ward by their father. While Kpirigh was in the army during the war, his father had died and his ward had grown up. His brother therefore took her, married her off, and received bridewealth for her. When Kpirigh returned, he did not live in his native *tar*, but went to Makurdi where he had a job. However, when he got short of money, he remembered his ward and went to ask her husband Abaji for further payment on the bridewealth. Abaji refused, saying that, as he was not the man from whom he had got a wife, he intended to pay him nothing whatever. Kpirigh talked to his sister, Abaji's wife, and convinced her that he was in the right and that Abaji was trying to keep her for nothing. She consented to return with Kpirigh to their brother's compound in their native *tar*. Abaji did not come immediately to fetch his wife, so Kpirigh gave her to someone else and accepted bridewealth. Shortly afterwards Abaji came to demand his wife. When told that she had gone to another husband, he called a case before the *mbatarev*.

Kpirigh said that, since he was the woman's guardian, and since he had not received any bridewealth from her first 'marriage', it did not constitute a true marriage. The *mbatarev*, however, informed him that his brother had received bridewealth, and the marriage was thus valid; if he wanted to collect the debt from his brother, he could do so, but he could not disregard the bridewealth which Abaji had paid.

In this case Kpirigh was 'given the fault' and was also fined 5*s*. He was fined, not *because* he had eaten the fault, but because he had accepted two bridewealths. Thus Kpirigh had 'fallen on the *tindi*', on which all Tiv agree, that it is wrong to accept two bridewealths. He also 'ate the fault' in the *jir*.

However, it sometimes also happens that a man 'eats the fault' in a decision when he has not 'fallen on *tindi*' at all.

[1] I shall expand this discussion of fault and righteousness in my book on Tiv religion.

JIR NO. 25. *Husband's mother calls guardian*
Eating the fault need not imply wrong-doing

Mbatuna called a *jir* before the *mbatarev* against the guardian of the woman she had 'married' (*er*) for her son. The *mbatarev* asked the guardian where the girl was. He said that he didn't know: Mbatuna had *kem* this girl as a wife for her son, but as the son was away and had not come home for six months, the girl had run away. He added that he had sent her back twice, she had then run away a third time and now he did not know where she was.

He was 'given the fault', and was made to return the bridewealth paid to him.

Although 'given the fault', he had not 'fallen on *tindi*', because he had done nothing that was not in accordance with an injunction or *tindi*. Thus, 'guilt' of having broken a law or *tindi* is not the point in deciding which of the litigants eats the fault.

'Winning the case' or 'losing the case' does not translate 'to eat the right' and 'to eat the fault'. Although the man whom we would consider the winner of the case does, in fact, usually eat the right, this translation cannot be reversed, for the man who eats the right need not always be, because of that fact, the man whom we would consider to have won the case. The Tiv phrase 'the *jir* seized him' means approximately 'he lost the case'. I do not know another phrase which might mean 'he won the case' in our sense.

Tiv say that some *mbatarev* are corrupt, and that in some Native Authority Grade-D courts it is possible 'to buy a *jir*' (*yam jir*). They add that there are some courts indeed which do not 'hear' (*ungwa*) *jir* at all, and that if you want a *jir* settled there the only way to have it done is to buy it. However, it is also said to be much more difficult than in the past for an *ortaregh* to be corrupt. One man explained to me that in order to bribe a Native Authority court today, it was necessary to bribe the *mbatarev* separately, as almost surely there was rivalry enough among them to make them unwilling to accept bribes in one another's presence. At least so far as MbaDuku was concerned, this observation seemed correct. Besides the *mbatarev*, Tiv continue, it is also necessary today to bribe the scribe and the policeman and messengers. All in all, it becomes a very expensive business. It is my opinion that most cases, in MbaDuku at least, were heard on their merits, and that bribery and corruption were at a minimum. Tiv have told me of one court in which rates for 'buying the *jir*' were discussed and haggled over in open session, but they declared this to be the exception.

Although I cannot, obviously, document this sort of thing, I believe that corruption in Grade-D courts is much less common than Tiv think. It is even less common than their European administrators think. This does not imply that Tiv are more honest than other peoples, but merely that their social organization and the organization of their courts are such that bribery becomes difficult because one must bribe so many people: as one of my friends put it, 'Whenever you try to buy a *jir* you find that it includes your opponents' kinsmen who cannot accept any offer, no matter how high.'

The task of the *mbatarev* in 'ending' a *jir* is not to make a decision, but to make suggestions for settlement. In a properly run *jir* the principal litigants must also play their parts: they must both concur (*lumun*) in the judgment.

Tiv litigants would seem to believe that the proper and correct solution of a dispute 'exists'. It 'is'. The task of the judges is to find it. In the old days the principal litigants would go from one elder of the community to another until they discovered one who could penetrate the details of the case and emerge with this 'correct' solution. To a lesser extent, they still do so today. It is obvious to Tiv that when a right decision has been reached, both litigants will concur in it, even though the particular judgment may not be wholly in favour of either.

The importance of such concurrence by the litigants cannot be over-emphasized. It is to misunderstand the Tiv view to say that Tiv courts have or have not the 'authority' to 'enforce' a 'decision'. 'Authority', 'enforcement', and 'decision' are all Western legal concepts which spring from our notions and ideas of authority hierarchies. They are part of the Western folk system concerning our jural and governmental institutions. If Tiv judges make a settlement in which both parties can concur, there is no problem of 'enforcing a decision'. If they do not, they have not, by Tiv definition, 'ended the *jir*' satisfactorily. The correct solution is known to have been found when all the judges and the litigants concur.

Tiv *jir*, then, discover a solution to a dispute which is in accordance with the *inja* of the Tiv, and in which all the persons concerned in the *jir* concur. This is comparable to, but vastly different from, the fact that Western courts make a decision in accordance with the facts of the case and with the 'law', and have the authority to enforce that decision. It is very difficult to discuss the acts and values of either system in the words and concepts and language of the other.

Concurrence of the litigants never occurs without concurrence of the entire community: no one is ready to make concessions while any portion of public opinion still supports him. It is the opinion of the community which forces concurrence. Judging, like all other activities of Tiv leaders, consists largely in the timely suggestion of what the majority thinks is right or desirable.

The 'correct solution' changes as the situation of both litigants changes. Tiv, therefore, tend to deplore 'final decisions', which their European administrators, of course, prefer. Tiv feel that making a final decision, in the English sense, often perpetuates conditions which will eventually become unjust. It sometimes appears to foreigners that Tiv do not want their courts to make decisions at all, but it seems more accurate to say that they want the judges to point out a *modus vivendi*, which will endure while the situation endures.

For Tiv judges to settle a *jir* by any standards other than the concurrence of the litigants, and eventually of the community, is to settle it 'by force' (*sa apela*). This literal translation might be more meaningfully rendered 'settled by despotic action'. If a Tiv Native Authority court uses its government-backed authority to enforce a decision in which the litigants do not concur, and in which community opinion does not insist that they concur, that court is said to have 'heard the *jir* by force'. This is the worst thing that can be said of any *jir*. It is much worse, in the Tiv view, than the acceptance of bribes. Bribery is at least not capricious.

Even though judges might be able to defend their decisions on the basis of Tiv custom, unless the litigants, pressed by the community, concur, a settlement is described as one made 'by force'. The way in which community opinion brings concurrence is interesting:

JIR NO. 26. *Combo, wife of Yaji, calls Zege*
        Concurrence in a decision

Combo called a *jir* because Zege beat her. She said that she went to her farm and caught Zege stealing cassava from it. When she questioned his right to be on her farm, let alone take cassava from it, he told her it was his land and therefore his cassava, beat her, and tore her blouse.

The *mbatarev* turned to Zege, who listened meekly to a long lecture on deportment. 'Zege,' Chenge said, 'you are a woman's child (*wan kwase*). This is not your place (*ian*).' One of the others took it up, 'Why have you come to make trouble among your mother's lineage? Your *igba* have allowed you to hoe farms here. If these farms are disputed, it is your *igba* who should take up the dispute—not you.' Another added, 'And to steal things from your *igba* is indeed very heinous. They are your kinsmen (*angbianev*) and have given you land to hoe, and a place to build a homestead, and you have stolen from them!' Chenge now asked, 'Zege, who was it who gave you place?'—that is, a place to farm and build. Zege replied quietly that it was Agber.

'Agber, come!' Chenge shouted. Agber was in the crowd—as everyone knew. Agber came to the centre of the *jir* circle. 'Agber,' Chenge asked, 'did you show Zege place?' Agber admitted that he had done so. 'Agber,' he continued, 'why have you let him fight and beat the wives of our *ityó*, our lineage?' Agber said nothing. 'You have dared (*chihi*) much,' Chenge said. 'And you must pay £2 fine for harbouring a thief, and for showing him a house site and for giving him farms. You have given him a place amongst us where he can sit and from which he can steal things from people!' Agber paid unprotestingly.

Chenge turned back to Zege, who admitted to ripping the blouse but not to stealing cassava, and told him to pay a shilling for repair of the cloth. Zege paid. Chenge added, 'Besides this, Zege, you must bring ten shillings as fine for fighting in the fields.' Again Zege paid the fine without a murmur.

The purpose of these moral lectures is not so much admonition as repetition of values held by the entire community. The statements may be 'laws', seen from one point of view. But the more important point is that they are truisms, and the litigant cannot deny them. He must concur that they are right because the community considers them irrefutable. He must eventually concur in the judgment they represent.

In this case, Agber knew that he was responsible for the wrongs committed by his sister's son so long as that sister's son was living with him. Zege knew that his rights in this community were tenuous. Both paid their fines because they knew they were wrong, but, more importantly, because they knew that their relationships with their neighbours would continue to be strained until they made some sort of move to admit that they were wrong.

The fines paid in this case were aligned with the idea of *tia*,

Litigants before the *jir*

A witness, with *swem* beside him

PLATE III

Uta 'about to be in contempt of court' (*Jir* No. 23)

Mtswen and his people came to Chenge's compound to 'drum the scandal'

PLATE IV

which is usually translated inaccurately as 'fine'. *Tia* is an animal which Tiv bring to the judges or arbitrators of their cases in order that the animal may be butchered when the case is settled. In the traditional system, the *tia* is provided by the man who calls the case, not the man who loses it. The meat is shared by the entire community; in recognition of the fact that one has had one's affairs and relationships renovated and harmony now reigns.

When a man brings his wife back to her natal *tar* so that her elders may perform a ceremony on her behalf, they require that he kill them a *tia*: the animal is butchered and amounts both to payment for services and, at the same time, indication of a 'repaired' relationship. Similarly, when a man summons the elders of his lineage to a moot, he must sometimes provide them with a *tia*. When he does so, it pays them for coming and means also that the members of the lineage rejoice because another difficulty has been resolved. The elders will usually set the value of the *tia* to be provided, in accordance with their notion of the importance of the occasion and the service.

Tiv have, without signal success, tried to bring fines into line with their ideas of *tia*. A fine, as we think of it, is called 'the words of the *jir*' (*zwajirigh*), and was, I believe, introduced with the Native Authority courts. Tiv, however, saw similarities between the fine and their custom of *tia*. Insofar as a fine imposed by a court is seen as a payment for services and as the symbol of turning over a new leaf, it is called a *tia*. The same fine, seen as money payment which goes into the coffers of the Native Authority instead of being dispersed directly back into the community, is called 'the words of the *jir*'.

Another technique which the judges sometimes use to make the litigants concur is the threat to send the dispute to a higher court— that is, to the Grade-C court at Vande Ikya. Judges as well as litigants can send disputes to appeal.

Both fines and the judges' refusal to finish a *jir* are seen as penalties (*mtsaha*) inflicted by the *mbatarev*. They can also inflict another penalty: they can imprison wrongdoers for periods up to three months. It should be emphasized that, even here, the idea of authority to fine and imprison is not a Tiv way of seeing it. The man who is being fined must still 'concur' in that fine if the decision is not to be considered arbitrary. Before a man serves a prison sentence, he most often agrees that it is just punishment. If he does not concur, the *mbatarev* will either reconsider the sentence or appeal to the audience. Public opinion makes a man concur in a punishment. In moots, but never in courts, I have seen a group of agreed elders threaten to withdraw their protection from witchcraft in order to force a man to concur in a decision which was favoured by all save himself.

Tiv attitude to prison as a punishment is fundamentally different from our own. There is no disgrace involved in a prison sentence. They are cheerful prisoners and, according to their District Officers, are usually well-behaved prisoners. One official told me that if they did misbehave in prison it was very difficult to punish them further. He had, however, hit on the idea of making them do women's work—especially flour grinding—as the only infallible corrective.

We shall note other punishments: public ridicule is involved in a case of a young thief who stole shoes (*Jir* No. 61).

Tiv notions of concurrence are indeed comparable to European notions of enforcing judgment, especially in the light of penalties inflicted. They bring about roughly the same ends. But they must not be confused with them. To say that public opinion is the enforcing agent is to misunderstand the Tiv viewpoint, though it is, from our point of view, true.

VI. CONCLUSION

The subject matter of this chapter is a descriptive analysis of the Tiv institutions comparable with those of procedural law in European societies. I have not, however, stated the principles in terms of norms and rules, but have let social acts performed within the institution of the *jir* speak for themselves. The *jir* is the device by means of which Tiv settle many of their disputes; its rules are inherent in its organization.

It would, I suppose, be possible to elicit rules of procedure from the cases. The rules might be set forth: 'When a defendant or witness is outside the area of jurisdiction of a court, the *mbatarev* can send to members of the *jir* in whose territory he is to be found, and ask that the person be sent to them.' Or, 'The *mbatarev* can take possession of disputed goods and hold them until the dispute is settled'. Or, 'Tiv judges will not hear a marriage *jir* until all three of the principal parties to the marriage—husband, wife, and her guardian—are present.' Or, 'The judges can require a witness to take an oath.'

It would be possible, once one had elicited all the rules which one could find in all the cases, to arrange them into some sort of order and set them forth as the procedural law of Tiv courts (and indeed, I shall experiment with this method in the following consideration of substantive law). The error would be that the arrangement is not part of the Tiv way of looking at it, and hence would be false. 'The mere fact that a rule is reasserted in a fresh setting reinforces it and clarifies it, or throws new light upon it and this element is "additive" '.[1]

I have tried throughout this exposition to avoid this additive element. I consider it to be the cardinal error of ethnographic and social analysis: the grossly ethnocentric practice of raising folk systems like 'the law', designed for social action in one's own society, to the status of an analytical system, and then trying to organize the raw social data from other societies into its categories. I have also tried to avoid the equivalent error of raising the folk systems of the Romans or the Trobriand Islanders to the level of such a filing system for data which may not fit them. Such a doctrine is probably a counsel of perfection, impossible of attainment. But impossibility of attainment does not make it less desirable.

[1] C. K. Allen, *Law in the Making*, 5th ed., p. 146.

CHAPTER V

TIV MARRIAGE *JIR*

W E have outlined the organization of the *jir* and have described the folk system of the social action which takes place within it, then noted that procedural law would be the European equivalent of the latter. We have yet to consider what jurists would call the 'substantive law' which is handled by the *jir*.

There is, in Western civilization, or in any civilization with a developed law, a dual relationship between the court and some other institutions. The court, for example, enters into family institutions at some points, especially in matters of divorce and inheritance. Conversely, a portion of the folk system of family institutions has been, in our society, restated so as to form the substantive law which is part of the jural institution.[1]

Jir, like courts everywhere, not merely have folk systems for action, but they also make use of the folk systems of some other social institutions. In this and the next two chapters, we shall examine cases before the *jir* from the point of view of the substantive rules of the cases and the nature of those rules.

I. SCRIBES' RECORDS OF 'CIVIL CASES'

The scribes, with varying degrees of accuracy and skill, keep brief records of the cases heard by the *mbatarev* of the area; some of their case summaries will appear below. The categories into which they are required to classify cases or *jir* are derived by the Government from European law. The first division is into 'civil' and 'criminal' cases. The basis for this distinction has been the subject of much thought and effort by European jurists; I believe they fail to agree on definitions. Certainly the distinction is not always understood by the scribes, for it is not an easy one to draw

[1] I am using Malinowski's masterly conception of institution: a group of people, who have a purpose, an organization, and material culture to carry out the purpose; they also have what Malinowski called a 'charter' which is the web of idea, conception, and doctrine in which they see themselves, their purpose, their tools, and their organization—and indeed their doctrine itself. See *The Dynamics of Culture Change*, New Haven, 1945, pp. 49–50.

when discussing disputes in the Tiv language; it forms no part of the indigenous folk system. However, it is one of the basic categories of the Grade-D court; as such it has ethnographic validity. The 'civil' and 'criminal' cases are catalogued in separate books. Both registers make further classifications of cases.

In MbaDuku, civil cases are broken down by the scribe into three categories: (1) marriage, (2) debt, and (3) appeal. The third category—appeal cases—concerns the method of settlement, and hence may include cases which are, by subject matter, included in one of the other two. The only registers of civil cases available at the time this study was made were for two years beginning in September 1950. Only the numbers of cases which had been both 'docketed' and settled are given in these figures.

MbaDuku *jir* completes between 250 and 300 registered civil cases per year:

	Debt	*Marriage*	*Appeal*	*Total*
		Number of settled cases of		
1950				
September	19	21	1	41
October	7	7	1	15
November	2	2	—	4
December	18	29	—	47
1951				
January	7	3	—	10
February	19	16	2	37
March	—	2	—	2
April	16	28	—	44
May	6	8	1	15
June	—	—	—	—
July	19	18	1	38
August	2	7	—	9
September	10	15	—	25
October	3	2	—	5
November	17	31	1	49
December	8	14	—	22
1952				
January	28	13	1	41
February	—	—	—	—
March	14	15	—	29
April	5	5	—	10
May	—	—	—	—
June	7	5	—	12
July	—	—	—	—
August	43	61	6	110

II. LITIGANTS IN MARRIAGE JIR

Marriage is one of the most disturbed areas of Tiv life. There are several reasons for this, the most important being the abolition in 1927 by government decree of exchange marriage, in which Tiv were deeply involved psychically and socially. A further factor was the introduction of a money economy, which upset the normal spheres of exchangeable commodities and has had a profound effect on exchange of rights in women, and hence on marriage. It is small wonder that a large proportion of *jir* concerns women and marriage.

There are three, not merely two, persons of importance in a Tiv marriage: the husband, the wife, and the wife's guardian (*tien*). It is not possible here to go into all the intricacies of Tiv marriage custom. It must suffice to point out that Tiv formerly had a complicated system of exchange marriage based on the idea that the only commodity decently exchangeable for the fertility of one woman was that of another.[1] In explaining this system to Europeans, Tiv put it in its simplest terms: two men exchange sisters. Actually, the situation was seldom so simple.

Exchange marriage involved two sets of exchanges. It was customary for a small group of agnatic kinsmen, whom Dr. East has called the *ingôl* group,[2] and whom Tiv themselves call 'those who eat one *ingôl*' (*mbaye ingôl i môm*), to distribute their daughters equitably for use as marriage wards (*ingôl*, plural *angôl*). Each man then traded his marriage ward (who would be his daughter, his sister, or the daughter of a close agnate) for a wife, thus completing a second exchange. In this arrangement, one's ward married the man (or one of his dependants) who was guardian (*tien*) of one's own wife.

When exchange marriage was 'abolished', only one of the two exchanges ceased to take place. The exchange of wards between husbands was stopped. However, Tiv continued to form and to use *ingôl*-groups: today, the male members of such a group still distribute their sisters and daughters among themselves. But instead of exchanging their wards directly for wives, they 'sell' them for

---

[1] The idea is discussed in Paul Bohannan, 'Some Principles of Exchange and Investment among the Tiv', *American Anthropologist*, 1955, and in Paul and Laura Bohannan, *Tiv Economy*, Northwestern University Press, 1968.

[2] Rupert East, translator of *Akiga's Story*. East's and Akiga's discussions in Chapter III are helpful for understanding Tiv marriage. There is also a discussion of Tiv marriage, including exchange marriage, in Laura and Paul Bohannan, *The Tiv of Central Nigeria*, pp. 69–75.

bridewealth, usually paid in money. A woman's guardian receives the bridewealth instead of receiving a woman in direct exchange.

The result of the abolition of exchange marriage has been that two formerly enmeshed structures are now rendered discrete. In a social system characterized by marriage ratified by bridewealth one can see a kinship structure which has its nodes at individual marriages. There is, in addition, a network of debt relationships which is more or less coterminous with the network of marriage and kinship relationships, but which has its nodes in the individual contracts between women's guardians and their husbands. This logical separation was not possible under the system of exchange marriage, in which debts did indeed exist, but the debts themselves could be seen as potential future links in the kinship system, not a special system which stood outside it. In the exchange system, the debt owed was a woman—ward to one man, wife to the other. The debt one assumed at marriage was discharged when one's wife's guardian married one's own ward.

Today the debt structure and the kinship structure have become separated, for—with the introduction of money—a debt connected with a wife is of much the same nature as a debt incurred in any other manner. Tiv have tried to keep them separate, but have not found it feasible to do so. The ideology—and the usages—of Tiv marriage have become very much more complex since the abolition of exchange marriage. This point is ironical in that one of the main reasons for the abolition, given in contemporary files, was that exchange marriage was too complicated for British officers to understand: it has at least the advantage of being a single ideological system.

The debt aspect of marriage is summed up in the Tiv notion *kem*. One says, 'I *kem* my wife from her guardian.' *Kem* means 'to accumulate' and its only other common usage is in 'accumulating a farm'—that is, gradually over the years getting more and more seed yams so that one can have a bigger and bigger farm. The *kem* relationship of debt between a man and his wife's guardian is never broken, because *kem* is perpetual, the debt can never be fully paid. I translate *kem* 'to make payments'.

Among my notes there are 54 marriage *jir* which I consider of value; these include several recorded by my scribes when I was not present, and several taken from the MbaDuku scribe's records. It is possible to classify these 54 marriage *jir* according to which of

G

the three principal parties to a marriage calls the *jir* and against whom he calls it. When we make this sort of classification, we find:

Husband calls Guardian	24	
„ „ Wife	3	
„ „ Adulterer	9	
		36
Guardian calls Husband	5	
„ „ Wife's mother	1	
		6
Wife calls Husband	5	
„ „ Guardian	7	
	12	54

It must not be thought that the proportions indicated by this table correspond to the distribution of marriage *jir* in Tivland, or even in MbaDuku. It was not possible for me to record all *jir* equally carefully. I suspect that in my unconscious selection I omitted many of the guardian *v.* husband *jir*, because most of them were matters of debt and were simple, uninstructive, and dull. The sample is overweighted with *jir* called by women. I instructed my scribes to pay particular attention to such cases, did so myself, and selected several cases out of the MbaDuku Case Books which—though inadequately recorded from my point of view—were of a sort that my sample did not contain. Therefore the proportion of *jir* called by wives is almost certainly not so high as in this sample. It must suffice to say that by far the largest proportion of marriage *jir* which enter Grade-D courts are called by husbands against their wives' guardians or against their wives' seducers.

III. THE SUBSTANCE OF MARRIAGE JIR

I have arranged the *jir* in such a way as to bring out, in what Europeans would consider an orderly manner, as complete a listing as possible of the substantive rules of marriage, breach of which has led to *jir*. After the bulk of 'case material' and the rules have been presented, we shall be in a position to inquire in what sense we have reported a folk system and in what sense we have created an analytical system, and to examine the fruitfulness of the latter.

I. MARRIAGE AND PAYMENT OF BRIDEWEALTH

1.1 *Before a man has a right to live with a woman in his compound he must begin to make payments* (kem) *and certainly he must marry* (er) *her*

This principle is stated clearly in:

JIR NO. 27. *Tyukwa (guardian) calls Wanor (seducer)*
Husband required to pay bridewealth

Tyukwa called this *jir*, telling the *mbatarev* that Wanor had his ward and wouldn't return her to him. The *mbatarev* asked Wanor, 'Do you have Tyukwa's ward?' Wanor said he didn't have the girl; she was now in Gav (a lineage a score of miles to the north-west). Chenge impatiently told him that he had been told before to bring this girl back; since he had not done so, he must now be put in the hands of the policemen (*dogari*) until the girl was brought. Then they would hear the *jir*.

Wanor stayed in the hands of the policemen only about three days. He was released as soon as it was definitely known that someone from his compound had been sent to Gav to get the girl. This case never again appeared before the *jir*, as Wanor's father's brother, the head of his compound, made private arrangements for Wanor to make payments to Tyukwa for the girl.

Tiv men say that if you are a woman's guardian, you do all in your power to prevent her eloping; you require her suitor to come to your compound, with his people, to make a proper arrangement for giving presents to you and your people (the girl's father and mother, in addition to the bridewealth paid to the guardian); then, when you have reached an agreement on the amount of the *kem* payments, you insist on receiving some of the money before you let your ward depart with her husband. Tiv men also say that if you are getting a wife, the best thing to do is to elope with her and then to regularize the union, because you do not need so much cash in hand for payments on a wife who is already in her husband's compound. Tiv women sometimes use the fact that they eloped with their husbands—thereby saving them money—to get presents and special favours from them.

1.2 *If a man makes some* kem *payments on a wife, her guardian cannot remove her from him without her consent*

This rule was frequently stated in the MbaDuku *jir*. It is, however, a rule introduced with the new forms of marriage after 1927.

Under the rules of exchange marriage, it was precisely the power of the guardian to remove his ward from her husband which ensured the reciprocity of exchange. Even today, in those areas of Ityoshin where Grade-D courts are more distant and less used than they are in the crowded areas of the south, guardians in fact recall their wards from their husbands in order to get more money from the husbands.

JIR NO. 28. *Achii (first 'husband') calls Ivar (husband)*
  Achii loses his wife because he paid no bridewealth.
  [MbaDuku Case Register 1946: 28]

'Long ago, Achii stole a woman at Anuwe's and lived with her for seven years without making payments for her. So Anuwe finally took his child and gave her to Ivar. Achii then called a case against Ivar. The *mbatarev* found that, although Achii had been told to make payments, he had never done so. Therefore the wife was lost to (*bunde*) him. Ivar got the wife, and the case was finished.'

The rule is plainly stated: since no bridewealth has been paid, the guardian has the right to remove his ward. The rule is better illustrated with a positive instance:

JIR NO. 29. *Ityungu (second husband) calls Kunda (first husband)*
  Determinant bridewealth payment

My clerk's account of this *jir* begins with a fair summation: 'Ityungu called a case against Kunda because the latter had married his wife.' The *mbatarev*, scarcely letting either husband speak, turned on the guardian, 'To which of these two men did you give your ward as wife?'

The guardian said Kunda had first married (*er*) her, but he had paid only the miscellaneous gifts, and hadn't made *kem* payments for her; he had on several occasions asked Kunda for payments, but always in vain. This greatly displeased the wife, for she felt that Kunda was trying to use her elopement with him as an advantage against her kinsmen. So she ran home to her guardian.

A few weeks later Ityungu appeared, liked the woman and asked for her. The guardian gave her to him as a wife. Soon afterwards, however, she ran away and returned to Kunda.

The *mbatarev* now asked Kunda if he had made payments when he married her. He replied that he had given one *gbagir* cloth worth £2; he had given his mother-in-law beads worth £2, and had killed chickens valued at 10*s*. for his father-in-law.

The guardian, asked if this was true, replied that he thought so, but could not be sure. When the girl had first married Kunda, she was her father's ward; he had inherited her, as ward, on her father's death.

After discussion, the *mbatarev* gave Ityungu the fault (*ibo*) saying that he had 'married someone else's wife', because that other person had given money for her. It was indeed true that Kunda had not yet made payments for her, but since he had spent money on gifts for her father and mother it could be assumed that he intended to do so. The *mbatarev* told Kunda to take his wife and go.

In spite of the fact that the first husband had not made the *kem* payments, which Tiv say are those which ratify the marriage, he had made some gifts (called odds and ends, *aveghem*) which, because they are not always returnable at divorce, proved to Tiv that he intended to make payments or he would not have made the gifts. It was therefore decided that the guardian could not remove the woman, but must rather demand the *kem* payments for her.

The most illuminating case concerning this rule is one that we saw begun when we described a day in court:[1]

JIR NO. 4. *Lankwagh (guardian) calls Dagba (husband)*

Lankwagh called Dagba before the *jir*, telling the *mbatarev*, 'Dagba has my ward and won't return her to me.' Dagba, asked where the girl was, replied that she was at home as a good wife should be. The girl was sent for.

The *mbatarev* told Dagba to relate his side of the story. He said that while he was courting the girl, who had just passed puberty, her brother Lankwagh had suggested that he come and give her mother money to untie the shell.[2] He accordingly gave £1 for the shell, tied cloths on his mother-in-law for £4, and gave Lankwagh a pair of trousers and £1 for a *liga* robe: the whole, he said, came to £7. Then Lankwagh, who was searching for a wife, found himself in need of money; he turned to Dagba, demanding £5 as a *kem* payment. But Dagba had no more money. Lankwagh, angry, then took £6 from another man for the same girl.

Lankwagh admitted the truth of Dagba's statement. But, he insisted, he was in the right, for he had received no *kem* payments from Dagba.

The *mbatarev* asked Dagba: 'Do you want the woman, or do you want your money back?' Dagba replied, 'The woman pleases me; money never pleases me.'

---

[1] In two instances, I have recorded different aspects of the same case in different places. In each place emphasis and elaboration of detail are different. Each is complete for the purpose in hand.

[2] i.e. pay for rights of cohabitation, not marriage. See L. and P. Bohannan, *The Tiv of Central Nigeria*, p. 75.

The *mbatarev* then asked her: 'Do you want to stay with Dagba, or do you want to return to your brother?' She looked at Dagba. He reached into his pocket and gave her 6*d*. Without speaking, she handed it to the scribe, thereby paying the registration fee for her marriage to Dagba.

'In this *jir*,' Chenge said, 'Dagba shall keep his wife, but he must make payments.' The amount was discussed: the guardian demanded £18; Dagba offered £5. Gbegba asked, 'Dagba, what about your bicycle? Is it better than a wife?'

Dagba agreed to sell his bicycle and pay £10 at next month's court session. To the guardian's objections, Chenge replied that he was lucky to get so much. In any event, it was merely the initial payment; the total would be discussed when Dagba made the first payment.

Dagba later told me that he had paid the full £10, but that the matter of the total was not discussed. Indeed, I believe I have never heard a total bridewealth sum discussed in a *jir*.

1.3. *Once a guardian has accepted payments from a husband, he has a responsibility to see that his ward does not live with any other man.*

JIR NO. 30. *Gbachan (husband) calls Apev (guardian)*
        A guardian lets his ward elope

Gbachan called Apev before the *jir*, alleging that Apev, his wife's guardian (and also her father), had given her in marriage to a third man. The *mbatarev* asked him what payment he had made for his wife. He said he had made payment of £4. 5*s*. and another 5*s*. fine because he had 'stolen' the woman.

The guardian then asked him, 'To whom did you make payments for the woman—to me or someone else?' Gbachan answered that he had given the money to Hwande, Ihulen, and Aie (who are 'children' of Apev). The *mbatarev* asked the guardian if the girl was present. He said she had gone to a husband in MbaYongo.

Chenge asked, 'Apev, do you mean to say that this girl went to a husband following her own heart, and you have not gone to see about it?'

Apev admitted that his daughter had simply gone, and he had done nothing. Chenge said, 'Apev, the *mbatarev* will "catch" you for this, but first you must send somebody to get your child and bring her home, so that we can hear this *jir* properly.'

Chenge told me later that they would probably fine Apev, but this part of the *jir* occurred shortly before I left Tivland, and I have no further information.

The father/guardian was blamed for allowing his ward, while still married to one man, to go off and form a 'marriage' with another. He could have been fined for such behaviour.

1.3*a*. *A guardian can be called before the* jir *if his married ward commits adultery*

Although this rule is implicit in the case immediately preceding, it emerges more clearly in:

JIR NO. 31. *Anyon* (*husband*) *calls Humbe* (*guardian*)
The guardian is called because his ward committed adultery

Anyon called Humbe, his wife's guardian (and father), before the *jir* for having allowed and encouraged her to leave the compound of her rightful husband and bear children in adultery. Humbe replied that Anyon married his ward and took her home, where she bore him three children. Finally she ran back to her guardian because Anyon constantly beat her and all her children as well. Some time later, Humbe continued, she again became pregnant and bore a son, but her husband didn't come to name the child. Later she bore yet another child, whom her husband also failed to name. At this juncture, said Humbe, he began thinking he should get Anyon to make *kem* payments for the woman who had borne him so many children. But before he had done anything, Anyon called him to the *jir*. And on what grounds? The girl bore her children. 'Her husband says she has committed adultery. I, her father, have not seen that she has committed adultery simply by bearing her husband children. She has done well.'[1] He then turned to the *mbatarev* and said that Anyon should be made to come and make his payments for the woman here before the eyes of the *mbatarev*.

Chenge refused to follow this suggestion. In his opinion, Humbe should let Anyon return to his own compound and then follow him to receive the payments there.

The wife's mother now broke in: if they were going to send the woman and the children back to the husband, wouldn't they at least give her the fourth child to rear? Anyon constantly ill-treated this child, calling it an ugly child and a bastard, beating and cursing it. The *mbatarev* patiently, but plainly, told her that they would not do so; the child was Anyon's child (no matter who had begotten him). They

---

[1] Humbe did not mean, as it might appear in a European language, that the children had been begotten by Anyon, for indeed all concerned admitted that the last two were not. Since Anyon was the woman's husband, however, she was bearing his children in the sense that he is *pater* of all her children.

suggested that she go to Anyon's compound and ask to be given the child.[1]

This episode finished, the *mbatarev* told Anyon that he had behaved very badly; he had been neither a good husband nor a good son-in-law, and he ought to make a conciliatory gift to his father-in-law because he had been impertinent to him. Anyon, still surly, took 4s. from his pocket and gave it to Chenge to give to his father-in-law. Chenge refused, commenting that in these circumstances 4s. was scarcely enough. Humbe now spoke up: Chenge ought to make Anyon give him £1 as a conciliatory gift. Chenge would not set the sum; he recommended that Anyon go to Humbe's compound and present his gift there in a seemly fashion. Chenge also insisted that the husband was to have his wife and children; Anyon was to complain to him, the chief, if the guardian refused. With that, they left.

This *jir* raises the interesting question of the nature of adultery: apparently it is not adultery if the wife's purpose is to bear children that her husband will not give her. This view is borne out by the fact that the word for adultery (*idiar*) is the same as that for sexual passion.

1.4. *If a guardian's kinsman takes money for his ward, the matter becomes a debt among kinsmen which does not concern the husband*

This rule is vividly illustrated by:

JIR NO. 32. *Akol (husband) calls Yua (guardian and father)*
       A guardian's kinsman accepts bridewealth

Akol stole Yua's daugher, without her father's knowledge. The girl's mother had known of the elopement and had helped to bring it about. Afterwards, an elder kinsman of the wife went to Akol, who gave him a goat 'for the shell' and 10s. 'to open the hut'.

Some months later the girl, having become pregnant, visited her father's compound. There her father 'caught' her and gave her to another husband. Thereupon Akol called his *jir*.

When *mbatarev* asked Yua for his version he said that he, his daughter's guardian, had never accepted bridewealth from Akol; therefore he had acted correctly.

The kinsman was called, and readily admitted that he had received the goat and the 10s. On hearing this, the *mbatarev* turned on Yua,

---

[1] When there is more than one child, it is morally almost impossible for a son-in-law to refuse such a request. It means only that the child's mother's mother rears him; it does not affect his agnation.

'You! Your child is pregnant, and did you ask who impregnated her? Your kinsman took money for your child, and you took her and gave her to another husband. You have committed a fault.'

Yua sent his son to tell his daughter to return, and she was again given to Akol.

1.5. *A child who has no* pater *outside his mother's lineage can, through payments by his genitor, be filiated to his genitor's lineage*

A Tiv child whose mother has not had payments or exchange made for her is 'agnate' (*ityô*) in his mother's agnatic lineage. In some lineages genitors of such children can make payments for them, thus filiating the children to the agnatic lineage of the genitor.

JIR NO. 33. *Utsa of Shangev (pro-husband) calls Samber of MbaDuku (pro-guardian)*

A genitor makes payments for his child

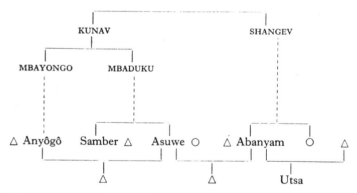

Abanyam came to MbaDuku many years ago, to marry Asuwe and took her away with him. He made *kem* payments for her—in brass rods and *gbagir* cloth—to his intermediary. However, there was a dispute within Asuwe's ward-sharing group, so that it was uncertain which of her agnatic kinsmen should be her guardian. Therefore none of them would accept the bridewealth from the intermediary, and he—long since dead and in any case not of the same lineage as either guardian or husband—eventually 'ate' it. This meant, in effect, that Abanyam never made payments for Asuwe, because no one in her lineage had received the bridewealth. She bore him one son; then Abanyam died. Since she did not want to be inherited, Asuwe came home. Samber had by now become her guardian. He accepted money from Anyôgô of MbaYongo, who came, courted, married and made payments for her. However, when she became pregnant by him she slipped away in the night and went to Abanyam's to bear her second child.[1] Several months after the birth, she departed, taking both her children with her. Abanyam's people now called a case against Samber, her guardian, asking for their 'wife'. Actually, they were not demanding her bodily return, but were making a claim to the paternity of both her children; they also hoped to get back some bridewealth.

The *mbatarev* decided that Samber was not at fault for accepting bridewealth from Anyôgô, because no one in MbaDuku had accepted bridewealth from Abanyam when he married Asuwe. They decided, further, that since Anyôgô had not been Asuwe's legal husband at the time she bore her eldest son, his heirs should be allowed to make payments to MbaDuku, thus affiliating the child to his lineage. The second son, however, was begotten by Anyôgô after he had become Asuwe's legal husband; he was, therefore, Anyôgô's lawful child and filiated to Anyôgô's lineage, MbaYongo.

It is, thus, possible under some conditions for a genitor to make payments for his child to the agnates of its mother, thereby becoming its *pater* as well as its genitor.[2] It is usually *not* possible if the mother was married to some other man at the time of the child's conception or birth.

I have known several instances in which a man, whose genealogical position was in question because bridewealth payments or exchange had never been made for his mother, had himself gone to the heirs of her guardian and made payment for himself. This is usually £2 or £3, corresponding to the amount deducted from returnable bridewealth for a son.

The *jir* also indicates that responsibility for a wife's conduct does not depend upon the husband's payment but upon the guardian's acceptance. Had any of Samber's affines in this *jir* actually accepted the bridewealth which Abanyam had paid, and had Samber *then* married her off to another husband after he became her guardian, he would have been culpable.

---

[1] Tiv women often do this sort of thing. Their motivation is in the congeniality of the women of the compound. I have recorded many times that Tiv women bear children to subsequent husbands in the compound of the first husband, especially if the first child lived.

[2] These terms and those which follow are discussed and defined in E. E. Evans-Pritchard, *Some Aspects of Marriage and the Family among the Nuer*, Rhodes-Livingstone Papers No. 11, 1945, and in Laura Bohannan, 'Dahomean Marriage: a Revaluation', *Africa*, October 1949, pp. 273–87.

2. PROTECTION OF RIGHTS IN WOMEN

Rights in a Tiv woman can be said to be the 'property' of her agnatic lineage, and more particularly of that part which forms her ward-sharing group. Certain of these rights are transferred to her husband and his lineage on marriage. In a recognized Tiv marriage, both rights *in uxorem* and rights *in genetricem* are transferred to the husband in exchange for similar rights in another woman or in exchange for bridewealth.

It is possible to protect one's rights in a woman by calling the violator of the rights before the *jir*.

2.1. *'Stealing a woman'* (i a ii kwase), *be she wife or girl, is a finable offence*

JIR NO. 34. *Pev (guardian) calls Ortese (husband)*
[MbaDuku Case Book 1944: 114]

'The *mbatarev* called Ortese and asked him whether he had Pev's ward. He said that he had. The *mbatarev* told him to make payments on the ward of Pev, but Ortese had no money. Ortese was then fined 5*s.* for having stolen Pev's ward and failing to make payments for her. The *mbatarev* said he was to make a £3 payment for the girl and bring £1 for [that part of the wedding celebration called] the *kwase amar* dance. He has not brought it yet.'

There are many *jir* in this chapter in which a man is fined or otherwise penalized for 'stealing a woman'.

2.2. *Adultery with a married woman is a finable offence for both man and adulterous wife*

JIR NO. 35. *Maji (husband's mother) calls Agim (seducer)*

Maji, a widow living with her grown sons, called a case against Agim, and told the *mbatarev*, 'Agim took my [son's] wife.'

The *mbatarev* asked Agim, 'Did you marry this woman's wife?' He said that he had met the girl at market and had asked her, 'Are you anybody's wife?' [i.e. shall I get in trouble if I try to have an affair with you?] When she replied that she was not, he asked her to come home with him. She had come, and had made no move to leave. That was all he knew about the matter.

Cross-questioning of the girl and her guardian revealed that she had been 'married' (*er*) by Maji for one of her sons who was away from home indefinitely, and had got bored living without a husband.

The *mbatarev* fined Agim £3 for stealing another man's wife, and fined the girl 10s. for leaving her husband's compound and living in adultery (*idiar*). Agim had no money, so he was sent to prison for three months. The woman also had no money, so her husband's brother paid her fine.

Tiv use the terms 'stealing a woman/wife' and 'adultery' for the same situation—the former of a man, the latter of a woman.

2.3. *It is a finable offence to be accessory to adultery*

JIR NO. 19. *Nguhar (husband) calls Tarkighir (adulterer)*[1]

Nguhar briefly announced to the *mbatarev* that Tarkighir had seduced his wife by offering to take her to her natal compound. Tarkighir said that one day this woman, whose name was Ierun, came to his compound accompanied by another woman named Girgi. Ierun had told him to go and tell another young man (who was never named) to come and lie with her. She then went into his hut while the other woman sat in the reception hut. Tarkighir said that he went and called the man who also went into the hut.

The *mbatarev* here interrupted him and told him he had committed a transgression (*er kwaghbo*) because he was 'spoiling somebody's wife'. They readily agreed that he should be fined £2. He asked whether the fine was because the woman had sent him or because he had gone. Gbegba, the oldest of the *mbatarev*, asked him patiently, 'If it were your wife, and someone had gone and got another man to lie with her, how would you like it?' Tarkighir replied that if his own wife told him to go and fetch one of her suitors to fornicate with her, he would do so. The entire court laughed and called him a fool (*bumenor*). Gbegba again became serious and said that the woman in this particular case was not his wife and all men were not such fools. Since he had gone on an evil errand, he would be fined £2.

The *mbatarev* then turned to the wife and asked her to tell what she knew of the matter. She said she had not sent Tarkighir to fetch anybody nor had he fetched anybody. She had gone with her co-wife Girgi to weed her farms, and while she was weeding Tarkighir had come to her and said, 'You woman, are you a fool or not? Here poverty and trouble keep on at you with your husband. Why don't you leave him and go join your mother?' When she told him she had no money to buy food on the road, he offered her 6d.—and even offered to go with her. He told her that he very much wanted to marry her, so he would take her to her mother's compound and then return home and begin courting properly. That, she said, was all she knew about the matter.

Turning back to Tarkighir, one of the *mbatarev* asked, 'Is that the

[1] Details concerning the oaths in this case are given above, p. 44.

way it was?' He said it was not, and repeated that the woman had sent him to fetch another man. If the *mbatarev* weren't satisfied with his story, he suggested that they call Girgi, the co-wife, and ask her to tell what happened.

The case was adjourned, while the *mbatarev* sent for Girgi. When she arrived, she was with some difficulty made to take an oath. She stated that she and Ierun often went to Tarkighir's compound to rest while working on their farms, which were nearby. On this particular day he had asked Ierun to go into his hut, and she did. After some time, she (Girgi) had rapped at the door and told Ierun to come out, so that they could go back to their farms.

The *mbatarev* asked her, 'Where did Ierun get the 6*d*.?' After much persuasion, she said that Ierun had admitted being given it by Tarkighir.

The *mbatarev* now decided that, having first fined Tarkighir £2 for assisting a woman to commit adultery, they must also sentence him to two months in gaol for committing adultery with her. He said he couldn't pay the fine, so they gave him three months in gaol.

The case appeared to be concluded when the husband shouted for attention and asked if it wasn't usual to fine a woman in such cases. Chenge said that they sometimes did, and asked, 'Do you want your wife to be fined?' 'She has done a very bad thing,' the husband said. Gbegba then suggested that they fine her 10*s*.; Chenge agreed. The woman said quietly that she had no money. The husband told her that she had 6*d*., but himself paid the 10*s*. fine. He got a receipt from the scribe, and the case was ended.

I tried on several occasions, but without success, to discover how the husband collected the 10*s*. debt from his wife, for I have no doubt that he did collect it; Iyorkôsu, my clerk, suggested cynically that perhaps it was worth 10*s*. to him to have something to hold over her.

Tarkighir, although the full story proved that he did not in fact connive at the woman's adultery with any man save himself, was fined, on the basis of his original statement, for having done so. When the *mbatarev* heard the truth, the fine was not rescinded.

3. DISSOLUTION OF MARRIAGE

Just as those rules concerning the regulation of marriage which become evident in the course of various *jir* centre on notions concerning bridewealth and rights in women, so the *jir* which concern dissolution of marriage are mainly disputes about bridewealth.

3.1. *If a woman leaves her husband, the guardian (and some others) must refund certain parts of the bridewealth*

JIR NO. 36. *Adugba (husband) calls Ahidi (guardian)*

Adugba called a *jir* against Ahidi, his wife's guardian, because she had run away to Ahidi's compound.

Ahidi admitted that what Adugba said was correct. The *mbatarev* told him to restore Adugba's wife. He said that since Adugba paid no attention to her, wouldn't dress her properly, or provide her with adequate farms, he had given her as wife to another man and had no intention of making her return to Adugba.

The *mbatarev* asked Adugba, 'How much did you give when you married this woman?' He replied, 17 score brass rods and £1. The guardian did not dispute the amount. The *mbatarev* said that 17 score rods would be about £1. 5s., which made a total of £2. 5s. Ahidi took £2. 5s. from his bag and paid it before the eyes of the judges.

This case, besides showing that it is possible for a man to take his former wife's guardian before a *jir* in order to have his bridewealth refunded, indicates that once a guardian has made an arrangement with his ward's husband, he must show grounds for removing her similar to those which she must show if she seeks a divorce (Rule 3.4).

Sometimes there are disputes about which parts of the bridewealth are returnable. The amount paid for a woman is always returnable, less deductions for children she has borne. Although the amount to be refunded may be disputed, I have never heard the rule disputed. There is, however, much dispute about which other payments are returnable.

Return of the gifts made to the wife's parents is not always required. I saw one instance in which a mother-in-law herself repaid £3 for cloth 'under the eyes of the *jir*'. I did not record any case in which similar gifts to the father-in-law were returned, but was told that it was often necessary. I have no record of any other case in which a man requests the refund of money he has spent on ceremonies for the benefit of his wife, and I was told that only a foolish man (*bumenor*) would make such a request.

Several payments, I was told, can never be returned once they have been made: those for the 'shell' which buys the right to first intercourse with the girl (Tiv do not see this as a matter of virginity); what we should call 'bribes' or 'gifts' to the mother to 'open the hut door'; and another to 'open the girl's legs', which is a thank-offering for the girl's mother's consent to the marriage.

3.2. *A widow who does not want to be inherited can return home, and her guardian must return bridewealth (minus allowance for children) to her husband's heir*

Today—and Tiv say that it was always so—a widow sometimes does not want to be inherited in her dead husband's compound. She is then free to return to her own home. Many widows choose not to be inherited, but the dead husband's agnates always tend to resent their behaviour—especially if they are of child-bearing age or have young children.

Widows are inherited about a year after the husband's death. Those who elect to stay are asked to name their levir; their wishes are in most cases taken as final (but see Moot II below). Those wishing to leave are 'distributed' to the men entitled, but not chosen, to inherit a widow from the dead man. Tiv folk theory on the subject is that these men can go to the widows' guardians, demand the return of bridewealth, and marry new wives with the proceeds. We saw in *Jir* No. 33 above that a young heir was calling a case concerning an old widow whom he had inherited from his father. An even clearer case is to be found in:

JIR NO. 37. *Pro-husband calls guardian*
A widow chooses not to be inherited

Before 1927, when Tiv were still practising exchange marriage, an MbaGbera man made an exchange with an MbaDuku man.

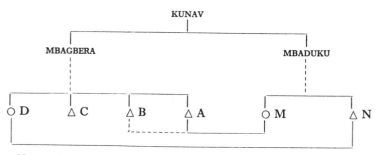

Note: I do not know the actual kinship relationship of A, B, C, and D, and have presented it here in its simplest form. The only thing of importance is that they are agnatic kinsmen and members of the same ward-sharing group. M and N were paternal half-siblings.

In this exchange A took his ward D and gave her to N in exchange for N's ward M, whom he married. When A died several years later, his wife was inherited by his 'brother' B. When B died, M returned to MbaDuku. At this time, she had borne four children to MbaGbera, either to husband A or to B. Her exchange partner, D, had borne only one child in MbaDuku and had since died.

The present case was called against N by C, who had inherited M as a wife in the distribution of B's goods, made about a year after his death. C asked the *mbatarev* in the correct, formal way to 'return his wife and child' (the youngest child had returned with his mother to her home).

N, the woman's guardian, told the court that he was willing to give his ward back to C, as she was their wife. He grasped her wrist, formally to do so, when the woman said, 'Wait, I have not spoken.'

The *mbatarev* asked the woman why it was that she did not want to return to MbaGbera. She replied that she had been inherited once in MbaGbera, and that she preferred not to be inherited twice. In any case she had borne four children in MbaGbera. Thereupon the *mbatarev* took the youngest child by the wrist and handed it over to C, its father's brother.[1] They then told the woman that, since she had borne four children in MbaGbera and her exchange partner (*ikyar*) had borne only one child in MbaDuku, and was dead, the exchange marriage was completed, and she was free to marry again.

In checking this matter later, I was told by the *mbatarev* individually (not by the *jir*) that the woman would probably marry again, and that her guardian N would collect bridewealth for her—that the exchange marriage was finished because her husband was dead and no further change in the filiation of the children would be made. One of the *mbatarev* ended our discussion with, 'In any case, she won't fetch over a couple of quid.'

3.3. *If a woman dies, her husband cannot recover bridewealth from her guardian*

I have not myself seen a case in which a widower tried to recover his bridewealth, but found this case while examining the records kept by MbaDuku scribes. I give a translation of that entry.

---

[1] This was a boy of 7 or 8 years. This did not mean that the boy must return to MbaGbera immediately to live, and I do not know whether in fact he did so. The meaning is a reassurance to all that the child is filiated to MbaGbera, not to MbaDuku, his mother's lineage.

JIR NO. 38. *Mela (widower) calls Timbir (guardian of deceased wife)*
[MbaDuku Case Book, 1944: 102]

'The *mbatarev* told Timbir that Mela had said that he had married a
ward of Timbir's, that she had died and he wanted his money (£3)
back. The *mbatarev* told Mela that they had heard this case in the days
when Gbegba was chief of the MbaDuku and they did not intend to
reopen a *jir* which had been previously ended, especially as the *jir*
was very old and Mela had never appealed. They also added that there
was a *tindi*, written on paper,[1] that if a woman dies, a man's bridewealth
was not to be returned to him and that this had always been the custom
of the Tiv in *kem* marriages [as differentiated from exchange marriages
where the exchange was either 'finished' by the return of the dead
woman's exchange partner, or was reaffirmed by giving a new woman
for her]. Mela wailed that the money and the woman were both lost
to him.'

Bridewealth, although of the utmost importance, is not the only
consideration in the dissolution of marriage. One partner or both
(or the guardian) must have grounds.

Tiv tell the investigator that men never divorce their wives.
This is not, strictly speaking, true. I know two instances in which
men (or their fathers) have driven wives out of their compounds.
Jir already cited show instances of men stating that they do not
want their wives to come back to them. It is true, however, that
husbands do not call *jir* for divorce. Such *jir* are always called by
women or by their guardians.

Divorce *jir* called by women are easily divisible into two sorts:
(1) the woman calls her guardian for making her stay with a
husband whom she finds distasteful; (2) she calls her husband
himself. In the first case, the dissolution of the marriage is called
kwase bunde. *Kwase* means both 'wife' and 'woman'. *Bunde* refers
to a breakdown, as of negotiations; it means 'to be cancelled', as of
a meeting or journey; it means 'to annul', in the sense of taking
back something which has been said or done. However, it is
dangerous to translate the word as 'annul', for it bears relatively
little relationship to European ideas of marriage annulments. A
marriage breaks down or *bunde* because of a breakdown in some
relationship *other than* that between husband and wife.

[1] I am assured both by Tiv and by Captain Downes that some of the marriage
rules were written down in the early 1930's and attempts were made to apply
them as law. I could not find a list of them in the files or from extensive inquiry
in Tivland. Captain Downes provided some of them from his personal notes.

H

Many Tiv women bring their guardians to court rather than their husbands, because it is considered more seemly to do so—it reflects less, it is said, on the husband. It reminds one of American women who sue for mental cruelty instead of naming the 'real reason'. Another important factor is that if a woman calls her guardian, she is calling the *jir* before her own *mbatarev*. If she calls her husband, it must be heard by his *mbatarev*.

It is, however, necessary for a woman to present grounds in order to be divorced. I heard one *jir* in which a woman sought divorce on inadequate grounds:

JIR NO. 39 *Bukwagh (wife) calls Adetsô (husband)*
    Divorce refused on inadequate grounds

Adetsô, of Shangev Ya, married Bukwagh, an MbaDuku girl. She left him and returned home. He came after her. Because he would not stop annoying her in her kinsmen's compound, and kept trying to induce her to return to him, she called a case before the MbaDuku *mbatarev*. She said that her husband had given her sufficient cloth (a more or less literal metaphor for caring for her material wants), he had not fought with her and he did not beat her much; she simply did not like him.

The judges gave her a lecture to the effect that she was lucky to have such a husband, and told her to go with him. She said she would not. They told the husband to take her and get her out of there. She said nothing more, but she put up a pretty good fight. In the long run, it took two of her husband's kinsmen to carry her off: one grasping her arms, the other her ankles. There was no noise, but she was still kicking and struggling as they carried her out of the compound.

The grounds which this woman mentioned (but admitted that she lacked) justify divorce (*mpav*). As we shall see, the grounds in the marriage *bunde* are somewhat different:

3.4. *A woman can dissolve her marriage, with grounds, by calling her guardian before the* jir.

All the cases in my samples in which a woman brings her guardian before the *jir* and achieves the dissolution of her marriage centre on the barrenness of the marriage, insufficient sexual attention to provide children, or the death of all or most of the children of the marriage.

JIR NO. 40. *MbaTôô (wife) calls Ataka (guardian)*
Sterile marriage [MbaDuku Case Book 1945: 62]

MbaTôô called Ataka complaining that she had not borne a child to her husband and didn't want to return to him. Her guardian, Ataka, said that MbaTôô was no longer his ward, although she had been when she married her husband (Goramise), and that it was true that she had never borne him a child. The *mbatarev* adjourned the case until they could hear what Goramise had to say in the matter. The husband came and the case 'caught' Ataka. That is, Ataka was ordered not to force or persuade his ward to return to Goramise but to allow the marriage to lapse, break or be cancelled—to *bunde*.

Barren marriages are usually dissolved (*bunde*) rather than ended by divorce (*mpav*). Marriages in which all the children die at an early age are treated similarly. I have never myself seen a *jir* called on these grounds. Several occur in the case books, of which a good example is the following, in the terse language of the scribe:

JIR NO. 41. *Ikyuji (wife) calls Alaji (guardian)*

'The *mbatarev* called Alaji and asked him about the matter of Ikyuji. He said that she had borne children to her husband but that they had died. So this wife *bunde* her husband.'

The death of all the children of a marriage very often comes up in those *jir* we call moots, for it is most often thought to be associated with witchcraft activities in the husband's lineage, and the N.A. courts do not deal with witchcraft.

3.5. *A woman can dissolve her marriage, with grounds, by bringing an action against her husband*

When a woman calls her husband before the *jir* to get a divorce, her usual grounds are not barrenness or death of children (charges which tacitly imply witchcraft), but rather what Tiv see as the obligations of husband to wife as wife, not as mother. The metaphor in which a husband is usually charged with being inadequate is that he does not give his wife cloth. Some husbands try to make the judges take the metaphor literally, by proving that they have indeed given their wives cloth: but once the judges begin the investigation, it is usually simple to discover the real inadequacies of which complaint is being made. The use of the metaphor is well illustrated in:

JIR NO. 42. *Kusana (wife) calls Tar (husband)*
[MbaDuku Case Book 1944: 99]

'The *mbatarev* asked Tar, "Your wife, Kusana, has told us that you are keeping her in want, not clothing her or making farms for her, and that you are controlling her with fetishes; therefore she won't return to you." Tar said that he had done nothing; his wife had been caught in adultery, and he was shocked that the *mbatarev* should suggest that he had done such things on the basis of her false accusations. The *jir* caught Kusana [was decided against her] and she went with her husband. The case is finished.'

In bringing her complaint, this wife alleged (apparently without grounds) the three most common charges against a husband: (1) that he will not clothe her; (2) that he does not make her farms properly so that she can feed herself and her children from them; and (3) that he is restraining her by charms and fetishes. It is my opinion that divorce by 'mutual consent' is usually obtained on such grounds—the woman who brings the action accuses her husband of being inadequate by referring to the list of things that a good husband does. She does not necessarily mean that he actually did or did not do them.

There are a few grounds for divorce yet to be considered. One is a husband's leprosy.

JIR NO. 43. *Kwaghmande (husband) calls Ibu (guardian)*
Divorce from a leper

Kwaghmande called a *jir* against Ibu, alleging that he had married Ibu's ward, and when she had returned to her home, Ibu didn't send her back. The *mbatarev* told Kwaghmande that this case had been brought to their attention before. Gbegba said, 'Kwaghmande, your wife tells us that you have leprosy,' and added that it was for this reason that they had divorced her from him. 'Is it,' Gbegba finished, 'your money that you want? for if it is money, Ibu must bring it and give it to you.'

Kwaghmande cried out that he didn't want money, he wanted his wife. The scribe now interrupted and told Kwaghmande to give him his 'paper' (court receipt) so that he could cancel the *jir*—unless he wanted to call a *jir* about money, in which case he would change the entry. Kwaghmande repeated that he did not want his wife divorced from him. The *mbatarev* told him to give his receipt to the clerk. He did so, and the *jir* was cancelled. Chenge told Ibu to pay within a month the money he owed to Kwaghmande and the *mbatarev* turned to the next *jir*.

Divorce may also be sought on grounds of desertion:

JIR NO. 44. Jir *concerning desertion, called by a wife*
[Text written by Iyorkôsu Ageva]

'A woman named MbaVaan called a *jir* before the *mbatarev* because she had no husband. The *mbatarev* asked her where her husband had gone. She replied that he disappeared into the bush five years ago [i.e. he ran away]. The *mbatarev* divorced her from this man so that she could look for another husband. They gave her a paper to which they had attached their thumb-prints, as evidence [literally, as a witness] that they had divorced this woman from her husband.'

A woman can also get a divorce if her husband has used medicines and charms on her. This is usually called 'illegitimate juju', in English, in the scribe's record books.

JIR NO. 45. *Alaghga* (*husband*) *calls his wife's guardian*
Divorce on grounds of 'illegitimate juju'

Alaghga came before the *mbatarev* and said that his wife had gone home several months before and would not return to him. The *mbatarev*, as usual in such cases, asked if he wanted his wife or his money. He said that he wanted his wife. The *mbatarev* called her from among the spectators and asked, 'Why is it that you won't return to your husband's compound?' She said that he had cut off bits of her hair and fingernails and that she wanted them back. These are ingredients of a charm called *ichuu* which, buried before the hut in which the woman sleeps, prevents her from running away, or, if she does run away, draws her irresistibly back. The husband denied making the charm and asked his wife when and where he might have got hold of her hair and nails. She replied that he had taken them while she was sleeping. She told the *mbatarev* emphatically that this was taking unfair advantage of a wife and that she had no intention of returning to him, so they granted her divorce.

This *jir* completes the examples illustrating the various grounds on which Tiv say that a woman can claim a divorce. It does not, however, complete the survey of *jir* that may be heard at the time of dissolution of a marriage. Two other classes of marital problem come before Tiv judges: those concerning filiation and custody of children, and those concerning property.

3.6. *Filiation of children is to the lineage of the* pater. *Custody of children may be given to persons other than the* pater

I have no record of any good *jir* dealing with filiation of children.

None in the scribe's Case Book gave sufficient detail to be of value. Such *jir* are usually concerned with trying to determine which of two successive husbands begot a child.

I have, however, several *jir* in which not the filiation but the custody of the child is at issue. Such a case was described in Chapter III. Tiv judges, in my experience, always give custody of the child to the mother if she is a good woman. Her custody lasts until the child is about thirteen, when fathers come for their daughters in order to arrange marriages and sons go to live with their fathers because men enjoy full citizenship rights only in the *tar* of their natal agnatic lineages.

3.6a. Custody of a nubile daughter is vested in the pater, *following on filiation, though before nubility it may be given to the mother or some other kinsman*

JIR NO. 46.   *Ayila (husband) calls Aungwa (guardian)*
             Custody of a child

Mbatese had been given by her guardian to a first husband, who had not made *kem* payments. The guardian therefore demanded her return and married her to Ayila, who made the initial payments. She bore Ayila a daughter and, a few months later, ran away from him and returned to the compound of her first husband. Thereupon Aungwa, the guardian, went to the first husband and got £2 in *kem* payments. He had thus taken money from two men for the same woman.

Ayila called a *jir* against Aungwa saying that he wanted his small daughter but not his wife—he would like his money refunded instead.

The *mbatarev* asked the woman to state her position in the matter. She denied none of the facts, as presented by Ayila, and told the *mbatarev* that if they gave him the child she would return to him, as she wanted to live with the child. Ayila broke in here and said he did not want his wife and would not have her; it was only his child that he wanted. The *mbatarev* told him that if he refused his wife in this way, he could not now take the child. They offered to give him a written statement that the child was his, so that when she reached puberty he could come and get her; but since Mbatese was not a bad woman, and since she wanted the child, they intended that she and the child should have the pleasure of living together until the child was old enough to be married.

Ayila said he could not possibly accept this arrangement. Chenge said that in that case he could leave; the woman was to stay in his own compound, under the eyes of one of his senior wives, until the *mbatarev* met again and determined what to do in this case.

Thereupon Ayila said that he would take the £3 he had given for Mbatese. The *mbatarev* told him to go to his father-in-law's compound and ask for his money in a seemly manner. If it was refused, then a case for debt could be called. They all left. I could not ascertain what settlement was finally made.

Lastly, there is the matter of property settlement. In general it is true to say that a Tiv woman has no property rights whatever except as a wife. Before her marriage, and after its dissolution, she has rights in her natal lineage to property or land only as she utilizes those of her mother (who has or had rights as her father's wife). Once married, she has property rights in her husband's lineage and *tar* so long as she remains married. When she leaves her husband, she forfeits those rights.

3.7. *When a woman leaves her husband, she must take nothing with her save the property which she brought with her on marriage*

This principle is best illustrated in:

INSTANCE NO. 47. *A woman's property rights on divorce*

A woman, born of MbaDuku, came before the *mbatarev* and said she wanted to ask them about her divorce in MbaYongo. She had, she said, been married for many years to an MbaYongo man; when she left him, she took £2 with her. He had called a *jir* against her, and the *mbatarev* of MbaYongo had made her give him the £2. She wanted to know if this was right; she had got £1 by making and selling beer, and the other by trading yams, sweet potatoes, and other produce.

Chenge told her: 'My child, the water which you drew to boil the beer was the water of your husband's *tar*. The soil that grew the yams, the sweet potatoes, and millet which you sold for the other pound, was the soil of your husband's *tar*.'

Huwa capped the illustration: 'If you kill an elephant in your husband's *tar*, and you leave him, it is his elephant.'

Chenge finished by instructing her that any goats or fowls she bought with money she had got from her husband, or from produce of his *tar*, she could not take with her when she left him. Only the money which she had brought with her from her compound could she take back to it.

It should be repeated, however, that so long as a Tiv woman is married she controls a major portion of the food and a not inconsiderable proportion of the monetary wealth of the compound. So long as she is a wife she has generous rights to a livelihood and sufficiency of goods. Only when she leaves her husband must she forgo all her property except what she got from her own kinsmen.

IV. MARRIAGE IN THE JIR

Representative *jir* which concern marriage have been arranged so as to elicit, from the total cluster of rights and obligations of the parties, those that can be claimed with the aid of the *mbatarev* and their *jir*. These rules are not merely implicit in the cases, but are very often made explicit by the Tiv themselves. They are rules of the sort that Llewellyn and Hoebel have called 'legal norms'.[1]

Legal norms are those norms or rules of an institution which enter into the jural institutions. Jural institutions in all societies use and work with folk systems, whether they be overt and stated, or whether they have validity only in vocabulary and habitual action. However, the jural institutions of some societies—including our own—create a second folk systematization, be it a codification or some other form of *corpus juris*, which is erected between the judges and the institutions to which the rules apply.

In our own society, there are norms of family life and of marriage, the organization of which is to be found in social action within the family, and in our moral and ethical statements and ideas about it. There is also the 'substantive law' concerning marriage, in which some norms of family life and marriage have been reorganized for the specific purpose of action in courts. The two organizations use much of the same material, and can be made congruent on most points, but they are still two organizations, each with a different purpose.

My organization of the rules that emerge in Tiv marriage cases is of still another sort: it is an analytical system for determining some of the norms of Tiv marriage. It is not a folk system either of Tiv marriage institutions or of Tiv 'substantive law'. Tiv ideas and actions concerning family and marriage form the folk system of their family institutions. They do not codify or in any other way reorganize any of these rules to make a special body for jural purposes, as do the Code Civil and the Japanese Civil Code. In a sense, the entire institution enters into the *jir*, not just a specialized part of it.

When we study jural institutions, we must be sure that we do not attribute more to them than is actually there. Among Tiv, the *jir* settles disputes. The judges or *mbajiriv* do so in terms of their knowledge of Tiv institutions; they do not do so in terms of rules

[1] *The Cheyenne Way*, Chapter II.

of those institutions which have been resystemized specifically for the purpose of jural action. The 'rules' in Tivland are the norms of institutions. The organization of the rules is the institution itself. There is no second organization for specifically jural purposes, no discipline of law and no *corpus juris* in the Tiv folk system. There are only laws and the norms of institutions, which may be considered to form a *corpus juris* in an analytical system if it is fruitful to do so.

V. THE JIR IN MARRIAGE

Having seen that marriage enters the *jir* in that the folk system of the entire institution is brought to bear, rather than a re-interpretation of part of it for specifically jural purposes, we must now look at the obverse problem: how does the *jir* enter into the institution of marriage? We can best ask this question by asking, 'How do Tiv use their *jir*, and for what purpose?'

The most important use that Tiv make of the *jir* is as a threat or lever to impel social action. Nowhere is this better brought out than in:

INSTANCE NO. 48. *The* jir *as a threat in the marriage dispute between Tyokyer and Tyumnya*

Early one morning, Orihiwe (one of my clerks) and I started out to spend a few hours with Tyokyer, a man with whom I could talk comfortably for hours about things in general. Tyokyer was almost always willing to be interrupted, and seemed to enjoy our talks as much as I did. I had in mind discussing Tiv notions of physiology, in which I was particularly interested at the time.

Tyokyer was willing and eager to talk, but he was not interested in physiology that day. He had trouble. He had given his ward (his daughter) to a Shangev man who, he said, gave him £4. 'He was', Tyokyer said, 'a nice, clean boy and I liked the look of him.' The boy, named Hindan, took Tyokyer's daughter home with him as his wife. Within a few days, Hindan became ill and soon afterwards died.

When Tyokyer heard the news, he sent his son to fetch back the girl. The son, aged about twenty, arrived at Hindan's compound and saw his sister, but Hindan's kinsmen refused to give her up. When his son returned with this message, Tyokyer became very angry, and again sent him to bring the girl home, this time ordering him unconditionally to do so. The girl ran away, joined her brother on the path, and came home with him. Tyokyer said that some days later he had sent a message that Hindan's kinsmen should come and discuss the matter of refunding the bridewealth.

Hindan's kinsman (named Tyumnya) set out for Tyokyer's compound, but on the way turned off to Chenge's compound to 'tell' him about the matter in the presence of witnesses—that is, to make Chenge publicly aware that the situation existed. Chenge sent a message to Huwa (of MbaYar, Tyokyer's smaller lineage), telling him to get Tyokyer, the girl, and the Shangev people together and ask them to agree on a story; if Huwa could do so, he was to settle it himself, otherwise he was to bring it before the assembled *mbatarev*.

At the time when Orihiwe and I heard Tyokyer's story, we did not know who the Shangev people were. The next afternoon, however, Orihiwe told me that a kinsman of his wife had come to see him, and that Hindan (a common Tiv name) had been his (Orihiwe's) affine.

Tyumnya, said Orihiwe, was his wife's kinsman, so he went thoroughly into the matter. Tyumnya claimed that Hindan had paid £10. 17s. to Tyokyer for the girl. When Tyumnya went to Tyokyer's, the latter told him to get the marriage intermediary; when he went to do so (Tyumnya said) the intermediary refused to go to Tyokyer's compound under any circumstances, claiming that Tyokyer had tried to get him to concoct a lie about the amount of bridewealth and split the profit.

When at last they all met at Huwa's, Tyokyer said that Hindan had given him £4; Tyumnya said that the amount was £10. 17s. The intermediary, called as a witness, said on oath that the amount was £9. 10s. Tyokyer said that that was wrong, it was really £8. Tyumnya said he did not believe £8 any more than he did £4.

Huwa eventually got the £9. 10s. from Tyokyer and gave it to Tyumnya, both transactions taking place before several witnesses. Tyokyer's daughter was then courted by and married to another husband in MbaYongo, the lineage in the opposite direction from Shangev.

The main point revealed by this case is that the *jir* can be used as a threat to force people to perform their obligations in a manner coinciding with the way most people think that they should be performed. The threat of the *jir* was used to bring about a settlement which was considered fair by all.

Reference to the cases reviewed earlier in this chapter will indicate that far the greater number of them lead to a correct set of actions and relationships within the institution of marriage. The *jir* points out the correct action, and assumes that the principals will carry it out. The assumption is usually correct. Thus, in

Jir No. 31, it was suggested that Anyon should give his father-in-law a conciliatory gift because he had, in Tiv eyes, maltreated his wife by not giving her children and then beating those she bore him by other genitors, and because he had insulted his father-in-law by dragging him before the *jir* when actually he himself was at fault. The gift was a recognition of wrong and a basis for re-establishing the relationship. It was atonement, but not what a Tiv would call punishment or penalty. The *jir* here reiterated the norms and made suggestions for the social action that would comply with them. The gift counteracted the breach. But the *jir* was not really interested in whether or not the gift was actually made, because it was not a penalty.

In the same case, Chenge and the other *mbatarev* refused to order that one of the children be given to the mother's mother. It is usual—it is, in fact, considered a norm—for a man with several children to 'give' one to his wife's mother to raise if she asks for this privilege. Chenge was anxious that the people should carry out their obligations in such a way that it would look as if the *jir* had not entered into the matter. He did say, however, that if any of the persons concerned did not carry out their obligations correctly, the *jir* was to be notified. It is difficult to say what the *mbaterev* would have done had any of those involved refused to carry out his obligations. It is an idle question, for, except in suits for debt, I have never known the issue raised.

Jir cannot, of course, make people carry out the conditions which society imposes as part of marriage. There are, however, some basic norms in the marriage relationship, the breach of which, when followed by a *jir*, can be repaired, as Tiv put it, by penalties enacted by the *jir*. The most stringent of these penalties is divorce, and we have seen above that the judges can order or grant a divorce.

In *Jir* No. 19, in which Tarkighir was tried for having committed adultery, the court fined him both for adultery and as accessory after the fact of adultery, and imprisoned him in lieu of a fine. Fining and imprisonment are social acts that follow on action by the *jir* and are penalty and retribution for the original breach, which cannot be undone. That such a fine is seen as a penalty is strongly suggested by the fact that the wife's husband requested the *jir* to levy a fine against her as well as against her lover.

In *Jir* No. 46, we found that Tiv judges not only attempt to

H

get people to carry out their obligations, but sometimes threaten penalties if they do not carry out *all* the obligations of a relationship. In that case, a man said that he wanted his child but not his wife. The wife was declared not to be a bad woman and therefore, if she wanted to return to him, the husband must either accept her or forgo the custody of the child until it was adult. The husband said he would forgo the child.

We can elicit from all the instances a series of three social actions which can be presented simply as a diagram:

I am obviously using norm as 'a rule or authoritative standard', and never in the sense of statistical norm or average.

Breach of norm must not be confused with the norm itself. It is not merely its opposite. A 'norm' is a rule or authorized standard —it is *not* an act. A social act may proceed in accordance with the norm, but it can never *be* the norm. A breach of norm is always a social act; it is followed (and therefore defined) by the type of social action we have called a 'counteraction'. The relationship between the two is very like that between 'proaction' and 'reaction' as defined by Murray.[1] The type of 'counteraction' in which we are specifically interested here is the *jir*, as it is purely a jural type of social action. There are, obviously, within the institution of marriage, many other sorts of social action that counteract breaches of norm.

The counteraction, if successful, is followed by a 'correction'. There are two types of 'correction': the first is action in accordance with the norm originally broken; the other is a substitute action, which is said to atone for the original breach.

In the cases discussed in this section, the breach of norm and most of the corrections are social acts within the institution of marriage. The counteraction is the *jir*, the jural institution. A few of the 'corrections' involve penal institutions.

I have, in this short discussion, avoided as irrelevant the difficult problem of 'sanctions'. In Austin's definition, 'sanction' is the ultimate force behind the counteraction and correction; 'the

[1] In Talcott Parsons and Edward A. Shils, *Toward a General Theory of Action*, p. 439.

evil which will probably be incurred in case a command be disobeyed'.[1] Radcliffe-Brown, who follows Leon Duguit, says that sanction is itself a social action; his definition reads: 'a reaction on the part of society or a considerable number of its members to a mode of behaviour which is thereby approved (positive sanctions) or disapproved (negative sanctions').[2] Taking this definition alone, a sanction would fall merely into the 'counteraction' category and the *jir* itself would be a sanction. If we take the technical usage of the word 'sanction', which refers to that portion of a law which sets forth the penalty to be expected for infringing the rest of it, the word would seem to refer wholly to what we have called the 'correction'.

'Sanction' is one of the very complex concepts used by Western lawyers and jurists for examining Western systems of law. But it seems to me to obscure more than it clarifies when used to examine the jural activity of alien, especially African, societies. Explanation in terms of a series of social actions which show the interpenetration of institutions, such as we have set forth in this section, seems more comprehensive and economical.

[1] John Austin, *Lectures on Jurisprudence*, 5th ed., pp. 91–92.
[2] A. R. Radcliffe-Brown, 'Sanction', *Encyclopædia of the Social Sciences*.

CHAPTER VI

DEBT *JIR*

I. DEBT AND LIVESTOCK

THE second major class of cases found recorded in the scribe's 'Civil Case Book' are those *jir* described as 'debt'. The Tiv word for this classification, *injô*, covers a wider range of phenomena and social relations than the English word 'debt' usually does. If I borrow money or goods and fail to repay, I have 'fallen into debt' (*gba injô*). Furthermore, if I have agreed to care for some of my kinsman's livestock, this stock and its natural increase are my debt or *injô* to him. Still further, if my animal damages a neighbour's field the matter 'becomes a debt' (*hingir injô*). Many Tiv personal relationships are expressed in terms of debt. If my ward has married into a lineage which has not provided me or one of my close kinsmen with a wife, it is their *injô* to do so, even though there may be no actual bridewealth debt. The matter of 'flesh debts' (*ikpindi*, which Tiv themselves correlate with *injô*) covers one of the primary problems of social relationships as expressed in terms of witchcraft and religious belief.

Rather than fit Tiv cases into European categories like tort, contract, property rights, etc., thus hiding the most important thing about them, I have organized the cases in such a way as to illustrate the Tiv notion of debt or *injô*, while allowing us to make finer distinctions in the analytical system outlined in the preceding chapter.

The simplest sort of debt *jir* called by Tiv involve livestock: disputes over ownership of livestock and disputes over the damage caused by livestock.

In Chapter III, when examining a day in MbaDuku *jir*, we described a dispute about some goats (*Jir* No. 2). Akpalu had 'released' a nanny goat with WanDzenge and, when he had come for her and her kids, a dispute arose about the number of kids the goat had borne. This case illustrates a general principle of Tiv stock-keeping: one seldom keeps one's own goats, lest their number be decimated by the rightful demands of one's kinsmen for sacrificial animals. It also illustrates the rule that the person who looks after another person's goats can claim one kid in three (with adjustments of this number according to the individual case). The *jir* concerned the debt resulting from such an arrangement.

I have in my notes other well-documented *jir* concerning ownership of goats. Tiv seldom dispute ownership of cattle, which are rare among them because of tsetse, and which enter entirely into the system of prestige and only incidentally into the system of subsistence or that of ritual. Tiv keep pigs, but since pigs are butchered rather than sacrificed, the moral rights of kinsmen to one's pigs are weak, and the animals are usually kept in the owner's compound. Sheep, used in only one rite so far as I know, are also often kept by their owners. These are some of the reasons why most livestock cases are disputes over goats.

JIR NO. 49. *WanIgarwa calls Gbilin about the ownership of some goats*

WanIgarwa told the *jir* that three or four years ago she was going to Asawa market in Obudu town to sell her two goats—a young billy and a nanny. About halfway to market, they became more and more difficult to lead. Then, 'since the goats were giving me trouble, and since I am only a woman, and therefore didn't know quite what to do, I turned into the compound of Gbilin's father because I knew him and I knew his wife.' When, she continued, she told of the trouble the goats were giving her, Gbilin offered to bring them the rest of the way to market on the next day. She accepted gladly. She went on to market and spent the night with her kinswoman. Next day, when Gbilin came to market he had only her billy goat and made excuses about the nanny. She sold the billy goat. Several months later, she said, Gbilin sold the nanny. She ended by asking the *jir* for the nanny goat and the two kids it should meantime have borne.

Gbilin said that WanIgarwa had indeed brought the two goats to his father's compound, but had told him that only the billy was to be sold and that she wanted to 'release' the nanny with him. Therefore he had not brought it to market. Moreover, the nanny was sickly, had never borne kids at all, and had perished soon after he had accepted it. Thus, he claimed, he owed nothing whatever to WanIgarwa.

Chenge thereupon told Gbilin to bring the nanny goat and one male kid and give them to WanIgarwa, and to stop lying. 'Did you,' he asked, 'go to WanIgarwa when her goat died and tell her it had died, and settle the matter then and there?' Gbilin said that he had not. 'Did you,' Chenge continued, 'let the matter drag on, with WanIgarwa not knowing that her goat was dead?' Gbilin repeated that he had not told her when the goat died.

'Then,' Chenge finished, 'you must give her a goat and a kid—it is a debt.' He continued that the goat had [Europeans would say 'would have'] borne two kids in this period; therefore Gbilin must pay for the young male, and would be allowed to keep the equally hypothetical young female. The scribe was instructed to write this decision on the back of WanIgarwa's receipt. The judges then asked Gbilin whether he chose to pay his debt to WanIgarwa in goats or in money. He elected to pay in goats. The *mbatarev* asked her to set a value on the goats. She replied that the nanny was worth £3 and the billy £1. Gbilin immediately replied that this was far too much; he agreed to admit goats worth only £1 and 10s. Chenge announced that WanIgarwa's figure was indeed too high, and Gbilin's too low; he was to repay her a nanny worth £1. 10s. and a young billy worth 16s.

This *jir* shows far more than the norms of 'releasing' livestock with friends and kinsmen. It is of considerable analytical importance because it illustrates vividly one technique by means of which Tiv argue their *jir*. WanIgarwa can be said to have cited an act by Gbilin—his failure to bring one goat to market—which is a breach of norm. Gbilin sought to establish his act as of a different sort, and to bring it into accordance with another norm: that of 'releasing livestock'.

Gbilin sought to change the norm involved, so that his actions would seem to be in accordance with *some* norm. This process seems to be similar to the English 'admission and evasion'. In English and American law—or, at least, lawyer's culture—this technique of argument is recognized, named, and forms part of the jural system. It is *not* explicitly stated by Tiv.

It would be possible to consider *jir* which concern 'releasing livestock' as cases of breach of contract. Little purpose would be served by so doing, for Tiv do not have a concept 'contract', and if we do so classify them, there is very grave danger of forgetting that we have applied the notion 'contract' from our own culture.

Like the term 'law' itself, 'contract' must be given two definitions: one in European law, the other in comparative jurisprudence. I am interested in explaining the Tiv notion, in which a word like 'contract' does not enter. If, later, we want to compare the Tiv notion either with contract in English law or with some more generalized notion of contract used by comparative jurists, it would no doubt be illuminating. I am not saying that Tiv do not 'have' contract; I am merely saying that they have it like M. Jourdain spoke prose.

Similarly, it might be possible to consider the next group of *jir*—those concerning one's responsibility for the actions of his animals—as 'tort'. We have, I think, sufficiently indicated the reasons for believing that it is preferable not to do so. The simplest of these *jir* represent the substantive norm that the owner or keeper of an animal is responsible for any damage it causes.

JIR NO. 50. *Dzungwe calls Timin*

Damage to crops by Timin's pig

Dzungwe called a *jir* against Timin, saying that Timin's pig had completely ruined his field of peanuts. He asked the *mbatarev* to make Timin pay him £3 for the damage. They asked Timin if it was true that his pig had eaten Dzungwe's groundnut crop. Timin said he did not know—he had not seen the pig do so, nor had any of his children, but it was in the nature of pigs, so perhaps it had. The *mbatarev* thereupon sent Gberihwa, a young and intelligent tax-collector, to look at the field. He was to count the number of rows, the number of mounds per row, and the total number of mounds which the pig had destroyed. Then, they said, they would be able to assess the amount that Timin should pay. A few days later, when the case was resumed, Gberihwa said that the field consisted of 16 rows of groundnuts, each containing 18 mounds. The number of mounds destroyed by the pig was 60 [out of a possible 288—less than one fourth of the field]. Dzungwe objected, but when told that he must either accept £1 or get nothing, he agreed to the decision. The next day Timin brought £1 and handed it to Dzungwe 'under the eyes of the *mbatarev*'.

In order to include the initial action in this *jir* under 'breach of norm', we have to say it is a norm that Tiv must keep their live-stock under control. In spite of this proposition, to which Tiv assent, stock is never herded (though animals are occasionally tethered), so that disputes of this sort are common.

The next *jir* illustrates the fact that in some cases Tiv resort to counteraction other than *jir* to protect their fields from the live-stock of their neighbours.

JIR NO. 51. *Yaji (of MbaAji) calls Batur (of MbaKov) for shooting his pig*

In the course of several days' bickering about land and boundaries between the *utar* of these two men, Batur shot one of Yaji's pigs,

I

alleging that it was eating his cassava. The *mbatarev* asked Batur if he had gone to tell Yaji that his pig had eaten the cassava. Batur replied that he had many times—and vainly—warned Yaji that this pig was in danger if it kept eating cassava from his fields. The *mbatarev* asked Yaji if the pig had died, and he replied that it had not. The *mbatarev* then turned back to Batur: 'Why didn't you come and tell *us* that Yaji's pig was eating your cassava, and call a *jir* as you ought?' Translated into the analytical language of the anthropologist, this question would read, 'Why did you counteract this breach of norm by means of self-help rather than by means of the *jir?*'

Batur could only say that it was indeed true that he had not come to report the matter to the judges. They fined him 5*s*. for shooting the pig instead of calling a *jir*. Yaji received no damages—called by Tiv a 'debt'—for the pig. When I asked Chenge why, he said that since the pig had eaten Batur's cassava, and hadn't died but had only been wounded, the two men had lost equally, and there was no further cause for dispute between them.

The interest in this *jir* is that it relates to what is usually called 'self-help' in anthropological literature. We shall investigate self-help in the next chapter. Here we need note only that it arises in *jir* classified as 'debt' as well as in those classified as 'criminal'.

II. DEBT AND PAWNING

It is possible to pick out of the scribe's records quite a large number of Grade-D court cases which would appear to be matters of simple debt. In my experience, such *jir* usually are not so simple as they seem. Here is an example of how the scribe of MbaDuku recorded a debt case:

JIR NO. 52. *Hingir calls Iko*
    Recovery of a debt [MbaDuku 1945: 72]

'The *mbatarev* called Iko and asked him about this debt of £3.15*s*. which he is said to owe Hingir. Iko said that he knew about £1. 13*s*. 4*d*. Thereupon the *mbatarev* asked Hingir to bring witnesses. He said that Agber was his witness, so the *mbatarev* called for Agber to come. When they asked him to make the ritual motions and swear, he said that he knew about £2. 6*s*. 8*d*., so the *mbatarev* caught Iko to come and pay this amount, but he has not brought it yet. [Added later:] The *mbatarev* took £2 and gave it.to Hingir but there is still 6*s*. 8*d*. which is not paid.'

Such a record makes it appear that the *jir* is used as an agency for collecting debts. This does occasionally happen, but usually the judges will not act unless they hear the whole story of the origin of the debt; they then judge the original action rather than merely the matter of debt.

A more nearly accurate account of a simple *jir* is one reconstructed from my notes and those of one of my clerks:

JIR NO. 53. *Rumun calls Faga about pawned clothing*

Rumun told the judges that several months ago Faga had fallen into difficulty and, needing money, had come to him for help. Faga was his 'best friend' (*hur-or*) and one cannot refuse one's best friend. So Rumun had asked, 'How much money do you need?' Faga had replied that he needed only 15*s*. Rumun said that he had no money, but he had a Hausa gown (*liga*) and a fez worth more than that, which Faga could take. Rumun's wife had objected, advising him to give only the fez and to keep the gown; however Rumun was adamant that you cannot refuse a best friend when it is in your power to give.[1] Faga took both garments and pawned them. Rumun ended by saying that he hadn't seen them since, and wanted them back soon or they would be worn out.

Faga agreed with this story, but said that he was still in need of money and hence could not redeem (*paa*) the articles. The *mbatarev* told him to get money from his kinsmen and redeem them immediately. This ended the *jir*. As usual in such cases, Rumun was left to enforce the decision himself.

This is the simplest debt *jir* that I recorded. It involves pawning. Simple borrowing is rare in Tivland. One does not lend to close kinsmen—one gives to them (tools, the obvious exceptions, are borrowed only rarely and for short periods). One does not lend to distant kinsmen or to non-kinsmen: one pawns to them. For this reason alone, debt *jir* are complex. Some of them vividly illustrate Tiv notions of pawning and borrowing:

JIR NO. 54. *Apev calls Iyoadi about a pawned gun*

Something had been stolen from Apev. A day or two afterwards, Iyoadi sought him out and told him that for £1 he would tell him who had stolen his property, help him recover it, and act as his witness. Apev had no money at the time, so he gave Iyoadi a home-made gun, with the understanding that he could redeem it for £1. Iyoadi took the gun and acted as Apev's witness in the *jir*, which Apev won. Iyoadi

---

[1] Capt. Downes tells me that he once dealt with a case in which a man came to serve his 'best friend's' prison sentence.

then took the gun and pawned it with one Ayam, who gave him £1. 12s. for it. When Apev took £1 to Iyoadi to redeem his gun, Iyoadi couldn't —or, at least, didn't—raise the other 12s. to redeem the gun from Ayam, who said that he had meanwhile had it repaired at the cost of an additional 12s. which Iyoadi would also have to pay, making a total of £2. 4s.

Iyoadi, in reply to the *mbatarev*, substantially agreed with the story, but said that he got only £1. 6s. from Ayam, and that furthermore he ought not to have to pay the repair bill, because he had never fired the gun. The *mbatarev* said, however, that since he had taken the gun as surety, he would have to pay for its repair. Iyoadi then said he had no money—the point at which such cases always arrive when the evidence is all in, the judgment given, and a settlement about to be reached. Tyukwa, the acting *ortaregh* of MbaPwa, said that since Apev was his kinsman, he would himself redeem the gun from Ayam, and he gave him £2. 4s. which settled Iyoadi's debt. He then accepted the £1 from Apev, and told Iyoadi to bring £1. 4s. within a month, take the gun (which would remain with Tyukwa), and return it with his own hands to Apev. Iyoadi agreed, after some hesitation.

Besides illustrating the chains of debtors that a pawning transaction can involve, this *jir* contains a reference to hiring witnesses which was considered in Chapter IV.

The practice of using intermediaries, even in such matters as redeeming pawned articles, leads to further complications and disputes:

JIR NO. 55. *Ayaiko calls Kwentse, his intermediary in a pawning transaction*

Ayaiko said that he had pawned his gun and three goats with Gum in exchange for £4, which he used to get a wife for his son. Subsequently he sent Kwentse with £4 to redeem his property. Kwentse returned with the wrong gun and with three small, sick goats instead of the large, healthy animals which Ayaiko claimed to have given originally. Ayaiko refused to accept them and told Kwentse to go back to Gum for the right animals and the gun. Now, several years later, Ayaiko called a *jir* because he had never got either his £4 or his property from Kwentse.

Kwentse replied that the fault was not his. He had taken the property from Gum, before a witness, and given the £4 in return. Then, when Ayaiko refused the property, he took it back to Gum, who said that the debt had been cleared and that he did not propose to enter into it again. Therefore Kwentse was left with the property rejected by Ayaiko and what, he asked, could be expected of him more than he had already done?

Gum on being called and interrogated, said that the debt had indeed been as reported, and that when the £4 was brought he had handed over the property, also before a witness. He had seen or heard no more about it until that day. To a direct question he replied that Kwentse had never come back with the goats and gun.

The *mbatarev* decided that they must hear the witnesses. Kwentse said that his witness was dead. Some of the audience tittered—Tiv usually assume that a man who says his witness is dead is lying. Gum said he could bring his witness. Neither witness was ever named, for at this point Chenge turned to Kwentse and said, 'Kwentse, bring Ayaiko's gun and his goats. You have eaten his debt.' He then turned on Ayaiko: 'You too are lying. You forgot which goats and which guns were yours.' Both declared themselves to be innocent: Ayaiko said that perhaps Kwentse had substituted small goats and a cheap gun for those which he had taken from Gum. Kwentse countered that Ayaiko was apparently trying to get something for nothing (*elen likichi*), which surely was no way to treat one's witness and middle-man.

The *mbatarev* set a value on the goats and told Kwentse he must pay within two months either goats worth that amount, or the cash, and Ayaiko's gun. Reluctantly, he agreed.

It is becoming evident that Tiv rules of property management and financial transaction are not nearly so rigid or so generally agreed as those of marriage. There may be differences of opinion about marriage norms; there are seldom differences of principle. In regard to property, however, the rules are very imprecise, and rights and duties are not nearly so clear-cut. This observation may be correlated with another: marriage is highly important to Tiv, and involves very broad-scale and far-reaching relationships. These relationships are themselves very dense, each having many strands and many implications. Debt, on the other hand, is much less far-reaching in its social consequences. The relationships between debtor and creditor and between pledger and pledgee involve fewer people and can be broken with less disruption to the social order and to the lives of individuals and families.

Since land cases do not enter into the jurisprudence of debt— Tiv do not consider land a commodity and all land cases are boundary disputes—debt cases tend to concern relatively trivial matters. Even a dispute about a cow is considered of minor importance compared to one about marriage.

It is possible, however, to make some generalizations, to elicit some implicit 'norms', in regard to *jir* about pawning. We can see, for example, that, except in the case of goats, Tiv do not have any overt policy of interest on loans. They are not morally opposed to interest (except on loans among kinsmen) and are learning from Hausa traders and from their own young men who have been abroad. But they are not above trying to get more than they gave, as almost any *jir* concerning pawned property can illustrate. The rules, however, are vague, and each instance is a test of one's ability in bargaining and one's 'market luck' (*ikol*). Any piece of property which is pawned can be used by the person in whose custody it has been placed.

It is evident also that very complex debt structures may arise over what we might consider fairly simple property matters. Tiv, as a matter of prestige, willingly enter into the debts of others. In *Jir* No. 54, an *ortaregh* entered into the debt relationships of some litigants. 'Rich men' (*or nyar*) often assume debts in order to increase their followings, a practice which sometimes leads to their undoing:

JIR NO. 56. *MbaAsor calls Wanshosho, who had tried to help her recover a debt*

MbaAsor called Wanshosho, the market master of Atsar market, in the matter of her cloth. She told the *mbatarev* that a new cloth disappeared from her hut, and she knew someone had stolen it, but not who. A week after missing it, she had gone to market and seen a young man wearing it. She asked him for it and, when he refused, went to Wanshosho for help. Wanshosho sent one of his assistants to get the youth.

When he arrived, Wanshosho asked him where he had got the cloth. He replied unhesitatingly that he had won 8s. gambling at snail shells and had taken the cloth in lieu of the money. He added that if it belonged to MbaAsor he was willing to give it to her if she produced his 8s. Wanshosho asked from whom he had won the cloth. He named a youngster who lived in MbaAsor's compound, and who was therefore probably the thief.

Wanshosho took 8s. from his own bag and handed it to the boy, telling him that his claim on the cloth was finished. The boy took the money and departed happily. Wanshosho then told MbaAsor that she could redeem the cloth for 8s., meanwhile he would keep it. The cloth was, of course, worth well over 8s.

She went off to try to get the money from her husband's nephew, who had gambled away the cloth. Meanwhile someone else came to Wanshosho and said that MbaAsor had sent him to redeem the cloth. Wanshosho took his money and gave him the cloth. Soon after the stranger had disappeared, MbaAsor came with her 8s. Wanshosho, in great surprise, asked her if she had not already sent an agent to redeem her cloth. She said that she certainly had not. She was, therefore, now suing Wanshosho for the return of her cloth.

The *mbatarev* deliberated considerably on this case, but decided that Wanshosho was indeed at fault, for he had been gulled. They said he must therefore pay for the cloth, and asked MbaAsor to set a value on it. She said her husband had bought it for £1. 15s. (which was obviously too high). The *mbatarev* said that, since it had been worn a few times, Wanshosho need pay her only £1 (approximately its true value) and that he would also forfeit the 2s. court fees. Wanshosho at once paid over the £1. 2s., and the case was finished.

I discussed this *jir* with Chenge at some length. He said that Wanshosho would have a case for the recovery of his money if he ever discovered the man who had tricked him into parting with a 20s. cloth for 8s. He said that it was a general rule in Tivland that anyone who buys from a gambler or a thief (a new interpretation of Wanshosho's action in English, but not in Tiv) stands to lose both his money and the property if the rightful owner discovers it. I asked about the matter of the original thief. Chenge said that since this was a matter involving a single compound, the compound head must go into the question. Affairs within the compound, even such affairs as stealing, are the business not of the *jir* but of the compound head.

III. CONCLUSION

The purpose of this chapter has been twofold: to present the Tiv notion of debt in such a way that its unity becomes apparent, and to carry forward some small distance the analytical system hypothesized in the preceding chapter.

We have discovered that Tiv use a single concept 'debt' (*injô*) to cover instances and cases which we, in our folk system, classify into several different categories. Tiv take those *jir* which, in our classification, might be called contract and they see the debt aspect rather than the contract aspect as the most important point. From the viewpoint of the comparative jurist, there is a contract between a man who owns a goat and the man who keeps it. One could also speak of a contract between a pledgor and a pledgee. Tiv agree with such statements if made and explained to them.

But they do not use this aspect of the relationship for purposes of classification. In their own folk system, the idea of contract takes, for purposes of classification, a subordinate position to the idea of the debt involved.

Tiv can be said to have a right against the world for their crops to be protected from molestation by other people's livestock, and it can be said—accurately in one sense—that it is a tort for a man to allow his livestock to harm another's crops. But Tiv classify this idea also under debt: if a man's livestock injures a farm, he falls into debt to the farmer. Debt is an aspect of both this sort of contract and this sort of tort: it is the aspect on which Tiv classify. Needless to say, our categories of contract and of tort are not coterminous with the Tiv category of debt.

The main analytical point which has been put forward in this chapter on debt is that, if the *jir* is a counteraction following on a breach of norm, it is possible—and is often done—for Tiv to defend themselves by attempting to maintain that their action was not a breach of norm—that it was an act in accordance with some norm or another.   It is therefore up to the judges to decide which norm has been broken as well as whether or not the action was actually a breach of norm.

CHAPTER VII

'CRIMINAL' *JIR* AND THE PROBLEM
OF SELF-HELP

I. CRIMINAL JIR IN MBADUKU

EARLIER in this book I stated that I adopted the classification of
the cases heard by the MbaDuku Grade-D court into civil and
criminal, not because it was a standard European distinction, but
rather because the scribe of MbaDuku *jir* classified them in that
way. The fact that the distinction is of European origin is momen-
tarily beside the point—it is, today, a distinction found amongst
Tiv.[1]

The only records of criminal cases available in MbaDuku at the
time I was working there were those from 1946 to 1950.[2] The
classification in the following table is that of the court scribe.
Most of the terms he used were in English; I have put into
inverted commas those I have translated. The arrangement into
five categories is my own, and not a folk division.

The first category includes illegitimate juju, adultery, illegal
marriage, bigamy, and kidnapping, which were discussed in
Chapter V. Illegitimate juju, although it may apply to cult objects,
is usually the finable offence of making magic in order to keep
one's wife faithful—it is also grounds for divorce. The *jir* is sometimes entered in the criminal book if a fine is involved; an exactly
similar case may be entered in the civil book and called divorce.
Similarly, adultery cases, particularly those ending in fines or
prison sentences, are often entered in the criminal rather than the
civil book. Illegal marriage and bigamy occur in the same way:
the scribe's accounting for fines levied upon guardians who accept
two bridewealths, or occasionally upon a woman for having
blatantly, and without adequate grounds, disregarded both her
husband and her guardian, to live with a lover. In a polygynous

[1] Nadel's analysis in terms of social range elucidates the Tiv material, but is
not essential. S. F. Nadel, *The Nuba*, pp. 499 ff.
[2] Case books after 1950 were at Central Headquarters being checked and
audited for several months of that spring, and illness prevented my returning
later in the year to complete the record.

community, obviously, bigamy is a misdemeanour only on the part of a woman; the charge is usually one against guardians who have accepted bridewealth 'on two paths'. The one kidnapping charge was a case which might better have been called seduction.

		1946	1947	1948	1949	1950
I.	Illegitimate juju	1	2	1	4	
	Adultery	9	11	4	6	19
	Illegal marriage	5	12	8	10	14
	Bigamy	5	8	11	6	16
	Kidnapping		1			
II.	'Contempt of court'	9	13	10	13	28
III.	N.A.R.	8	13	20	13	16
IV.	Arson			1		
	Gambling				3	
	Fraud	2	1	1	2	
	'Robbery'	1	2			
	Slander		2	2		3
V.	Stealing	6	7	8	8	44
	Assault	9	17	19	5	41
	'Fighting'					2
	Miscellaneous	1	2	3	7	14
	TOTALS	56	91	88	77	197

The second category, 'contempt of court', was discussed in Chapter IV. The third category, Native Authority regulations, consists primarily of cases of bush-burning (which the Government, acting through the Native Authority, has made illegal) or of felling hardwood trees without permit. These cases are almost always brought by the forestry assistants assigned to the district, and the fines vary from 2s. to 30s. depending on the nature and magnitude of the offence.

I have grouped into Class IV cases of a sort that I have never seen or about which my material is wholly inadequate. I have never been present at a case concerning arson. It is a crime which is rare in Tivland.[1] Nor have I ever seen a trial for slander, though I know that in Gboko and Makurdi they are fairly common, and the amounts claimed for damages are rising.

Gambling was made illegal in Tivland by a regulation of the Native Authority, which was passed by the tribal council. Nevertheless, Tiv gamble a great deal. More sophisticated Tiv play a form of blackjack; other card games are less common. Almost all young men gamble with one of two indigenous games: one played with snail shells, the other with cowries. The one instance of gambling which I recorded concerned the game played with cowry shells. Six youngsters of about seventeen or eighteen years were brought before the *mbatarev* for playing it. Each was fined 5s., and the one in whose hut they were playing 5s. more. They had been arrested by Chenge himself. I never determined the criteria by which gamblers were arrested. There were three gambling 'houses', so to speak, each one hundred yards or so outside Tsar market, within a mile of Chenge's compound. Every market-day games were going from early morning until late; the stakes were sometimes high. In one 'house' playing-cards were used, in the two others cowries. No one in MbaDuku was unaware of their existence, but no attempts were ever made to close them. One was left to draw one's own conclusions.

I have never been present at a *jir* which tried anything that I would call fraud. I should find it difficult in Tiv to distinguish fraud from the stealing that usually goes with it. I doubt if there is a Tiv word for fraud. One instance, which never came before a *jir*, is worth mentioning as it illustrates Tiv ways of combating what we should call fraud.

INCIDENT NO. 57. *Ugo is left holding a bag*

Ugo, son of Ukpoepi, had gone to market in Obudu, in Udam territory a few miles south of Tiv country. Another Tiv, whom he did not know, came up to him in the market-place and asked if his father had come to market. He said, No. 'In that case,' answered the man, 'you must come help me buy some cloth.' Ugo did not wish to, but as the man insisted he finally agreed to help him. They went into one of the permanent canteens, kept by an Ibo. The man picked out three cloths

---

[1] This belief is confirmed by the fact that arson is so common in the parts of East Africa which I know. I have never heard a Tiv express fear that his house would be burned while he was sleeping in it. Capt. Downes remembers no cases save those during a war.

and told the shopkeeper that he would like to show them to his wife, who was selling vegetables on the other side of the market-place. He handed Ugo a small bag and said, 'I will leave him here with my money.' The shopkeeper agreed.

Ugo stood holding the bag for almost an hour. The shopkeeper, growing impatient, finally asked, 'When will your father return?' Ugo replied that the man was not his father. 'Then who is he?' asked the shopkeeper. 'I have never seen him before,' replied Ugo. The Ibo, immediately suspicious, opened the bag and found that it contained not coins, but pebbles. He at once called the police, who took the boy and the bag to the police station.

There were many Tiv in the market that day and Ugo's father knew of the incident within a few hours. He asked many questions, and soon discovered that the man who had tricked his son was from Utisha in the south-east of Tivland. He went to Udam and bailed his son out of gaol for £3. He then disappeared for a few days. He was not popular in the community, and the uncharitable said he had left to avoid paying his tax. But within a few days he returned with the cloth. He took it back to the shopkeeper, who said it was worth 25s. (all he ever claimed for it). Ukpoepi called a case in Udam to recover his £3, but said some two years later that he never got it.

In discussing this occurrence, Tiv said of the Utisha man who had tricked Ugo that he stole (*i a ii*) and that he lied (*er yie*). So far as I am aware, no more specific name was given to his action.

The case is also of special interest because Ukpoepi did all his own police and detective work, and all the enforcement of the law and of his rights. It brings us up squarely against the problem of rights and the problem of self-help, which are discussed below. The remainder of the chapter will deal mostly with those classes of *jir* that I have put in category V—stealing and assault. These are the most common types of *jir* which the scribe classes as 'criminal'.

II. THE TIV CLASSIFICATION OF 'WRONGS'

Sir Henry Maine has written at some length of the difficulties which men of ancient society experienced in perfecting the distinction between delict and crime. He found that if 'the criterion of a delict, wrong or tort be that the person who suffers it, and not the State, is conceived to be wronged, it may be asserted that in the infancy of jurisprudence the citizen depended for protection against violence or fraud not on the law of crime, but on the law of tort'.[1]

We have seen, in the last few pages, that Tiv scribes also have difficulty in making this distinction. Tiv, other than the scribes and a few of the most informed *mbatarev*, do not make the distinction at all.

They also have trouble in making overt the distinctions of a jural nature which their vocabulary and their very actions contain. They have trouble in making and maintaining distinctions among their own words, and among their various classes of faults. This difficulty in clarifying distinctions seems to be one of the most thorny difficulties in all situations of social control.

To understand how Tiv use their *jir*, it is necessary to investigate the distinctions which they make among wrongs. In order to make this investigation, it will be simpler to change our point of analytical focus. Hitherto we have focused on *jir*; but, in order fully to understand the notion *jir*, we must investigate other institutions that are used in its place. The best means of doing so is to change our focus to the wrong which is the breach of norm or the first social act in the series. In this section we shall investigate Tiv distinctions of wrongs, and in the next we shall be in a position to compare *jir* with other social acts of the sort we have called 'counteraction', which can and do follow on the commission of wrongs or the breach of norm.

There is probably no language that does not contain words for bad and reprehensible acts. The substantive content of these several words and categories varies from one language to another— if it did not, we could not speak of cultural variation.

We must examine three Tiv words: *ifer*, *kwaghbo*, and *kwagh-dang*. Now, there are two Tiv dictionaries, one by a missionary and the other by a linguist-cum-administrator with some anthropological training. It is interesting that all three words are translated by the missionary with the notion of sin or wickedness, and by the administrative officer by the notion of crime, fault, misdemeanour. Thus, to the missionary an *ifer* is a 'bad, wrong, sinful thing'; to the administrator it is a 'crime, fault, misdemeanour, mistake'. The missionary defines or translates *kwaghbo* as 'a wicked thing, a sin', whereas the District Officer as 'a bad deed, a

---

[1] Henry Sumner Maine, *Ancient Law*, 10th ed. London: Murray, 1912, pp. 380-1.

crime', though he gives one—just one—example of the notion 'sin' in translating *U gba shin kwaghbo* as 'You sinned or committed a crime'.

Such translations tell one more about missionaries and administrative officers than about what Tiv mean by *ifer* or *kwaghbo*. Their most obvious lesson is that Tiv do not differentiate between a sin and a crime as Europeans can; it is not possible to translate *ifer* with one English word and *kwaghbo* with another. The field of meaning is cross-cut in a somewhat different way, and I should say that administrative officer and missionary are both right. How then do we go about differentiating these words?

First, let us examine the composition of the words *kwaghdang* and *kwaghbo*. *Kwagh* is a substantive meaning 'thing' or 'affair' or 'matter', modified by adjectives *dang* and *bo*, which are the crucial variants. Both dictionaries translate both *bo* and *dang* as 'bad'. Both add some examples which allow us to say that *bo* also means 'ugly' and 'stingy'.

Dang, on the other hand, extends to 'unhappy' or 'useless', and a man of *dang* is a bad person or a profligate. More important, one can say that a disease is *bo* or serious, but not that it is *dang*, for to say it is *dang* would be to imply that it is morally at fault, whereas to say that it is *bo* means that it is dangerous. One can say of drugs or medicines that they are *bo*, or dangerous, but not that they are *dang*, morally bad. One can also say that witchcraft substance (*tsav*) is *bo*, dangerous, but it need not be *dang*. Mischief of a minor sort, on the other hand, can be *dang*, but need not be dangerous or *bo*. If you ask a Tiv to differentiate between *bo* and *dang*, he will tell you that they are the same thing; but if you use one incorrectly, he will tell you to use the other. It is from such corrections and from hearing, very occasionally, a Tiv say that something was *dang* but not *bo* that one can arrive at definitions. A *kwaghbo*, with reference to human activities at least, is something dangerous and anti-social. A *kwaghdang* is a thing—person or act—which is morally reprehensible.

Both dictionaries list another word, *ishor i bo*, as meaning 'bad deed, sin, evil' (Malherbe) or 'crime, sin, fault' (Abraham). I myself recorded this word only in connexion with supernatural evils performed by witches (*mbatsav*). The *bo* is obviously the same *bo* as in *kwaghbo*, but since I am not certain what *ishor* means, I am not prepared to say that its meaning is limited to the supernatural. At least, it is not in everyday use for ordinary wrongs in the areas that I know best.

None of these three terms necessarily implies, it seems to me, a jural context or any sort of jural activity. It is true that the act which a thief or criminal performs can be said to be both *bo*, or mystically dangerous, and *dang*, or morally bad, but in neither sense because of their jural associations.

The jural associations are to be found in *ifer*. I find my material on this concept thin, because I had no difficulty in understanding it. When I was among the Tiv I used the word *ifer* to mean 'crime', and I do not remember ever having been corrected for so doing. I find that I made no specific references to it in my notes (as I always did with any word whose meaning or use proved recalcitrant), and that it is used comparatively infrequently in my texts. I remember (though I cannot find that I noted) one instance in which a woman called her child an *or-ifer*, a 'person [who has committed] *ifer*', when he took food from her hut without permission. I asked her about it after the child had left; she told me it was a little *ifer*, but that one must discipline one's children.

I used the word *ifer* in Tivland almost exclusively in jural contexts; either in discussing thieves or wrongdoers before a *jir*, or else in contexts in which the breach of norm is sanctioned by self-help rather than by jural procedure. We may say that an *ifer* is that wrong of which the accused stands accused.

In short, the *ifer* is the very breach of norm which must be counteracted. Either the wronged party uses self-help against the *or-ifer*, the man who committed the *ifer*, or else a ritual must be performed or a *jir* held, or both. At the very least, it will be considered by Tiv that one of these sanctions *should* have taken place.

Let me repeat that I am not establishing three 'boxes' and tossing various acts into one or the other. Obviously, a wrong can be put into two or into all of these categories: an act of murder is *kwaghdang* in that it is morally reprehensible; it is *kwaghbo* in that it is anti-social and mystically dangerous to the whole community; it is an *ifer* in the sense that some sort of counteraction should be taken to set it right.

If we may continue to formalize Tiv words into a doctrine— and realize that it is an analytical formalization, based on correct meanings and connexions but not done by Tiv themselves—we can see that insofar as an act is *kwaghdang*, it may be followed by punishment (*mtsaha*). Insofar as it is *kwaghbo*, it may be followed by ritual reparation (*kwagh soron*). Insofar as it is *ifer* it is followed by a counteraction, either *jir* or some other.

Incest, homicide, and sometimes adultery, require ritual reparation. Any form of homicide is an offence against the fetish called *swende*. Homicide is *kwaghbo* in that it is followed by a ritual. It is also *ifer* in that it is followed by *jir* or some other counteraction. It is *kwaghdang*, so it may be followed by punishment. Incest is *kwaghbo* which is repaired by ritual separation of the two culprits. It is *ifer* in the sense that it brings the *jir* (the moot, not the court) into action. It is *kwaghdang* in that it carries a severe punishment, at least for repeated offences. Similarly, adultery is an *ifer* in that it can be brought before the *jir*, as we have seen. It is *kwaghdang* in that it can be punished—husbands are expected to beat their wives for adultery, and we also noted that the *jir* fined adulteresses and sometimes their guardians. It is always *kwaghbo* in the sense that it is anti-social, and if the husband is a master of the *akombo megh* it is doubly dangerous and must be followed by a ceremony for repairing this fetish.

Tiv do not make the distinctions that Europeans make between wrongs which injure the entire community and those which injure individuals. Many of our own jurists have pointed out that there is no delict which is not in some sense harmful to the community, and no crime which does not harm some individual's rights. The distinction which Europeans draw is a folk distinction. The distinction which I have drawn between *kwaghbo*, *kwaghdang* and *ifer* is a folk distinction. We can compare the two sets of distinctions. But it is just as wrong and just as uncomprehending to cram Tiv cases into the categories of the European folk distinctions as it would be to cram European cases into Tiv folk distinctions.

III. THE INSTITUTIONS OF SELF-HELP

The remainder of this chapter deals with some *afer*. One serious *ifer*, the practice of witchcraft (*tamben or*), has, owing to the nature of Nigerian law, been made impossible of counteraction by the Grade-D court. The *ifer* of witchcraft is handled by that sort of *jir* which we shall call a moot and investigate in later chapters. The *afer* of homicide, slave-dealing, and rape have been taken out of the hands of Tiv and will be reviewed briefly in the final section of this chapter.

Tiv still carry out their own jural counteraction on two numerically important sorts of *ifer*: theft and assault. This being the case, the events and *jir* which we have utilized to illustrate Tiv institutions of self-help will, for the most part, concern these two fields.

Stealing (*iin a ii*) is an *ifer* which can be followed either by self-help or by reference to jural institutions, but so far as I am aware it is never followed by ritual reparation. The point is the return of the stolen object or objects or their equivalent. There is, moreover, usually some sort of punishment—either revenge or ridicule—associated with it.

INCIDENT NO. 58. *Gu deals with a thief*

This instance is one which I did not see—it would never have occurred had I been present. However, it occurred in a compound in which I was living, during a short period when I was absent. My clerk, Orihiwe, whose text and comments form the basis of my information (although I later discussed it with members of the compound), was there and saw it all. The text which he wrote starts by explaining Kuvishar's lineage connexions. It goes on to say that Kuvishar came to stay in our compound with Abum, a half-brother of Gu, the compound head. He was also a distant agnate of one of the wives of Atsegher, Gu's father's younger half-brother's son:

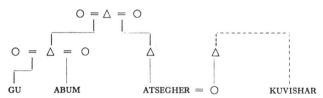

The text continues: 'When everyone was asleep, Kuvishar got up and entered the hut of Gu's wife, MbaAgor. He took a big carrying tray and brought it outside. He then went and entered the hut of a woman named WanIshwa. He took 4*d.* and a piece of cloth from her hut. He came out with them into the night and started to leave. Gu chased him almost to Mbesev and brought him back [a distance of some three miles]. So Gu got a rope, tied it around his belly, and tied him to the foot of the *konkuagh* tree here in the compound. He took off the thief's cloth and left him naked. I [the clerk] told Gu to give him a cloth of some sort to cover himself with, so Gu did. To get the cloth on him, he again untied the rope, after which Gu again tied the man around the middle, and tied his feet. He tied him to the foot of the tree and went off.

'About three o'clock the next afternoon, the thief started to cry. So

K

Gu [asked him what the trouble was, and when he said that he was hungry, Gu] went and took some pig faeces and put it in his mouth for him to eat. He began to beseech Gu, and Gu stopped. But others came and beat him. Oh, but he cried.

'When Atsegher [Gu's half-brother, whose wife was the thief's lineage-mate] returned, Gu released the thief. Atsegher asked him, "Why did you do this? What has this man done?" Gu told him about the stealing, but did not say why he had treated the thief in this way. Atsegher told Gu to let him go, because the boy was a youngster of Atsegher's father-in-law. But Gu took a big cloth which Kuvishar already had and kept it, because one of his [Gu's] wives was not there. Gu said that if that wife returned and said the cloth was hers, he would give it to her. If she said it was not, he would give it to Atsegher, who would send it to his affines for re-delivery to Kuvishar.'

This is an instance in which a wronged man, in face of an *ifer*, took matters into his own hands. He was his own police, judge, and jury. The thief was punished and the goods were recovered. In this case the breach of norm was followed not by a *jir* but by another counteraction: self-help.

I have noted several cases from the district files in which thieves have been killed in the course of such beatings administered as self-help. It is sufficient here to cite the evidence of one witness from the Preliminary Inquiry in connexion with Rex *v*. Agaga of 1941 [File 1706 in District Office, Gboko]. In this case, a woman, Awadzenga, had been caught stealing yams:

'This woman, Awadzenga, is past child-bearing age [the witness said]. She is an habitual yam-stealer—she has been in gaol for it several times. She stole some yams from Hummaren on this occasion. Hummaren and her mother-in-law were watching the yam field at night, and saw her digging them up.[1] Her mother-in-law raised the alarm [by ululation] and Hangen, Tar, Igba, and Kaan came and threatened to beat her. The mother-in-law objected, and said, "No, let her pay", but they took her to the compound where Agaga said, "She and her son trouble us too much with their stealing—you boys beat her." They staked her out and beat her with *ficus* branches, which they used one at a time until they broke. Igba struck her with the flat of a matchet on the back. This went on until Afaaka [the mother-in-law] told them to stop. Kayen [a woman] put pepper in her eyes, because she had robbed her farm [on earlier occasions]: that was the next morning while she was

[1] Both men and women often pass a night and sometimes weeks in the farm shelters.

still tied up. Tar threw dirt in her eyes—no, that was at night during the time she was being beaten. They left her tied until morning so she couldn't move. The next morning Ikar released her and washed her and took her to his reception hut, where she died in the doorway when he put her out and told her to go home.'

The accused in this same case is reported [in a questionable translation] to have put the matter thus:

'I was following a rule made formerly that if a man caught a thief he should kill him. If I was wrong, then kill me, but first pay for my wife's yams.'

Tiv say today that in the past any thief who was caught red-handed was beaten by the persons from whom he stole. Many of them express the opinion that such a procedure is more effective than calling the thief before the *jir*.

In the next example, taken from my own material, it is not the wronged man himself who acts, but the compound head of the wrongdoer.

INCIDENT NO. 59. *Waniwa stole a chicken and was punished*

A boy named Waniwa stole a chicken from a woman of another compound within his small lineage segment. Someone saw him pick it up and put it under his cloth. His compound head, Uhimbir, was in the immediate vicinity. When he was told, he caught Waniwa, grabbed the chicken from under his cloth and killed it by wringing its neck. He then announced loudly that a child of his own compound had stolen, and would pay 3s. to the owner of the chicken in compensation. Waniwa took the dead chicken and slunk away, spending the rest of the morning trying in vain to sell it for 3s. He wondered aloud what he should do with the chicken and where he should get the 3s. to pay for it. A man of the compound told him he didn't have any idea where he could get 3s. because he had done a very foolish thing and forfeited the help of his kinsmen. But, the chicken being there, he had better eat it before it spoiled. Others took up the idea: Yes, Waniwa must eat that chicken. But none of the women of the compound would lend him a pot in which to cook it; he had to roast it over the fire in one of the reception huts. No one would help him eat it, for none would eat stolen meat. He sat alone and ate the chicken inside a ring of his jeering brothers and kinsmen. Nothing for Tiv is so indicative of a man's social ostracism as his being made to eat alone. If Waniwa had refused to eat that chicken, to the last scrap, they would have forced him to, and he knew it. He ate the chicken.

In this instance, it was the boy's own kinsmen who took action. He had committed one of the most heinous of *afer*: he had stolen within the minimal lineage segment. His act was also, of course, *kwaghbo* and *kwaghdang*. It is said that, in the past, the elders might have sold into slavery a man who repeatedly stole within his minimal segment. Certainly they would have withdrawn their mystical protection against his being bewitched.

Theft from those far removed in the lineage system is held to be a less serious offence than stealing within the minimal segment. Stealing at a distance is sometimes compared to warfare.

Tiv hold two conflicting notions about thieves and stealing. They say that Tiv are the best thieves in the world, and that a good thief is one who can break through the mud wall of a hut, enter, and take out all the contents, including a bicycle, without waking the sleeping occupants. They admire the technical skill of any thief who can come close to this achievement, and on one occasion in MbaDuku when it was accomplished they were open in their admiration (although the thief was unknown). At the same time, Tiv say that stealing is an *ifer* and cannot be allowed to go unpunished. The usual way of punishing a thief is to beat him and take back one's goods.

Tiv say that thieves seldom reform. One man, in discussing this subject with me, said: 'Thieves steal (*Mbaiiv mba ii*)', that is, 'Once a thief always a thief'. Most of the accomplished thieves in Tivland are known. If they do not steal too close to home, they are usually allowed to live in peace. But no lineage brother would consider taking a thief's side in any case where he is accused. He has forfeited his good name and the right to assistance from his lineage, not only in this, but also in some other matters. But he has not been totally rejected from the lineage. 'Thieves steal', and must be watched; but some of them are good farmers, good fathers, and helpful kinsmen.

Which of these two attitudes to stealing is uppermost in any given situation depends on the position in the lineage system of the persons involved. It is a serious offence to steal within one's minimal *tar*. On the other hand, mutual stealing is the normal relationship between some socially distant but neighbouring lineages. People who live on such borders expect those on the other side to steal from them, and they make plans to protect themselves accordingly, and perhaps to steal back.

Although Tiv still embrace such a morality, the consequences of theft are changing. With the introduction of Native Administration policemen, there is for the first time in Tiv society an institution, other than the markets or the clumsy arbitration of kinsmen, which can be called upon to correct the breach of norm.

INCIDENT NO. 60. *A thief is caught*

This event occurred very shortly after our arrival in Tivland, so that we know only what we saw: our steward called us to come and see the thief. The thief was led by another man by means of a rope round his middle, and was carrying a heavy raffia sack containing the yams he was alleged to have stolen. All the women and children of the chief's compound in which we were living came rushing to see him. Women pushed their children forward and said, 'Look closely, so you will know him. He is a thief!' Others reminded their children, 'You see what happens to people who steal!' The thief was turned over to the Native Authority policeman who tied his wrists to his waist. He asked him if he had stolen the yams. The man did not answer, so the policeman slapped him once on each cheek. Then both accuser and accused told their stories to the policeman and several elders who had collected. I understood very little of it. The thief was taken, roughly, to the compound of the policeman to await the arrival of his elder. By the next day he had been released—at least, so I was told—and I don't know what happened to him.

Thus some people, at least, bring a captured thief to the British instituted authorities rather than try to deal with him themselves, as Gu did with the theft in his compound.

Such authorities are new, though in the past there were some occasions on which groups of elders could act. Some markets were organized in such a way that representatives of several lineages participated in erecting a fetish to protect the people who patronized them and to attack persons who violated the norms of the market or of everyday Tiv morality in the market-place. These organizations were sometimes used to recover stolen goods, and members of such a market pact might punish a thief among their own people, just as Waniwa was punished for stealing a chicken. Only with the introduction of officials by the British administration has a procedure of referring thieves to tribunals or to bodies of authorities become at all general.

However, most markets today, as in the past, have authorities who deal with any local petty theft that may occur during the hours when the market is open. These 'market courts' (*jir kasoa*) handle such a variety of disputes that we shall have to deal with them in a separate chapter. They arbitrate in only very minor accusations of theft; if a dispute is considered to be at all serious, it is referred to the *jir* of the *mbatarev*. Large markets are usually policed nowadays not only by their own organizations, but by the Native Authority policemen of the district in which they are held. These officials not only help to maintain order, but also act as agents of the *mbatarev* and often as what we should call prosecuting agents in the *jir* that follows the arrest of wrongdoers at market.

I recorded many instances of market theft, but two or three will serve to indicate the principles involved. One of the simplest and most instructive is:

INSTANCE NO. 61. *Iyornumbe stole shoes*

One of the two N.A. policemen stationed with Chenge, and on duty at Tsar market when they were not away on official errands, apprehended a boy named Iyornumbe who had stolen a pair of cheap tennis shoes in the market. The Ibo trader who had been robbed reported to the policeman and to the market authorities that a pair of canvas shoes had been stolen from him; the policeman, when he saw this boy with shoes which tallied with the description and which did not fit him, arrested him. The trader identified the shoes, down to the right size, so the policeman told him to come back in two days' time, when the *jir* was meeting. Meanwhile, he put Iyornumbe under arrest in his own compound.

At the *jir* it was this policeman who backed up the trader's shouts for attention. The four judges asked Iyornumbe, 'Do you know this Ibo?' and he answered that he did not. The judges then asked, 'Is this the man you stole the shoes from?' Iyornumbe—who had already admitted, quite readily, that the shoes were stolen—said, 'The day I stole the shoes, this man wasn't about; I didn't see him at all.' He went on to say that a small child had been looking after the goods in the market stall from which he had stolen.

The judges then asked Iyornumbe: 'Have you ever stolen before?' He said that he often stole. Asked what he did with the things that he stole, he said he traded them for food which he ate. Formerly, when he was in Makurdi, he had stolen £10 from an Ibo. An N.A. policeman had caught him, and he was in gaol for two weeks, after which he was sent home to stay. But he went back to Makurdi, and they caught him stealing a pair of shorts, and again a policeman arrested him. He was in gaol another two weeks, and then was released because someone had said he was too young to be locked up.

The judges handed the shoes back to the trader with all but an apology. They sentenced Iyornumbe to two months' imprisonment in Gboko gaol. However, it was some time before he could be transported there to serve his sentence. Next market day, he and another thief were still in MbaDuku. The N.A. policeman took them to the market place. There he made them shuffle about, penguin fashion; first Iyornumbe was made to cry out at the top of his voice, 'I stole shoes!' and then the other would bawl, 'I stole yams.' It was then Iyornumbe's turn again to shout, 'I stole shoes!' It was the general opinion that Iyornumbe would probably not return to this market for many, many years, and that if he did, everyone would know him and know that he was a thief.

Here we have the extreme opposite to Gu's apprehending and punishing his own thief. Iyornumbe was apprehended by a policeman and was tried and punished by a Grade-D court. We have thus, within Tiv society, the *ifer* of theft handled in some cases as a 'delict' counteracted by self-help, and in others as a crime counteracted 'by due process of law'. It is plain that the main difference is to be found in the counteraction. The Tiv system is changing towards the European model.

We can distinguish another form of self-help which lies between the two extremes already cited. An example is found in:

JIR NO. 62. *Shirsha calls Ungwachi for taking his bicycle*

Shirsha called Ungwachi before the *jir* for the recovery of his bicycle. The *mbatarev* asked Ungwachi, 'Do you have Shirsha's bicycle?'

He replied, 'I took (*tó*) Shirsha's bicycle and went to Makurdi with it.' It had 'broken' in some way and he had left it, temporarily he thought, in the compound of his affine while he went to Makurdi to get money to pay the repair bill. When he returned he found that the bicycle had disappeared; somebody had stolen (*i a ii*) it.

The judges decided that Ungwachi must pay for Shirsha's bicycle. He said that it was not he who should pay for it, but his affine. He himself had only taken (*tó a tó*) the bicycle—he had not stolen (*i a ii*) it. It was someone in his affine's *tar* who had stolen it.

Chenge told him that he must proceed to the *jir* of the *tar* in which his affine lived and call a case against him to recover his money; all they knew here was that he had taken Shirsha's bicycle and had not returned it. 'How much,' he asked Shirsha, 'do you want your brother to pay?' Shirsha said that the bicycle was worth £20. Ungwachi immediately said that this was too much, that the bicycle was worth only

£10. Huwa asked Shirsha what sort of bicycle it was. Shirsha replied that it was a 'Lali' [Raleigh]. Gbegba suggested that since it was not new the sum should be £14. Chenge said that he knew that a 'Lali' was a very expensive and fine bicycle, because his sons told him so, and he suggested that the sum should be £16. The decision was that Ungwachi should pay Shirsha £16 within three months, and do it before the court.

The distinction which Ungwachi pointed out between 'taking' and 'stealing' is a vital one in Tiv thought and jural procedure. Ungwachi did not steal this bicycle from Shirsha, even though he did not ask permission to go off with it. This was so because he was Shirsha's 'brother'; both admitted that, since he was a brother, he had intended to return it. He had merely 'taken' it. But while the bicycle was in the compound of his affine, it was stolen—removed by someone who did not, because of relationship with the owner, *ipso facto* intend to return it. Tiv consider it polite to tell a kinsman if you are going to 'take' something which belongs to him. However, they often do not do so, for fear of being refused.

There is another form of 'taking' which Tiv call 'taking for debt' (*tôn a tô sa injô*), in which the 'thief' takes something and proceeds immediately with it to his agnatic lineage area. He convenes his agnatic lineage—or, at least, as many members as he can interest—tells them what he has done, and shows them the stolen articles. He tells them further that he has taken the articles in compensation for a particular debt, which he specifies. The lineage will then decide whether to back him or to make him return the goods. In such cases there is usually no secret about who took the property, and if the lineage members consider the debt just they will probably support the man, and in meetings and by diplomatic calls will eventually convince the victim's lineage that what has been taken is just payment of the debt. However, if they do not agree that the debt is just, or that the method of collecting it was correctly resorted to, they will withhold their support, whereupon the owner of the goods can probably come and 'take' them back.

Tiv say that a man cannot count on the assistance of his lineage if he frequently 'takes' things in repayment of debts, as it is no longer worth their trouble. One's lineage brothers, they add, almost always grudge the bother, and perhaps expense and potential trouble, that they have had in such a matter.

Tiv will tell one that 'taking something for debt' is not a crime or *ifer*, as stealing is. In terms of our analytical system, we can see that stealing is a breach of norm; taking in a matter of debt is a counteraction using self-help. It is the social circumstances and the situation which determine whether or not Tiv apply the word *ifer* or the word 'steal' to a specific act. Similarly, it is the nature of the preceding and succeeding social acts which leads us to determine whether an instance of this sort is a breach of norm or a counteraction.

Even in cases of theft in markets, it is often held by the thief that he did not steal but merely 'took' something, implying a prior debt to himself or one of his kinsmen. Most disputes, by the time they reach the *jir* of the *mbatarev*, involve this distinction.

In the Tiv view, the ultimate correction following upon a counteraction is much the same whether that counteraction be self-help or resort to a *jir*: the goods are recovered and the thief is punished. There is, thus, a very wide range in the superficial aspects of handling cases of theft. In many instances, one or other of the desired results was not obtained—all these instances are inadequacies in what the English call 'the certainty of the law'.

Tiv do not, like some other peoples, require that double or more than the amount stolen be refunded.

JIR NO. 63. *Aboshin calls Kwaghnyiman and Tor for restitution of a stolen cow*

Aboshin called a *jir* against Kwaghnyiman and Tor, charging them with stealing his only cow, which they had taken to market in Obudu and butchered. There were witnesses in the matter and, though the case dragged on for several days, the guilt of the accused was firmly established. The *mbatarev* told Aboshin to place a value on the cow; he said it was worth £56, an absurd figure. The amount eventually agreed upon for repayment was £15: not because the cow, on the hoof, was worth so much, but because that was presumed to be approximately what the thieves had received from selling the meat once it had been butchered. Two days after the judgment they brought £12 in part payment, and asked for an extension of time on the other £3. After Aboshin had got his £12 (more than the cow was worth alive), he said that he had spent £8 for witnesses and assistants in looking for the cow and tracking down the thieves. The *mbatarev* told him that this was a separate *jir* and he could call it if he liked, once the rest of the money had been paid.

I examined this *jir* thoroughly and discussed it at some length with Chenge. The amount of money to be repaid was more than the price of the cow. The reason for the high price was that the thieves had sold the cow as butchered meat, not as a live animal. I asked specifically about the idea of repaying double the amount stolen. Chenge denied that Tiv ever did this sort of thing systematically, though he had heard of some judges who did it in particular instances.

In the preceding *jir*, the thief was not punished, only the goods were restored. Many *jir* for theft give this appearance:

JIR NO. 64. *Samber calls Ityo for return of stolen property.*

Samber told the *mbatarev* that during the war between the Tiv and the Udam in the late spring of 1950, his wife had taken a large bag full of black guinea-corn and hidden it in the tall grass. She had also put inside it a smaller bag containing 10s. in pennies and half-pennies, and had put with it a few other pieces of property, including a matchet of Samber's. After the fighting was over, they returned for the bag, but it was gone. Some months later, Samber was walking through the lineage area in which Ityo lives and came upon some people who were skinning a cow. Among those helping was Ityo, who was working with the matchet that Samber had lost. He asked Ityo where he got the matchet; Ityo replied that he had bought it in Gav.

Ityo told the *mbatarev* that he knew nothing about all this, because he had bought this matchet in Gav. However, several people identified the matchet as Samber's and Ityo was unable to produce any evidence that he actually had bought it in Gav. It was therefore returned to Samber, and the *mbatarev* told Ityo to return all Samber's goods, including the 10s. Without ever admitting his guilt, but also without denying it, Ityo returned the goods 'under the eyes of the *jir*'.

Again the 'correction' involved no punishment, but only restitution of the stolen goods. I once asked Chenge why the thief is sometimes punished and sometimes not. He replied that it depended on the magnitude of the crime. In the *jir* that Samber called against Ityo (which had occurred a day or two before) the mortification of having the whole community know he was a thief was sufficient punishment for Ityo. There are several cases cited above, however, which indicate that punishment is often a result of the action of the *jir* and a part of the restitution.

The instances of and *jir* concerning theft indicate that from the point of view of the individual, the end brought about by the *jir* is precisely the same as the result brought about by successful self-help. One's rights have been enforced. The point is somewhat clearer if expressed in terms of rights rather than in terms of norms.

A right, according to the *Shorter Oxford English Dictionary*, is a 'justified claim, on legal or moral grounds, to have or obtain something or to act in a certain way'. The right is, as it were, the actor's view of a certain situation in terms of the norm. When we speak about rights we are assuming the standpoints of the actors in the social situation.

Tiv, therefore, use both the institutions of self-help and the *jir* to enforce their rights. This is not, however, the way they put it. Their emphasis is on means of making others carry out their obligations. They discuss social acts by comparing them with what one 'ought' to do or to have done. Both the *jir* and the institutions of self-help are used for the same purpose, that of making people carry out their obligations towards one.

That the *jir* and self-help are alternative institutions can be seen even more clearly in the assault instances and cases than in those concerning theft. Instances of minor assault are usually handled by elders, for it is well known that if a *jir* is brought before the *mbatarev* in such matters, someone will probably be fined heavily for 'spoiling the *tar*'. However, my notes on informal settlements by elders do not contain illustrative instances as good as those heard by the *mbatarev*, so I have selected one of the latter for description.

JIR NO. 65. *Wantor calls Tarhemba for assault*

A woman named Wantor alleged that she had been beaten up by Tarhemba. She had been living for some ten months in the compound of an MbaDuku elder, but had no husband there or anywhere else. She complained that she had been brewing beer to make money for buying clothes; when she had gone to spread the news of her beer in the compound where Tarhemba was sitting, he called her a thief, insulted her, and beat her on the head and face.

Tarhemba was called and said tersely that it was Wantor who had caused all the trouble. A crippled woman from the compound in which they had fought was called as his witness. She said that Tarhemba had struck Wantor on the face, but that she had been insulting him and calling him names and shouting at him. Chenge asked if she knew Wantor to be a thief. She replied that, so far as she knew, Wantor was not a thief but was indeed an inveterate trouble-maker. The tenor of her evidence was that Wantor had behaved in such a way as to deserve a beating.

Chenge turned to Tarhemba and gave him a long lecture on spoiling the *tar* over so picayune a matter. Ikpokpo (*ortaregh* of MbaPwa at the time) noted that for a guest (*or va inya*) to cause brawling in the *tar* was very reprehensible payment for hospitality, yet it was undeniable that, whether or not Tarhemba had actually 'spoiled the *tar*', he had certainly 'spoiled her face', and it seemed to him that Tarhemba ought to give her 2s. as compensation. He was told to go and get the 2s. and to leave a piece of cloth as surety until he returned with the money. He got the money from kinsmen in the crowd and took it to Chenge, who immediately handed it to Wantor. She exclaimed petulantly that 2s. was little enough for the pain and humiliation she had undergone. Chenge interrupted and told the elder in whose compound she was living to shut her up and get her out of the way: she had got her just reward and more. The elder told her she had better cause no more trouble if she wanted to continue staying in his compound. She immediately stopped her complaints and faded into the background.

Wantor had used the *jir* as a counteraction to assault; the 'correction' consisted in her being recompensed for having suffered in the original breach of norm. The notion of recompense has been met before (*Jir* No. 31), when the judges suggested that Anyon should make a compensatory gift to his father-in-law. Reimbursement for 'damages' centres on the notion *wam*. *Wam*'ing a person means to make him a gift, thereby erasing a fault by compensation. If the gift is accepted, it serves both as an apology on the part of the offender and as a token of forgiveness on the part of the injured person. Sometimes a person himself makes the offer to *wam* another; but more often one of them forces an arbitration of their differences.

Tiv use the *jir* as a means of enforcing their rights against officials of the Native Authority as well as against private citizens. One can call such an official before the *jir* for breach of the norms of his job:

JIR NO. 66. *Ayo calls Mayange, an N.A. policeman, charging assault.*

Ayo told the *mbatarev* that he had called Mayange, the N.A. policeman, before the *jir* because Mayange had beaten his wife, who was pregnant, and had hit her belly, which had hurt ever since.

The *mbatarev* motioned Mayange into the court circle, but, apparently in recognition of his official position, did not require him to sit down on the ground before them. 'Mayange,' Gbegba asked slowly in his high, rasping voice, 'this woman says that you beat her in the belly. Did you do it?'

'I didn't beat her,' Mayange answered.

'What did you do?' Gbegba asked.

'It was in the market,' Mayange began. 'I had arrested a woman who was wanted in another *jir*, and this wife of Ayo came up and talked to her. I told her to go away, that it was not right to talk to a woman who was under arrest, but she paid no attention. I pushed her away and told her to be off. I did not beat her. I only pushed her.'

The woman broke in. 'Mayange was screaming and angry,' she screamed angrily. When he hit her in the belly with his night stick she had fallen to the ground, and had told him over and over again that he was mad to do a thing like this, that he had killed her child.

Mayange again interrupted and said it was a lie—he had not hit her in the belly, and she had not fallen to the ground. She had only got angry and abused him.

The *mbatarev* quieted them both. Then they asked the woman, 'What were you doing when Mayange started to beat you?' She said that she had only been talking to her co-wife whom Mayange had caught, and that she was doing so quite peacefully, when Mayange had come up and hit her without saying anything. The *mbatarev* asked her if she had had pains in her belly before being shoved by Mayange. She said that she had not.

Tyukwagh suggested that the child was not hurt, as he believed that 'a child who is injured while still in the womb will not stay there, but will come out immediately'. However, he added, when he himself had been a policeman in Gboko some years before, a similar case had occurred, and the District Officer had sent the woman to Mkar hospital for examination by the doctors; they had then decided the case after hearing from the doctor whether the woman had been hurt or not.

Chenge said this seemed a sensible idea. He turned to the husband. 'Ayo, you must come with 8s. on market day and take one of the lorries to Gboko.' He then told the scribe to write a letter to Tor Tiv, giving the details of the case, and asking him to make arrangements for the woman to be examined by the doctors in Mkar hospital. If it turned out that she was hurt, they would settle the case against Mayange; if she was shamming and trying to get money out of Mayange for nothing, they would hear a case against her and her husband. Meanwhile, they could do nothing.

Ayo agreed to take his wife to Mkar if they insisted, but said that she had never complained of pain in her belly until after being beaten by Mayange at market, and she had done nothing since but sit about crying. Therefore, it seemed to him that something must be wrong.

Huwa asked the woman, 'How long have you been pregnant?' She replied, ten months. He expostulated that a baby was in the womb only nine months, therefore she must be wrong. Gbegba added that a male child was in the womb nine months, a female child eight, and she must indeed be wrong. Her husband said that she had been pregnant for eight months. His mother spoke up from the crowd and said they were both wrong; her daugher-in-law had been pregnant for only seven months. The *mbatarev* accepted that figure and instructed the scribe to note in the letter that the woman had been pregnant for seven months.

Some ten days later Ayo and his wife came back to the *jir* bearing a note from Tor Tiv. The scribe read it out. It said that Tor Tiv had sent the woman to Mkar hospital as requested; there she had been examined by the lady doctor, who said that the child was not hurt in any way and that she could find no sign of bruises on the woman's belly or anywhere else. Ayo was thereupon fined 10s. for attempting to extort money from Mayange by making improper use of the court.

This example of the 'abuse of due process of law' is certainly not unique.

It is equally possible for a Native Authority policeman to obtain redress from private citizens if they have hindered him from carrying out his duty:

JIR NO. 67. *A policeman calls Apev for assault*

In February 1950, an N.A. policeman from a great distance away came before MbaDuku *jir* and lodged a complaint against Chenge's eldest son, Apev. He said that Apev had interfered with his delivering a message on which his chief had sent him. Apev was called into the court circle; Chenge asked the three other *mbatarev* to settle this case, as it concerned his son. Apev said that he had been walking along a path in MbaGbera when this man, dressed in a plain cloth, told him to get off the path and make way for him. Apev replied that there was no need to do so, but 'the man got offensive, so I threw him off the path. How should I know he was a policeman?'

The policeman answered that he had told Apev he was an official. Apev admitted as much, but said that the man was unable to show him a badge, a paper or any other evidence, therefore he had not believed his statement. The policeman now said that he had the papers which had been entrusted to him, but he shouldn't be expected to show them to just anyone. Gbegba agreed, but held that, on the other hand, the man should not have expected anyone to believe his bare statement that he was a policeman, otherwise every Tiv would claim to be a policeman whenever he wanted to throw somebody off the path.

After considerable discussion, Apev agreed to give the policeman 2s. because he had 'thrown him into the bush'. The policeman also received a long admonition from Gbegba to the effect that he must wear his uniform in future if he expected to be treated as a policeman—especially in strange parts.

There are, thus, some rights that might be said to be the prerogative of all, whereas others are the prerogative only of persons occupying specific statuses or offices. A policeman, for example, has special rights. Such rights also accrue to one because of genealogical position: in Chapter III we considered a *jir* in which a young man had claimed the rights of a sister's son (*igba*) to justify his taking five chickens from his mother's agnates in a single day. A similar *jir*, brought on grounds of assault, re-emphasizes this relationship and its special rights:

INSTANCE NO. 68. *Erkwagh injured his mother's brother's son's wife*

Erkwagh married a girl and, as is the custom, went to tell his mother's lineage and to demand and kill the chicken which they would give him on such an occasion. When he got to his mother's natal compound, he found no one there, so he took out his matchet from its scabbard and began to chase the largest cock, intending, he said, to kill and eat it on the spot. Just then the wife of his mother's brother's son came out of a hut. He didn't see her in time and ran into her, cutting her hand with his matchet. She began to ululate, and people came rushing from neighbouring farms and compounds. They set upon Erkwagh and beat him rather severely. They also took his matchet away from him. On returning home after the beating, his mother's father's brother, the compound head, took Erkwagh to Chenge. He said that he had not been present, otherwise he would have caught the chicken himself and given it to his sister's child, and even if the accident had occurred there would have been no beating. He did not know, he said, what to do when a group of people beat their *igba* for something that was doubtless an accident. Chenge refused to pronounce on the point, and left it until the next meeting of the *jir*. The *mbatarev* (unofficially, for no entry was ever made in the books) decided that nothing further should be done. They lectured all present on the immorality of beating one's sister's son, especially when he had done no real wrong.

It should be noted finally that Tiv do not grant the same rights to foreigners as they do to themselves. I was once told by a Tiv recently released from prison after serving four years for manslaughter that he thought European justice 'spoiled the *tar*' because the man whom he had killed was an Usô, not a Tiv. A further instance involving the rights of foreigners is:

JIR NO. 69. *An unknown Ibo is found and fined*

Early one morning in February 1950, a group of children from Ikpaor's compound found an unconscious Ibo at a cross-roads near their home. They ran to tell their father who, when he saw the man, quickly dispatched a child to Chenge's to tell one of the policemen. The policeman went with the child immediately, arrested the Ibo and about an hour later brought him to me for medical treatment. He had been beaten, and there was a large but shallow burn on his right shoulder. As I dressed the burn, the policeman told me, in Tiv, that the man had been stealing yams. He stated it as a fact. The Ibo himself said, in fair English, that he was employed on a lorry which had come to Obudu to trade, and that he remembered nothing between the time he sat drinking in a hut in Obudu and the time he found himself in a hut at Ikpaor's, where he had been taken to await the policeman. I asked him if he had been stealing yams, and he said he didn't remember.

Next morning, although it was not a regular session of the court, the *mbatarev* assembled to meet the District Officer who was on tour. They met before he was expected, and one of the *jir* to which they listened was the case of this Ibo. A large delegation of Ibo had come from the nearby trading community in Obudu. Their spokesman, one of the local carpenters, told the *mbatarev* that the man was neither kinsman, clansman, nor tribesman of any of the Obudu Ibo, and that none of them knew him. Yet, as he was one of their countrymen they would go bail for him, but first they would like to know who had beaten him and why. Chenge asked Ikpaor to tell them how his children had found the man. He repeated his story, adding that the man had been beaten before he was found. Chenge told the delegation that he did not know how or by whom the man had been beaten, nor what he had done to deserve beating, but he assumed that either he had been beaten by Ibo and brought by a lorry to a point near where he had been found, or else he had come to Tivland for no good purpose. The spokesman of the delegation agreed that no Ibo would come into Tivland at night unescorted unless he were mad or trying to steal. Eventually the man was fined £3 for 'stealing yams' (of which there was no actual evidence so far as I could learn) which was paid by the Ibo community in Obudu.

It seems probable that, had the same thing happened to a Tiv rather than an Ibo, nothing would have been done. Tiv consider Ibo their traditional enemies, and say that Ibo are always trying to cheat and murder them. One of my Ibo friends in Obudu once asked me to tell him confidentially why I lived with Tiv. I replied that I liked them and that I was studying their customs. 'They are savages,' he said—we were speaking English. 'They are tigers. They rob us and steal from us and eat us as if we were goats.'

We have learnt both from the instances concerning theft and those concerning assault that Tiv may enforce their rights either by self-help or by appeal to a *jir*. This is, indeed, true of European society as well. There is only one form of self-help so far examined which Tiv allow themselves and which we, in our legal system, do not: that is the 'taking in a matter of debt'. Taking someone's property is never, among us, an approved counteraction to a breach of norm. It is among Tiv, if one's kinsmen or the *jir* can be convinced that the act of taking a man's property in return for one's own does indeed lead to an acceptable retribution. The difficulty is, of course, that it may lead to a series of reprisals which are of the nature of feud.

IV. SELF-HELP: ENFORCEMENT OF RIGHTS AND REPRISAL

All institutions of self-help are seen, by the persons who use them, as mechanisms for obtaining one's rights or, perhaps more accurately, making other people perform their obligations. It is, however, possible to distinguish three sorts of self-help: (1) resort to jural institutions in which one must nevertheless do one's own detective and police work and oneself enforce the decisions of the court, (2) self right-enforcement, in which one takes direct action to protect one's rights, and (3) reprisal.

It has been noted in many of the instances recorded that the decisions of the judges are left to the principal litigants and their kinsmen to be carried out. In *Jir* No. 53, Rumun gave Faga a Hausa gown to pawn. The judges settled the dispute in his favour, saying that Faga should redeem and return Rumun's goods. But the implementation of the decision was left to Rumun. In instance No. 57, in which the cloth-buyer left Ukpoepi's son holding a bag of pebbles, we saw that Ukpoepi did his own detective work; he made inquiries at the market and among his friends and relatives to discover if anyone had seen his son with the man who had tricked him, and finally did determine his identity. He then,

L

unaided, proceeded to the compound of that man, recovered the stolen goods, and returned them. He was, thus, also his own policeman. We saw, in *Jir* No. 63, that when Kwaghnyiman and Tor stole a cow from Aboshin, the latter paid a 'disinterested' Tiv to act as his 'witness'—in other words, detective work was done by what we should consider private contract (as still happens among ourselves in some divorce cases). All these I would call self-help in a jural situation. It was summed up in a letter written to my cook by his brother, an N.A. policeman. The letter was in English, and the cook—whose English was more apparent than real— sought my help in deciphering it. The brother had just heard that the cook had, some weeks before, been robbed of two vests and a pair of shorts while taking his afternoon siesta in his hut. He advised him that the way to handle the matter was for him and his friends to ask around 'softly softly' and soon, the policeman brother said, we should 'come to know' who had stolen them, and then the matter could be taken before the *mbatarev* and the chief.

Self right-enforcement, on the other hand, is an action like Gu's when he dealt himself with the thief: no jural institution was involved. Self right-enforcement is acting in lieu of any jural institution.

Both these sorts of self-help can be contrasted with the third sort, reprisal. 'Taking in a matter of debt' is reprisal. Among Tiv it is a recognized counteraction to theft and debt, but it is not part of 'repairing the *tar*'. All instances of reprisal that I collected are referred to by another set of concepts, which might be called concepts of revenge.

Tiv concepts of revenge are many and varied. They overlap the even richer conceptualization of what we might call 'whittling people down to one's own size'.

When a man 'takes' a sheep from another, claiming that the latter owes him a sheep or its equivalent, he is said to be 'taking revenge', never 'repairing *tar*'. 'Evening out the score' might be a better translation of *iyev i oon*. *Iyev* is a noun meaning 'revenge or reprisal', and *oo* is a verb meaning 'to make *iyev*'—it is not used in any other context, so far as I know. My simplest text on this matter was written by Iyorkôsu, the less tame of my two clerks, as one of his first exercises:

'If a man beats your brother and you hear about it and don't like it, you say that you will certainly take revenge. So, one day when you see him, you beat him. He says that you have taken revenge. If a man steals your goat and you don't like it, you take his goat. He says that you have taken revenge.'

Iyorkôsu could write page after page on some subjects, but this is all he could think of to write on the matter of reprisal. 'It is very easy,' he said. 'It is not difficult to understand.'

Reprisal must be precisely equivalent to the original injury. If it is not—and, of course, it is seldom so considered by the person who suffers it—it falls into one of several other categories, of which *ifer* is one of the least common. One of the most common is *igya*, which means roughly an act of jealousy. Again a text from Iyorkôsu serves as illustration:

'If you are working in the same place as another man and he doesn't like you, he will begin to fight *igya* with you. You will do good work, but the man who is fighting *igya* with you will spoil your work. Now, take as an example, Sar and Ahwa [my wife's servants]. If Sar wanted to do *igya* to Ahwa, Ahwa would cook soup but Sar would get a lot of salt and pour into the soup which Ahwa had made. Then the soup would be too salty and not good to drink. If Ahwa didn't see what Sar had done, he would wonder why it was that Akimbi [my wife's Tiv name] scolded him—and he would know in his heart that it was Sar who poured salt into the soup, so Ahwa would begin fighting *igya* with him. Another day, when Sar had gone for his afternoon off, Ahwa would go into Akimbi's house and see her bottle of gin and take it and hide it in the bush. Then, when Akimbi didn't see her gin, she would ask Sar where he had put it. Sar would say he didn't know where the gin was, and Akimbi would say that he did know and she wanted him to bring it back! This would please Ahwa very much, because she had as good as said that Sar was a thief. Then Sar would be very angry, and he would go looking for medicine from somebody or other, and would come and bewitch Ahwa with it. So Ahwa wouldn't have the strength to work, and he could say to Akimbi that, because he hadn't the strength to work, he must go to Mkar Hospital to drink medicine. Akimbi would agree and give Ahwa a paper; he would go to the doctor who would completely cure Ahwa, who would return and take up his work. Ahwa would say he would never stop the thing—he would take revenge (*iyev*) if it was the last thing he did. Thus, he would frighten Sar who would be afraid Ahwa would kill him, so he would quit work and go home. Then Ahwa would be very glad and say that he had beaten Sar at *igya*.'

Before reading this text, I had not known the word *igya*, but I had certainly known households in which *igya* contests had taken place. I asked Iyorkôsu, 'If the servants in a household do *igya*, what does that make the master, who suffers from it?' He had never considered this problem. He thought for a while and answered, 'You can only say that his luck has spoiled utterly.'

The point of this text is, of course, that each person sees his own acts as revenge or *iyev* on the other, while he sees the acts of the other as unwarranted acts of jealousy (*igya*). What the initiator considers revenge or reprisal, the victim considers aggression, to be avenged or requited.

Tiv vocabulary and concepts centring on the notion of 'doing down' one's kinsmen and neighbours are exceptionally rich. The pivot of these notions (of which *igya* is one of the least virulent) is *iwuhe*. The word is translated by both Tiv dictionaries as 'envy, jealousy', a rather serious mistranslation. What we think of as envy or jealousy is expressed in the verb *tôm*. *Iwuhe* is a major anti-social act undertaken to bring about the discomfort or disgrace of someone else. It is easy to collect texts on *iwuhe*:

INSTANCE NO. 70. *Jealous acts lead to murder*

'*Iwuhe* is something which spoils the *tar* very much, and really has no purpose at all. One of my "brothers" killed his wife because of *iwuhe*— I know that it began with *iwuhe*. He went off looking for a wife to marry, and he saw the daughter of Dom, who pleased him very much —a girl named MbaTômon ("People will envy me")—who was very beautiful, and had many useful things like clothes and enamel-ware. My brother asked her, "Whose wife are you?" and she replied that she had no husband—she was the widow of an Ukan man. My brother asked her if her husband had been alone [i.e. had he no agnatic kinsmen to inherit her] and she replied that he had a brother who disliked her exceedingly. My brother asked, "Are you, then, going back to Ukan?" and she said, "No, I won't be going back." Whereupon my brother suggested to her that they should go to his *tar*, and MbaTômon asked him where his *tar* was, and he said it was MbaTiav, in the lineage of Chief Kuhwe. MbaTômon asked him what his name was; he replied that it was Kumaga. MbaTômon agreed to go with him.

'So Kumaga began to court MbaTômon and courted her for two moons, after which he married her and took her home. Almost immediately his senior wife began to do *iwuhe*[1] against MbaTômon. At that

[1] It is the fact that in many African languages the word usually translated 'jealousy' is the same as the word for co-wife. *Iwuhe* also means co-wife in Tiv, but Tiv scoff at the idea that there is any connexion save that which they use in jokes or puns. One of the favourite Tiv puns is *Kasev chii mba iwuhe*, which means (1) all women are co-wives; (2) all wives are jealous; and (3) all women are cold.

time, MbaTômon had no hut of her own, they all slept in one hut. Kumaga wanted to sleep with MbaTômon, but the senior wife wouldn't ever sleep: she would stay up all night, tending the fire until dawn, and Kumaga could never have sexual relations with his wife MbaTômon, who then snubbed her senior wife and wouldn't speak to her.

'MbaTômon was very upset because if she had known that this woman was one to do *iwuhe* like this, she would never have come. When the dry season arrived, Kumaga built MbaTômon a hut and also hoed her a farm.

'One morning MbaTômon went out very early to fetch water. She brought it and put it into her hut, and then went to the field to work. When Kumaga's senior wife saw that she had gone to her farm, she sneaked into MbaTômon's hut and defecated into the water. Then she left and went out to where Kumaga was clearing new farm-land.

'Kumaga came back from work and MbaTômon did too. Kumaga told MbaTômon to give him a drink, so MbaTômon got up to get the water to give him. When she first went into the hut, it was very dark. She took a gourd dipper and scooped up water in it to give to her husband. She got some faeces in it, but didn't see it in the dark of the hut. When she got outside, she discovered the faeces and threw it out and began to ululate so that people collected about her. They asked "What is it?" and she said that Kumaga had sent her to fetch a drink of water and when she came to give it to him, she had ladled up faeces out of the water. This surprised everybody. They thought about it, but didn't know, so they said it was the *mbatsav* who had done it.

'Another day, the senior wife went out and dug up MbaTômon's seed yams and threw them away. This time, they said it was the monkeys.

'That woman would not let MbaTômon leave anything about, for she wanted her husband to scold MbaTômon. The senior wife got worse and worse.

'One day, MbaTômon again went to her fields, and the senior wife again entered MbaTômon's hut to do some sort of damage in it. [She did not know that Kumaga was napping there.] She went in very softly and was just defecating in the water pot when Kumaga got up very suddenly from the shadows, grabbed a matchet and struck her on the back; he struck her so that he cut her very badly. She called out and all the people came and saw that she was dying. This is what *iwuhe* can do.'

Iwuhe is the point at which self-help and crime overlap. *Iwuhe* is always *kwaghbo* and *kwaghdang*. It is recognized that *iwuhe* is very often done in reprisal, but one never says that one has right on one's side. It always 'spoils the *tar*' if one resorts to *iwuhe*. *Iwuhe*, when performed by what we (but not Tiv) would call supernatural or non-natural means, is an important factor in Tiv witchcraft and religion.

The distinction is clear in the Tiv folk system. While both *jir* and self right-enforcement on the one hand, and reprisal on the other, may be utilized as counteraction for breach of right, both the *jir* and self right-enforcement are aspects of 'repairing the *tar*'. But reprisal is always a matter of 'spoiling the *tar*'—even when it is recognized as a legitimate means of counteraction. Tiv are unequivocal on this point.

Nowadays, however, the *jir* very often levies fines for reprisals that were undertaken as counteractions. In *Jir* No. 51, Batur shot an arrow at and wounded Yaji's pig when the pig ate his cassava; the *mbatarev* did not allow Yaji damages, because the injury to the pig was said to compensate for the injury to the cassava. They did, however, fine Batur for having taken reprisals instead of calling a *jir*—for having spoiled the *tar* further instead of having begun the process of repairing it. Other instances have also been cited.

Reprisal does not always depend on the exercise of mere force, though it often does. Tiv have an institution which they call 'drumming the scandal' (*kuhwan anger*), a reprisal type of action which almost always leads to spoiling the *tar*.

INSTANCE NO. 71. *Torgindi and Mtswen drum the scandal*

Early in the spring of 1950, an argument occurred between Torgindi of MbaYar and Mtswen of MbaGishi, both lineages contained within MbaDuku. Mtswen was the secondary marriage guardian of the wife of Torgindi's son, and had been guilty of some rather high-handed tactics that caused the marriage to fall through. Mtswen had then refused to act as intermediary to get Torgindi's bridewealth refunded, and the two men exchanged angry words. Torgindi went back to his compound and made up a song in which he said what a skunk Mtswen was. That night, when all was quiet, he drummed and sang the song as loud as he could, for the whole countryside to hear—including Mtswen, who lived a little over a quarter of a mile away.[1] The next night, he again sang the song, and all the members of his own compound and some from other compounds of his lineage joined in the chorus. The only thing for Mtswen to do was to make up a song of his own against Torgindi. But knowing that he wasn't much of a song-maker, he hired the best song-maker in Shangev Ya to stay at his place and compose scurrilous songs about Torgindi and all his kinsmen and wives.

[1] Some Tiv can pitch their voices so as to be heard up to three miles away.

Soon Torgindi's inventiveness was also exhausted, and he too hired a song-maker. By this time the two men were holding dances and song-contests every night. They each brewed beer and made food in order to attract dancers to come to dance and sing the songs directed at the other.

There are some specific rules for these songs. Chenge told me that if an act attributed in such a song was possible of human performance, it should be true, or the slandered person could call a *jir*.[1] However, if the act was not humanly possible anything could be said. In one of Mtswen's songs, he accused one of Torgindi's wives of stealing yams: this, by local consensus, was probably true because this particular wife was of the Udam tribe, and widely thought to be a thief. But if it was not true, Chenge insisted, Torgindi and the wife could call a *jir* against Mtswen and the song-maker. Another song, and one of the catchiest tunes which the contest produced, told how Torgindi changed himself into a pig at night and made it unsafe for every sow in the countryside. The Shangev song-maker (who later became a good friend and favourite guide) said that since even Torgindi couldn't actually do that, such a song couldn't be the basis for a *jir*. The song-maker said that he had thought of some much worse things to suggest that it was in Torgindi's nature to do, if it were only humanly possible, but that Mtswen had stopped him saying that all he wanted to do was to win the contest, not to 'spoil Torgindi's heart permanently'. They were, after all, neighbours.

The drumming contests continued every night for more than three weeks before the *mbatarev* took notice. Finally, Chenge decided that if the thing was allowed to continue it would almost surely end in a fight, for which he himself would be answerable to the District Officer. Therefore he sent word to both Mtswen and Torgindi that they and their people were to come to his compound the following afternoon, and both would sing and drum and he and the *mbatarev* would decide the case.

Both sides came fully prepared. Torgindi's group dragged a large *ilyu* drum for two and a half miles in order to accompany their songs and dances. Mtswen's song-maker and one of his sons hurried across to Udam and bought two small wooden figurines of the sort the Udam use in divination: a small male and a larger female. The male figurine they painted black; the larger female figurine they painted red. These two figurines represented Torgindi, a small and very dark man, and his tall, fat, light-coloured wife. They were tied together at the top of a long pole in a somewhat compromising position, and were waved frantically in accompaniment to all the songs.

---

[1] As I have stated earlier, I have never seen a *jir* for slander.

The *mbatarev* walked back and forth between the two performing groups. They noted this performer and that song. Then, about two hours later, they called for quiet and said that they would now hear the *jir*. As Torgindi began his story, the man carrying the two figurines put them up in the air and waved them—a roar of laughter followed. Chenge took them away from the offender and put them under his chair until the hearing was over.

The case, which was a simple marriage case, was very quickly settled, and both men—anxious to be rid of the vast expense they were incurring—concurred in the judgment. After the case was settled on its jural points, the *mbatarev* announced the winner of the song contest: Torgindi won the case, but Mtswen had the better songs. They then advised both song-makers to go home immediately and not return to MbaDuku for a couple of months until the feelings which had been aroused had died down.

Chenge and Mtswen's song-maker both told me that in the old days 'drumming the scandal' was a favourite method of settling disputes, and almost always led to fighting. Whoever won the fight won the dispute.

'But doesn't that spoil the *tar?*' I asked.

'Of course,' Chenge answered. 'But the *tar* was already spoilt by the fighting and lack of agreement.' He added quite candidly that the only reason he interfered was that he didn't want the District Officer to blame him if a fight occurred in his area. Some months later the song-maker, on the same assumption, commented that chiefs and District Officers spoil all the fun.

Another favourite form of reprisal is to take all the clothes of a debtor. An instance came to my notice when I was working in Iharev/Ityôshin.

INSTANCE NO. 72. *Anwase is stripped in settlement of a debt*

One day WanGbenger, the wife of a compound head of MbaAliko, told me that Anwase owed her 1*s.*, and asked me to help her collect it. Anwase was a happy-go-lucky and very intelligent youngster of about 22 who used to do odd jobs for me. The next time he earned a shilling I told him I was giving it to WanGbenger. He agreed readily, saying that he had meant to pay her sooner, but he seemed never to have a shilling. I asked him if WanGbenger was fool enough to lend him a shilling, and he replied that she had once been his best friend. He wouldn't tell me any more. That evening I walked over to give WanGbenger her shilling. She thanked me and I asked her if she actually did lend Anwase a shilling, and whether she did not know that if it weren't for someone like me she would never have got it back. She said this was probably true, but the day she had given him the shilling, 'Anwase walked into our compound completely naked, with his hand covering his penis, and he said, "WanGbenger, I'm naked", so I gave him a shilling to help buy a cloth.' She continued that Anwase had owed 9s. 4d. to a youngster over in Ukusu who had come with two brothers and forcibly removed his only cloth in payment, leaving him naked. She added that Anwase had collected more money in this way than he had actually spent on cloth, and she supposed that he 'ate' the remainder.

Taking a person's cloth in reprisal for a debt is fairly common amongst Tiv. In one instance, at least, it led to death:

DISPUTE NO. 73. *Stripping a man in reprisal leads to manslaughter*

In the 1941 case Rex *v.* Aloho (File 1568, Gboko Divisional Office), one of the witnesses is reported to have said at the Preliminary Inquiry, 'Aloho and I went off to hunt. We met the deceased and Kegh collecting mangoes in the ruins of an old compound in the bush. When [my companion] the accused saw the deceased, he told him to come down out of the tree and give us the thread which he had taken from him at a previous meeting. Deceased came down from the tree and replied that he did not know that they would meet here and so had not brought the thread. Accused then said, "I will take the cloth off your loins—that is my thread", and he did so. The cloth was new and I put it on, but gave him my old cloth to wear so that he would not be naked while we went to his compound to get the thread. We all started off. I was in the front, and a little later I heard deceased shouting "Let me go!" ' The debtor, in shame at having been stripped for debt, started a fight in the course of which he was killed.

In Tivland today, both self right-enforcement and reprisal are more common in those areas where Grade-D courts are inefficient or distant, than in areas where efficient courts are close at hand. Tiv agree with their European administrators that courts, because they are surer, are a much better way of asserting one's right than any sort of self right-enforcement. However, they often find the action of the court too slow.

In summarizing Tiv institutions of self-help, we have seen that they are founded on two principles. The self-help founded on the principle of reprisal (*iyev i oon*) is not a jural mechanism, for it often does not reach a stage of retribution by jural means. As Tiv put it, taking revenge is no part of repairing the *tar*. In fact, the second act in the series spoils the *tar* even more than the first.

The second principle, self right-enforcement, does lead to a stage of retribution. The initial act has spoiled the *tar*, and one is justified in taking action to set right the wrong.

We are left with the difficult problem of feud. Feud is the archetype of institutions resulting from reprisals. Institutionalized feud did not exist in Tivland. But such a statement needs qualification. Killings among Tiv did not lead to reprisals by kinsmen, but rather to war between lineages. At the end of such a war, the score was counted and remembered on each side and, when the next war broke out, a new total was added to the old. From what one can glean today, it would seem that all lineages lived in the possibility of warfare with their equivalent segments, and that reprisals for killings between segments were turned into this more general form of fighting.[1]

V. CRIMES SETTLED BY HIGHER COURTS

Tiv are not today in a position to deal with all the social situations which their European rulers term 'crime', or which they themselves call *ifer*. With the exception of witchcraft, all crimes that the Administration considers to be of a serious nature are dealt with by European courts, manned by European or European-trained Nigerians. These courts handle cases concerned with homicide, slave-dealing, rape, and theft or disputes involving large sums of money.

The only one of these with which we are greatly concerned here is homicide. Slave-dealing became a crime with the advent of Europeans; before that time it had its ethics and was an accepted part of social life. Tiv did not, I suggest, distinguish between rape and seduction—both are called 'spoiling women'.

The indigenous jural institutions for dealing with homicide are, for the most part, in abeyance. It is true that the ritual reparation for homicide is said to be still practised, but since the Administration has taken the jural settlement into its own hands, the ceremony has been somewhat curtailed in the interest of speed.

[1] Material on Tiv warfare will be published in a short monograph. In that place, I shall probably tackle the question of how it happens that Tiv, so like the Bedouin Arab and the Nuer in many aspects of their social organization, are not characterized by feud.

Homicide, like the other major crimes, is handled in accordance with the Statutes of Nigeria, whereas most of the offences so far considered in this book are settled by what the Statutes call 'native law and custom'. Therefore, in order to study major crime in Tivland, one must go either to the courts that deal with it, or to the records kept in the divisional office in Gboko and at provincial headquarters in Makurdi.

When a killing is discovered, *mbatarev* and their unarmed policemen arrest the killer, who is 'sent to the D.O.', as Tiv put it, with a note giving the circumstances and the names of witnesses. After that, it is out of Tiv hands. Many killers themselves go to the District Office to give themselves up. I believe, but have no actual evidence, that most of them attempt to have a shortened form of the *akombo swende* ceremony performed before doing so. This ceremony counteracts any evil that might befall the community; if necessary, however, it can be performed at any time, with a cloth or piece of property belonging to the killer, so it may be omitted until signs of the need have arisen.

After homicide is detected and the culprit has been arrested and charged, the divisional officers, who are also magistrates, carry out what is known as a 'Preliminary Inquiry'. They take statements and depositions from witnesses and, if he desires to make one, from the accused. These statements are then used by magistrates as the basis for briefs and preparation for trial before the Higher Court, as well as recommendations to the court by the Administration.

I do not intend to go very thoroughly here into the matter of homicide, for two reasons: first, it is today a part of the jural mechanism of the colonial society of Nigeria, not of the smaller society of the Tiv, and takes both its form and its aim from European law.[1] Secondly, my material on homicide and suicide appears in another, comparative study.[2] What is of most interest here is a brief statement of the counteractions which Tiv today say followed on homicide in the indigenous system.

Tiv elders have told me that they are content to leave the serious problems of homicide to the Government, for the only way that they could cope with murderers was to forgive them, sell them into slavery, or kill them. At the same time, many of them resent the fact that a man whose only serious fault is a single homicide may

[1] T. O. Elias, *Groundwork of Nigerian Law*, pp. 173 and 187–90.
[2] *African Homicide and Suicide*, Princeton University Press, 1960; (paper) Atheneum, 1966.

be imprisoned or executed, while Government has deprived them of their own methods (and not given them any new ones) of ridding the community of troublesome persons guilty of what Malinowski called 'the crime of being a bad lot'.

In the past, what was done with a murderer depended entirely on who he was and whom he had killed. As in many other African societies, fratricide was never punished, but merely 'ritually repaired'. If a man killed someone of another lineage, a general war usually resulted. It is said today that attempts were often made to avert such wars by employing as an intermediary a man related to both lineages. He was usually successful, it would seem, if the killing was accidental.

Tiv elders say that there were instances in which the murderer's lineage avoided war by deciding to give him to the lineage of his victim, to do as they liked with him. On other occasions, he could be made to hang himself in retribution for his deed. But the elders were unable or unwilling to cite cases in which either of these ways of handling the situation had in fact been adopted. More often, murder led to war between the two lineages. They fought until peace could be restored by the normal means. All Tiv today deny that killing ever led to a personal feud, but say rather that it always led to wars between lineages.

I was told of one case in which a madman, for no apparent reason, killed a woman who was married into a neighbouring lineage; a girl from his own lineage was handed to the victim's husband as replacement. This event occurred in Shangev Ya some time in the 1930's; I could not find any official record of it. All the Shangev elders with whom I discussed the case said that it was not the usual custom to give a girl to the murdered person's lineage. It had been done on this occasion because they were shocked at their brother's deed, and at themselves for having let him go free when they knew that he was mad—'But we thought it was only the small madness.' Another case, in which a woman was given as wife in compensation for murder, came to light in the files of murder cases, but my informants refused to consider it a normal procedure.

The presence today of a European Administration has had several effects on Tiv custom relating to homicide. It has shortened the ritual which follows on homicide and is performed for the benefit of the community, not simply of the killer. More important, it has taken the jural handling of serious crimes out of Tiv hands. The mechanism for handling disputes and *afer* in the Tiv community is not seriously affected so long as the Tiv concur in the view of themselves as part of the colonial society. It has, however, had the effect of vastly complicating the jural procedure found locally.

VI. SUMMARY AND CONCLUSIONS

We began this chapter with a review of the types of criminal cases heard in Grade-D courts. We ended it with a very brief review of the criminal cases heard by Nigerian magistrates and High Courts. We looked into the Tiv classification of wrongs and found that they differentiate moral wrongs (*kwaghdang*) from mystically dangerous acts (*kwaghbo*), and both from acts which are followed by a counteraction and then by correction (those acts known as *ifer*), and noted that the Tiv classification of wrongs was different from the English.

We also found that Tiv have three sorts of institutions of self-help, which may easily be confused because all of them are called, in English, 'taking the law into your own hands'. There are those cases which we termed self-help in jural situations, in which the principals must do their own police work and are left to carry out the decisions of the *jir*. There is another sort, self right-enforcement, in which the self-help, often in the form of violence, constitutes one's protection of one's own rights, and in which no jural institution is involved.

The third form of self-help, which we called reprisal, is not part of repairing the *tar*, but is described, in company with many other concepts, in terms of revenge. Vengeance or reprisal is a sort of social action that does not automatically end in restitution of the breach of norm which it was meant to counter. Its archetype is the feud, though institutionalized feud has never formed a part of Tiv culture.

This chapter also concludes our investigation of the subject matter of those *jir* that are heard by the *mbatarev*. A brief restatement of the analytical propositions and their refinements is in order.

In Chapter V we noted that Tiv scribes were required to separate and classify their cases into civil and criminal for record purposes.

We noted the subordinate categories of each class, and arranged our material roughly as the scribes arrange theirs. We have concluded, in the present chapter, that the distinction between civil and criminal law is one of several drawn by English law which cannot adequately be appreciated by Tiv, just as there are jural distinctions drawn by Tiv which English lawyers may find it difficult to appreciate.

Civil cases are divided (by scribes) into two main categories: those concerned with marriage, and those concerned with debt. In arranging marriage cases our first problem was the basis for arrangement. In Chapter IV we arranged some marriage cases to bring out and illustrate the norms of Tiv marriage, breach of which could be counteracted by the *jir*. We noted that this arrangement was an analytical arrangement, made for exposition, not for social action.

We investigated the way marriage entered the *jir*, and the way the *jir* entered the institution of marriage, and elicited another and more purely sociological type of analytical systemization of the case material. Our resultant system can be summarized in the diagram representing three social actions (see p. 100 above). We noted that a suitable and efficient counteraction was to be found in the *jir* or Grade-D court. The fines and punishments which it imposed, as well as the actions according to norm which it prescribed, are corrections.

When the debt cases were considered, in Chapter VI, we clarified the Tiv concept of debt and found it somewhat more inclusive than the English concept of debt. Many debt cases covered what we should call contract; Tiv emphasize the debt aspect of a contract (or, conversely, the English law emphasizes the contract aspect of some debts). We also determined that Tiv argued a *jir* in many instances by questioning which of several acts actually preceded it:

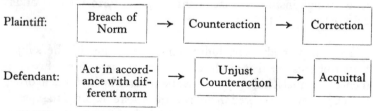

Finally, in the present chapter we have been investigating Tiv categories of wrongs and crimes, and the alternative counter-actions which Tiv may use to protect their rights. We have found several possible series of social acts which Tiv call repairing the *tar* or 'governing'.

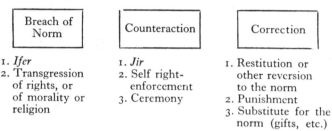

Breach of Norm	Counteraction	Correction
1. *Ifer*	1. *Jir*	1. Restitution or other reversion to the norm
2. Transgression of rights, or of morality or religion	2. Self right-enforcement	2. Punishment
	3. Ceremony	3. Substitute for the norm (gifts, etc.)

We found also that some social acts were in the nature of counter-actions, but that these acts were considered by Tiv to be reprisals, were discussed by them in the context of revenge rather than of repairing the *tar* and, unlike the other jural institutions, do not necessarily lead to correction and settlement of the matter in hand:

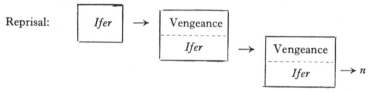

Reprisal:

$$\text{Ifer} \rightarrow \frac{\text{Vengeance}}{\text{Ifer}} \rightarrow \frac{\text{Vengeance}}{\text{Ifer}} \rightarrow n$$

In what I have called the jural institutions, a breach of norm is followed by a counteraction which (if successful) leads to reparation of the original breach or other sort of correction. Such is also the case with self right-enforcement. In what I have called reprisal, a breach of norm leads to a reprisal, which is interpreted as a breach of norm by the person who suffers it; he in turn takes reprisal, and so indefinitely. The state of correction, and hence of actions according to norm, is never reached.

It may be that institutions of reprisal are part of the 'legal' machinery in some societies. In Tivland, they are not part of repairing the *tar*, just as in present-day Europe and America feuds or duels are not part of the law.

CHAPTER VIII

MARKET *JIR* AND AGE-SET *JIR*

THE word *jir* is applied by Tiv to any dispute that is to be arbitrated. By far the greatest number are brought before the Native Authority court. Some of the more important disputes, even though their number is comparatively small, are brought before what we shall describe later as the moot. A few minor *jir*, however, are heard by market officials and by age-sets; they are briefly considered in this chapter.

I. MARKET JIR

A *jir* can be arbitrated by anyone before whom the principals are willing to discuss it. One of the places in which Tiv prefer to hear and discuss disputes is the market. We have already reported how preliminary hearings of disputes and *jir* are heard by chiefs and *mbatarev* in the markets. In addition, there is usually another *jir* in which market authorities settle those disputes that grow directly out of the trading or other events which occur in the market-place. There is a rather wide range of variation in the organization of markets among Tiv; the relationship of the market-masters to the officially recognized authorities varies even more widely. Every market in Tivland has either a headman, called the 'market chief' (*tor kasoa*), or a group of three or four elders who may be called 'Those who look after the market' (*mbanengen kasoa*). In the former case, it is often the market chief himself who hears disputes that arise in the markets, though he may delegate someone else to do it for him, especially if he is himself an important and busy man. 'Those who look after the market', in markets so organized, generally themselves hear disputes, either all together or two or three elders at a time.

I have records of disputes collected from five different markets, two in southern Tivland (Tsar and Iyon markets), one in eastern Tivland (Zaki Biam market) and two in central Tivland (Gboko market and the missionaries' market at Mkar). It would be impossible to distinguish the *jir* heard at any one of them from those heard at the others, with the exception of Iyon. Iyon might be called an 'international market', and most of the disputes among Tiv, Uge, and Udam peoples were aired at it. These disputes were of a sort which we might call 'international'. They will be more fully reported elsewhere.[1] Intra-Tiv affairs heard at this market were indistinguishable from those heard at other Tiv markets.

Most of the *jir* which I have selected to report were heard in Tsar market. Its market chief was neither the best nor the most popular judge in this part of Tivland, but the market was his by right of inheritance, and he did settle a great many disputes satisfactorily. The market met every five days, and was very large. It usually began with grain sales half an hour after dawn, and ended in the late afternoon when the final pot of beer had been either sold or, more probably, consumed by its makers. The market-master spent most of his time, on market day, in a rough shelter of bamboo and thatching grass erected for this purpose. Some half-dozen of his kinsmen—the number varied from week to week—acted as his messengers and market police, in addition to Chenge's two Native Authority policemen who spent the day there if they were not away on errands. Disputants and the market-master's friends all crowded into the small shelter.

The market-master charged a small fee—usually from 2d. to 6d.—for settling all the *jir* which he heard, except those brought in by his 'police'. He was busy most of the day. I spent comparatively little time in the market *jir*. One of my two clerks, who was both fond of markets and of a litigious disposition, reported these cases by the score. Although I have myself seen many cases like those reported here, most of them are taken from his notebooks, and from the notes I took while discussing them with him.

Here is a typical *jir*, from the clerk's notebook:

MARKET JIR NO. I

'WanAgayo bought 2d. worth of pepper at market. The man selling the pepper took the money, but as she was leaving, he got up and told her that she had not paid him. WanAgayo contradicted him, saying that she had given him the money, but he said she had not. Thereupon the man called a *jir* before the market chief against WanAgayo. The market chief asked her whether she had paid this man his money. She replied that she had indeed paid him. The market chief asked her whether she

[1] Paul and Laura Bohannan, *Tiv Economy*, Northwestern University Press, 1968.

M

would swear on the fetish. When she did so, the market chief said that it was the woman who had the right and he gave the fault to the man who sold the pepper.'

The fetish used was not *swem*, as in the case of a chief's *jir*, but a palm-frond, the symbol of the *akombo igbe*. Taking a false oath on this fetish is said to produce dysentery. The market-master was primarily interested in getting rid of a minor dispute, not in determining whether or not the money had been paid. He had one of the principals swear, thus acting as her own witness, in order to find a *modus placendi*.

Here is the translation of another text about market *jir*:

MARKET JIR NO. 2

'Ityavmough bought guinea-corn from a woman in the market. The woman poured the corn into an enamel basin, and gave it to Ityavmough so that he could pour it into his bag, after which he said he would return the basin to her. He went off with the basin, but didn't bring it back; she went and asked him for her basin, but he said he didn't know her, and hadn't bought any guinea-corn from her. She didn't like this, so she called a *jir* against Ityavmough before the market-master. The market-master asked Ityavmough, "Did you buy guinea-corn from this woman?" He denied it. The market-master then asked the woman, "There are many people in the market. Some are strangers. Are you sure it was Ityavmough here who bought the guinea-corn from you?" The woman said that he had a cloth tied around his waist in mourning fashion, and that he had worn a *gwarmo* cloth around his loins [as this man did], but since he was denying it she would call the woman who was with her. The market chief agreed.

'When this woman arrived, the market-master asked her, "Do you know this man?" She concurred, "Yes, I know him." The market-master continued, "Is he the man who bought guinea-corn from your co-wife?" "Yes," the woman replied, "he had a cloth tied around his waist and wore a *gwarmo* cloth and was chewing tobacco." The market-master asked her to swear on a fetish, and she swore on the Axe of Heaven. Thereupon, the market-master told Ityavmough that the *jir* had caught him, and that he must pay for the basin. So Ityavmough gave 4s. for it. The market-master had first asked the woman how much she wanted for it, and she had said 4s.'

This sort of dispute is very common in Tiv markets. Besides those illustrated above—disputes about payment and about property—the market-master is often asked to be witness to sales.

By no means all the *jir* heard in the market courts, however, arise directly out of market transactions. Market is, for example, a good place to catch one's debtors, so that a *jir* of this sort is fairly common:

MARKET JIR NO. 3

'Zenda, of MbaGbera, owed an Ute youngster 6*s*. So Zenda gave the money to the youngster's brother (*wangho*) and told him to give it to him. The brother, however, kept it, saying that the youngster had been in debt to him for a very long time. When the Ute youngster came to Tsar market and met Zenda, he called a *jir* against him before the market chief. The market chief called Zenda and questioned him. Zenda said that he had formerly owed this man 6*s*., but had given it to the latter's brother to deliver—he didn't know whether the brother had handed it over or not. The youngster said that his brother had never given it to him, and he didn't know what Zenda was trying to do. So Zenda got up and walked around the market. His luck was with him, for he met the man to whom he had paid the money. He brought him to the market chief. The market chief asked him whether Zenda had given him some money for his brother. He agreed that Zenda had given him some money, but since his brother was in debt to him—well, when it rains the trees can have a bath [take what comes your way and don't ask questions]. The market chief told them to be off.'

I have notes on many market *jir* in which people have discovered in the market property which they say was stolen from them, and have therefore called a *jir* before the market authorities in order to recover it.

MARKET JIR NO. 4

'Some thief stole a duck from Kwamande and took it to sell at Tsar market. When Kwamande came to market, he discovered it. Whereupon Kwamande asked Ukande, who had the duck, "Who gave you that duck?" Ukande said that he had bought it. Kwamande asked him whom he had bought it from, and Ukande replied that it was a man he didn't know. Kwamande then told Ukande to give him his duck, but Ukande said it wasn't Kwamande's duck and he wasn't going to give it to him.

'So Kwamande called a *jir* before the market chief, who told Ukande to bring the duck for him to see. When he had done so, the market chief asked Ukande from whom he had bought the duck; Ukande again said that he didn't know. Kwamande said that it was his duck, which had been stolen from him at night.

'The market chief told Ukande to give Kwamande his duck, but

Ukande said that Kwamande ought to pay for it, because it was not he who had stolen it. The market chief asked Ukande how much he had paid for the duck, and Ukande replied that he had bought it for 5s. 6d. The market chief asked Kwamande what he thought about it, and Kwamande replied that he didn't know who had stolen the duck, but it was his, and when he saw it in the market he resolved to get it back. The market chief told Kwamande to give Ukande 3s. and take his duck. Kwamande took out 1s. 6d., and said that was all he had, and he would give Ukande that. Ukande took the 1s. 6d., and Kwamande took the duck. The *jir* was finished.'

The difference between market *jir* and regular *jir* can be seen very quickly—the market *jir* are almost always compromises in disputes which do not really involve a custom (*inja*). Was this Kwamande's duck? My clerk thought it was, but was quite sure that Ukande was telling the truth when he said he hadn't stolen it. Had Wan-Agayo, in the first *jir*, actually paid for the pepper or not? No one knew, and they realized that it didn't matter.

Tiv say that fights start easily in markets, and that the market judges must settle every small dispute quickly to reduce the like-lihood of fighting. Still, fights often do break out in markets. Most of them are minor brawls which can be settled by the market chief and his assistants. Sometimes, however, a case of this sort is said to be 'bigger than' or 'to beat' (*hemba*) the market chief, and is heard in the '*jir* of the *mbatarev*'.

MARKET JIR NO. 5

'Ikyav called a *jir* against Iombur for shooting him with a gun in the market. [Ikyav had a powder burn on his arm, but the gun had had no ball in it.] The market chief sent for Iombur; when he came, the market chief asked him who had given him permission to shoot a gun in the market. He replied that it had all begun when an age mate of his from MbaYongo had met him in the market and they had begun a contest to see who could buy the other the most beer (*ihagh sha msor*). He had fired the gun merely to salute his age mate. The market chief told Iombur that he had done a very serious thing, and that he must bring a £1 fine. Iombur went immediately to tell Chenge, on the other side of the market place, and the *jir* "outgrew" (*gande*) the market chief and became a *jir* of the *mbatarev*.'

The market *jir* obviously, then, does not duplicate the work of the *jir mbatarev*, but settles the unimportant disputes which might make the work of the *jir mbatarev* too heavy. The degree of importance of the cases settled by market *jir* differs from one part of the country to another, usually varying with the distance from the compound of a chief or *ortaregh*, but also, though to a lesser extent, with their reputations for fair judgments and the dispatch with which they settle the cases brought before them.

Iyon market, for example, settles *jir* of greater importance than does the market chief of Tsar market. The reasons are twofold. First Iyon is some twelve miles by bush path from the *jir mbatarev* of Shangev Ya, the lineage which includes it. Moreover, Iyon market was already an important market in the settlement of disputes long before the arrival of the European Administration, and Iyon people have a tradition of settling their disputes at market. The market organization here is much more closely allied with other political activities than it is in many other areas of Tivland; moreover the *ortaregh* does not have as much influence as elsewhere; the elders who live in the neighbourhood of the court assist the market-master in settling many disputes.

The main business of the market *jir*, even in Iyon, is, however, to settle the petty squabbles that might well cause fighting in the market. It is a by-product of the market *jir* that they keep the *jir mbatarev* free from minor disputes.

II. AGE-SET JIR

In the past, age-sets had somewhat more influence than they have at present; there were formerly certain types of disputes which were settled by age-sets acting in concert. Akiga relates how, in the early years of this century, age-sets would assault and sometimes kill a man who was shown by the divining apparatus to have bewitched one of their members.[1] Today the jural activities of the age-set are almost wholly limited to pleading the case of one of its members before a moot.

The age-set can, very occasionally, still act as a *jir*, though only, so far as I know, in disputes among its own members. I have myself been present at only one such *jir*, which was carried out—or, more accurately, not carried out—by the men of the set aged about 45. The age-set's action in this instance grew out of a moot in which Kpoepi had accused his age-mate, Chovul, of seducing his wife—an even more serious charge among age-mates than

[1] *Akiga's Story*, pp. 329–30. R. M. Downes, *The Tiv Tribe*, 1933, pp. 24–26.

among others. In this moot, the elders of the lineage had decided that there was no truth in the accusation. What had probably happened was that Kpoepi had beaten his wife and she had gone home; at any rate, when Kpoepi went after her, he found Chovul in her father's homestead and assumed the worst.

Chovul was very angry about the charge, particularly because, when he was declared innocent, Kpoepi had alleged that Chovul's son Vihishima had seduced the woman. This charge was also considered groundless by the elders.

Chovul called together his age-mates within MbaWandia, and said that he wanted them to accompany him to the compound of Kpoepi, also their age-mate, to ascertain just why he had slandered Chovul and his son as he had. This action was the closest I ever saw to a case for slander. The age-set proceeded to Kpoepi's compound, but found that he had 'gone on a trip'. His senior wife, the only adult present, disclaimed all knowledge of when he might return. The age-set thought that their plans had become known, and that Kpoepi had discovered they were coming. They waited about two hours for him, to charge him with having maligned Chovul's good name, and to make him butcher a pig for them as a fine for an offence against one of their members. However, he did not return that day, and the men finally went home, having made plans to waylay him in another way. So far as I am aware, nothing further was ever heard of the matter.

To call this arrangement one of the jural institutions of the Tiv, is, perhaps, an overstatement. However, there is no doubt in my mind that, had the age-set caught him, Kpoepi would have killed the pig in expiation of his action in accusing without sufficient grounds his age-mate before a lineage moot. The activities of age-sets are limited today, but they are nevertheless very important associations in a man's life, and it is important that one's age-mates be trusted.

Age-set *jir* and market *jir* are included by the Tiv in that category of social acts which also includes courts and moots. Moreover they are counteractions that follow upon breach of norm: in the market these are often trading norms, often the norms of everyday life. In the age-set *jir* which we considered, the breach of norm occurred when Kpoepi brought a moot before his lineage against his age-mate. Even had the age-mate been guilty, this would have been considered bad form. Again, the market *jir* were followed by correction: penalties, 'appeal' to the *jir mbatarev*, reparation. The age-set *jir* considered here never actually occurred, but it was said that had it occurred, some sort of correction would have been exacted.

CHAPTER IX

MOOTS: THE *JIR* AT HOME

I. THE ELDERS OF THE MOOT

ONE major sort of *jir* remains to be investigated. It is held in the compound or homestead of the person who initiates the *jir*; all the elders of his lineage come as guests, to be his judges and mentors. Tiv call this sort of *jir* a '*jir* at home' (*jir sa ya*), or '*jir* of the agnatic lineage' (*jir ityô*), if it needs to be distinguished from the *jir mbatarev*.

Jir at home differ in many ways from those *jir* which the Administration calls courts. Three ways are of most significance. First, the personnel of the *jir* at home is different and differently organized from the personnel of the court; second, its institutionalization and procedure are conceptualized differently; third, the subject-matter of the disputes handled by the *jir* at home is different from the subject-matter of the courts. To put it another way, the personnel, the substantive law, and the procedural law are all significantly different in the two institutions.

The *jir* at home is made up of all the important members of the community. The 'community' can usually be taken to be the smallest or minimal *tar*, though on some occasions it may be larger and include a larger *tar*, and hence members of a more inclusive lineage; and on others it may be smaller and include only the members of one of those small lineages that Tiv call 'segments within the hut'. Collectively, the elders of such a group are called the *jir*, and can be summoned by any one of themselves to come to 'discuss matters'.

This *jir*, which is made up of all the elders of the community, I call a 'moot', to distinguish it from that *jir* which is called a 'court' by administrative officers. A moot, according to the *Shorter Oxford English Dictionary*, is 'an assembly of people, especially one forming a court of judicature'. A court is 'an assembly of judges or other persons legally appointed and acting as a tribunal to hear or determine any cause'. The difference obviously is that a court is a formal organization, with appointed and recognized judges and other officials. Its internal structure is quite precise; as a unit it is part of a larger structure. The moot is an assembly of neighbours and kinsmen who decide disputes. A court is an organized body with appointed officials; the moot is a community activity. The moot is a condition or mode of a social group (the lineage) which also exists in other conditions or modes; the court is a group of officials who have but a single mode or condition. Tiv moots are what Durkheim would have called mechanically solidary. They repeat themselves. The courts are organically solidary, and form a hierarchy.

For people to belong to the same lineage is sometimes expressed as their being 'those of one moot' (*mba jir i môm*). To be counted among those of the moot (*mbajiriv*—the same as the word for participants in a court action) a man must be an agnate in the lineage concerned, and he must be considered an elder (*or vesen*). In order to have influence in a moot, an elder must have a good memory for genealogies, for most of the cases touch on genealogies in some way or other. He needs an extensive and sure knowledge of the principles and details of Tiv religion, magic, and witchcraft. Perhaps most important, he must know all the ramifications of personal relationships within his small community, for most of these important factors are not brought out in the case, but are presumed to be known to all hearers.

'To sit in one moot' (*tema jir môm*) is a phrase frequently heard in Tivland. It refers to a group of people, but does not identify any particular group. Tiv may say of a lineage of any order, or indeed of a large compound, 'we sit in one moot'. The size of the group actually called to a moot depends, as in all lineage activities, on the importance of the people concerned in the situation, and on the magnitude of the situation itself. A smaller lineage 'sits in one moot' when the case concerns the illness of a young man than when it concerns an old man. A smaller lineage 'sits in one moot' for a minor illness than for a funeral.

The number and kinds of meetings of the *jir* of a community vary. In Iyon of Shangev Ya, a *jir* discussed two or three minor matters every week; a bigger and important case, for which representatives of all Iyon gathered, occurred every two or three weeks.

The other lineages with which I am acquainted convened moots less often than did Iyon. When I first worked in MbaDuku, few moots were held in MbaGôr, the minimal *tar* in which I lived. During our second tour, when we worked in Raav in north-western Tivland, there were almost no moots of importance within Ukusu, but many within MbaAliko.' We hypothesized that the difference was to be found in the effective leaders of the different communities. In MbaGôr there was one, in Ukusu there were two, effective leaders. All problems of the sort which Iyon and MbaAliko heard in moots were brought to them for consultation. In communities with no outstanding elders, there are many moots.

Our third trip was spent partly in Iyon and MbaDuku; we found that the leader of MbaGôr—Chenge's father, Kyagba—had died. There were moots almost every week; had I attended them all I should have been unable to complete my other work. The sort of problem which had formerly been taken to Kyagba was now discussed in open moots.

Those men who are considered the most influential elders of the community 'by day' are said to be the 'witches' by night. 'Witches' is not a good translation of *mbatsav*, even in the light only of other African data. Leadership—indeed, all ability—is an attribute, Tiv say, of a substance called *tsav* which grows on the heart of some men. A man of *tsav* (*or tsav*) is a man of talent. The talent includes mystical power.

The leaders of the community are *ipso facto* men of *tsav*. It is they who 'repair the *tar*' by daylight by sitting in moots and acting as peacemakers and by keeping the community running smoothly. They also 'repair the *tar*' 'by night'. The mystical aspect of repairing the *tar* is the subject of my next book, but it must be reviewed here briefly.

The elders who repair the *tar* by day—what we could call secular governing—form, Tiv say, an organization which meets at night in order to carry out secret rituals for the religious protection of the community. As such, they are called 'the *mbatsav*', those with talent. Tiv say that for the *mbatsav* to deal adequately with the supernatural forces of the universe there are some activities which require sacrifice of life—what our fathers would have called 'life force'. The sacrifice may be a chicken or a goat, but a few each year are said to demand the supreme sacrifice of a human being. 'Human sacrifice', I hasten to add, did not occur in Tivland as it did, say, in Dahomey, though it may have occurred sporadically.

Tiv say that in sacrificing a human being the *mbatsav* of the community, as a group, first decide on a victim from within the lineage. They then must 'kill him by *tsav*'. All Tiv profess ignorance of how this is done. But the intended victim dies and is buried. The *mbatsav* must then remove him from the grave and restore him to life. Only *then* can they perform the sacrifice of his body before the emblems of the fetish.

The *mbatsav* are 'dangerous' (*kwaghbo*); they are feared; they are also trusted. In times of political upheaval, the trust disappears. As Tiv put it, the *mbatsav* begin to use their talent to kill for personal gain and for the sheer love of the taste of human flesh. Tiv revolt always takes the form of anti-*tsav* uprisings. This usually means that the revolt is directed against the most influential elders of the community, who are 'by night' the *mbatsav*. In peaceful times, the *mbatsav* of the community protect its members from evil and from the *mbatsav* of other communities. That is the reason why times are peaceful. But protectors of the community have licence to destroy its individual members for purposes considered legitimate and for the good of all.

The elders who form the moot by day, then, form the *mbatsav* 'by night'. Death is either 'legitimate' killing by the *mbatsav* or else it is the illegitimate 'permitting' of the death by the *mbatsav*, or it is their weakness or the malice of some of them. Seen from the Tiv point of view, death is not merely caused; it must also be willed. They recognize the same causes of death as we do. But mere cause is for them insufficient explanation. They must also know who willed the death and who, by *tsav*, allowed the causes to cause death.

Tiv see all leaders in two lights: as their protectors and as their eventual vanquishers.

Moots are concerned with actions involving *tsav*, and hence often with charges against the elders of the community. The workings of *tsav* are known by the presence of illness, death, and evil omens.

Moots are also concerned with a lesser mystery: curses. The word here translated 'curse' is *ifan*. It is guilty knowledge as well as a curse, but the *ifan* must be uttered. Once uttered it can 'seize' someone—usually but not always the person against whom it was uttered. I know one instance in which a woman spun enough yarn for a cloth for herself. She gave it to her son and asked him to weave a cloth for her, because weaving is work for young men in Tivland. The son wove the cloth, but when it was finished he gave it to his new wife instead of his mother. In the circumstances, the old lady could say little. As mother-in-law and provider she could not rail at either her son or her daughter-in-law. Yet Tiv assumed that the loss of the cloth rankled. At a *jir* a year or so later, when the divining chains indicated an *ifan* or curse, she was told that she had muttered a threat or wish about this act of her son's which she resented, and this threat or curse, and especially the resentment leading to it, had created sickness and omens of ill feelings. Arrangements for restitution were made.

The ostensible subject-matter of the moots is thus different from that of those *jir* which can also be called courts. Moots deal with matters concerning *tsav*, and some of its accompanying or related beliefs: fetishes (*akombo*) and curses (*ifan*). All these beliefs and any of the practices that occur are called 'witchcraft' by the Administration and the missionaries. This being the case, all disputes concerning *tsav* come under the ordinance which makes witchcraft a crime.[1] *Tsav*, therefore, is recognized by administrative officers only as an evil—as 'witchcraft substance'. All disputes which turn on *tsav*, whether they be the activities of the *mbatsav* as a group acting for the benefit of the community, or of individuals of the *mbatsav* acting from motives of greed and personal gain, must be discussed before the moot. The court cannot concern itself in such matters.

Thus, to Tiv, the really important matters—matters of life and death—are heard before the moot, not before the court. The courts, they say, settle minor matters. The moot must exist to deal with major matters. The moots, as we shall see, also settle minor matters, but their doing so is considered incidental to their more important functions.

II. THE STRUCTURE OF THE MOOT

The action of a moot is simpler than that of a court, and has two main sets of components: the first is called 'convening (*lôhô*) the moot', the second 'discussing (*ôr*) the moot'.

[1] T. O. Elias, op cit. p. 203. The criminal offence of witchcraft is triable only in Magistrates' and Supreme Courts.

Convening the moot

The phrase 'to call a *jir*' refers only to courts. One never 'calls' a moot, but rather 'convenes' or 'invites' it. In both contexts the word *jir* itself refers to both the gathering and the cause: in order to put one's *jir*, one must convene the *jir*.

The moot is always convened by an elder who is an agnatic member of the lineage associated with the *tar*, and hence what we might call (but Tiv do not) a member of the moot. In most of Tivland no one else can convene a moot. There are several ways in which non-agnates can bring pressure to bear so that a moot must be convened. A woman can run away and precipitate a moot. A man can run to his mother's agnatic lineage and get them to take action on his behalf. Although I have not recorded it here, I attended a moot in the *tar* of MbaYongo to which almost two hundred MbaDuku elders went to 'ask' the MbaYongo agnates of their sister's son to explain the illness of the latter's children. A man who lives permanently in the *tar* of his mother's lineage cannot convene the moot of that lineage; he must ask his mother's close kinsmen to do so on his behalf. He is, Tiv say, a 'woman', because he is related to the lineage through women.

In Utisha, in the south-eastern part of Tivland, there is an exception to these restrictions on convening moots. Utisha people have a form of *swem*, called '*swem* of the treaty', which enables almost anyone to convene a moot. Anyone can get a *swem* by going to any *swem*-holder in a lineage with which his agnatic lineage has a treaty of the type known as *ikul*. Here the *swem* can be bought. With this *swem ikul* in his hand, the person convening the moot, or someone deputed to act for him, goes to invite or bid the elders to come to his compound to hear his case.

Threats by elders that they will not come to discuss a moot when invited are among the strongest weapons of social control. In Utisha, once the elders have seen the treaty *swem*, their failure to attend would be tantamount to piercing *swem*. If they have been summoned lightly, however, they can demand outrageous gifts and '*tia* fines'. Iyon elders often refused to come to a moot; MbaDuku elders seldom did so.

Discussing the jir

The first step in 'discussing' a moot is to decide on a programme of points. This is done by hearing reports from diviners and reconciling them. At least one person or group should consult a diviner before a moot is convened. Often several may do so. The remainder of the moot involves discovering how the general situation revealed by the diviner is to be 'applied' to the situation in hand.

Diviners do not tell facts. They tell mystical causes behind facts. The consultant tells the diviner the facts. The diviner then operates his mechanism, putting questions to it. Since all the facts are known to him (if he is a good diviner), and since the possible 'causes' of a recurrent situation are limited, he points out which of these causes may be present.

The questions that a diviner answers by means of his instruments are of four kinds: those concerned respectively with curses, with debts and marriage wards, with fetishes, and with *tsav*.

The suggestion of a curse is usually the only one that comes primarily from the instrument rather than from the diviner himself. The diagnostic portent of a curse is the position of the pods of the divining chains at certain stages of the consultation. Diviners are seldom asked who cursed whom: few would answer such a question, though there is a recognized means by which the divining chains can be made to give this information. Rather, the consultant merely 'knows'; even more often, the matter is left for the elders of the moot to discover.

The second point clarified by divination is the 'marriage ward'. Tiv expect difficulties to exist among brothers over the distribution of marriage wards. If the consultation is made on behalf of a sick man, the assumption is that he owes a marriage ward to someone or else that one of his 'brothers', perhaps mistakenly, believes that he does. If the sick person is a woman, the first assumption is that she has been assigned as marriage ward to the wrong man, and has been made ill in order to force a consultation and eventually a moot in which the elders will alter the situation.

The third point which a diviner clarifies concerns fetishes. A disease (more accurately a symptom) *is* a fetish. Therefore, when the consultant recounts the symptoms in detail to the diviner, the number of fetishes that may be involved is reduced. It is seldom possible to find a one-to-one correlation between a symptom and a given fetish. If the symptom is a cough, the diviner knows the names of several fetishes thought to cause coughs, and puts these to his apparatus. It is not surprising that different diviners can usually discover the same fetishes in a given instance. It does not in any case disturb Tiv if they do not, for it is always probable that more than one fetish is involved.

Finally, the diviner asks his apparatus if *tsav* is involved in the misfortune about which he is inquiring. This question must be understood to mean *tsav* acting in a mystical or psychogenic way—bewitching—and not *tsav* which activates the evil fetish rituals performed by individuals of the *mbatsav*.

All four of these questions concern mysteries: curses, fetishes, *tsav*. The point about the marriage ward is also a mystery; the implication is always that if a woman has been given as marriage ward to the 'wrong man' either a curse or some sort of witchcraft will result. This point is made difficult by the fact that there are several criteria for determining the 'right man' to be the guardian: every Tiv believes that a woman's guardian should be the husband of her exchange partner; every Tiv believes that for every daughter or sister he puts into the exchange group, he ought to get a ward in return, even though one of the express purposes of the group is equitable distribution of wards so that everyone may acquire a wife.

When the results of the divination are placed before the elders of the moot, they 'reconcile' the results if more than one diviner has been questioned. They are then ready to proceed.

Oaths, mechanisms and purposes of swearing in a moot differ considerably from those in a court. Although I cannot at the moment see any reason why witnesses should not be called before the moot if matters of fact are in dispute, I have never attended a moot in which they were in fact called.

I have never seen *swem* used for oath-taking in a moot. Oaths to repeat accurately the findings of the diviner are almost always taken on the *igbe* fetish, occasionally on the *iwa*, and rarely on the senior elder's wrist.

Evidence in moots is different from evidence in courts: what is *vough*, or precise and straight, is usually unknowable, because moots deal mostly with mystical acts, at least with situations described in a mystical idiom. This is not always the case, for in at least the first two of the moots presented below matters of fact are considered. However, the moot deals almost entirely in terms of *mimi*, the truth of right social relationships. Secondly, since much of the suspected wrong necessarily occurred on a mystical plane, if at all, the only thing that could be affirmed by oath is innocence of mystical activity, either 'bewitching' with *tsav*, or uttering curses or using fetishes for.anti-social and evil ends.

Protestations of innocence are not a matter of oath, but are made in a rite called 'blowing out the curse' which follows the hearing of the moot.

In the course of a moot, one's age-set, or occasionally the elders of one's mother's lineage, 'ask' (*pine*) the elders of one's agnatic lineage. In Moot IV below, the 'wives' of MbaGôr lineage 'asked'. Asking is usually put in the form, 'Why have you let our child be bewitched?' [1] or 'Why have you not protected our age-mate from the attack of the *mbatsav*?' 'To ask' does not mean to ask 'Why have you done this?' but rather 'Why have you not prevented it?'

Asking pits a social group which protects a person against that group of his agnates (or, occasionally in the case of a woman, her husband's agnates) who have failed to protect him. The asking group is most commonly the age-set; members of the age-set are also agnates, but in this situation they act against the rest of the agnates. In those moots in which the mother's lineage asks, two lineages are involved: no matter what the span of the lineage of the actual participants, it is always described in terms of the largest possible lineage—at the point where the agnatic lineage and the mother's agnatic lineage are equivalent segments. Such a situation invariably becomes involved in Tiv thought with the 'feuds by night' which are said to occur between the *mbatsav* of almost any two communities.

The contending 'parties' to a moot tend to be segments of a single social group: an age-set against the rest of the agnates; a man's mother's lineage against his father's lineage, though both are a single lineage at some point in the lineage system, and can be called the moot of that inclusive lineage; the wives of a lineage (who are usually a category, not a group) against the elders who are in fact their husbands. The group divides for discussion.

There is thus, in most moots, no person who is in fact the accused. There is no defendant. No one is charged. The exceptions are those instances (like Moot I below) in which it would be unseemly to take the dispute before the Native Authority court,

---

[1] 'Our child' in the case of the mother's lineage because 'we [a daughter of our lineage] bore him to your lineage'.

and therefore the elders are asked to come and arbitrate. Disputes within the minimal *tar*, Tiv say, should all be arbitrated by the moot rather than called before the court, but they do not always live up to their own precept.

This very fact—that there need be no accused—keeps the matter out of the courts which enjoy government tutelage, which settle cases in accordance with what Government thinks of as 'native law and custom'. The courts are established to handle items of debt and of wrongdoing against individuals who seek redress. They do not, and are not equipped to, handle instances in which a man charges his community with his peace of mind, the settlement of which is carried out in mystical language and involves the tacit, incidental settlement of many minor issues or disputes.

Moots overlap the actions of the courts only in a few instances: those in which individual rights are infringed, but in which the principals are close agnatic kinsmen.

Finally, the procedure of moots differs from that of courts in that moots are seldom said to be 'finished' (*kure*). Rather, Tiv merely use a past tense of 'discuss' to indicate that the moot has been held.

All successful moots end with the performance of a ritual. This ritual is a symbol that the elders have discussed the *jir* and reached a decision: they have repaired the *tar*. It is also symbolic of all the social and mystical acts that should follow the *jir* and re-establish the norm or correct its breach.

III. THE SUBJECTS OF THE MOOT

We shall examine five of the many moots I recorded. All those presented here occurred in southern Tivland, in Kunav, but the first and the fifth did not occur in MbaDuku. The first is a dispute which family solidarity prevents taking before a court.

MOOT NO. 1. *Ornyiman assembles his lineage*

One of my best informants in Tivland was a man named Ornyiman. He was clever and vastly conceited. He was, when I knew him, between 40 and 45 years old, a handsome extrovert who ran his seventeen wives and countless children with an executive's skill. The wives, at least, were devoted to him—it is a rare man who, not being a chief, can get and keep seventeen wives. Ornyiman was rich. Part of his wealth was acquired by

N

growing cash crops and by intelligent marketing. He was also a showy diviner who spoke half a dozen Udam dialects, several dialects of Ibo, and Ijaw. He would take his divination apparatus south and return, a few months later, with large sums of money.

Ornyiman lived some six miles from my compound, so I didn't see him more than two or three times a month. One morning in 1952, when I walked to his compound without sending warning, I found a moot about to begin.

Ornyiman, on a trip to Gav lineage several weeks before, had seen a good-looking, industrious girl whom he thought would make a good wife. He courted her and, when he returned home, decided he must have her. He gave £8 to his eldest son, Wannongo, and told him to go to Gav and get the girl. Wannongo, on arriving at the compound of the girl's father, discovered that he was too late, as she had already gone to a husband. He thereupon decided that, since he had £8 of wife-money in his pocket, it would be foolish after coming so far to return without a wife. He looked around until he found another good-looking, industrious girl and began to court her. Eventually, after several weeks, he 'married' (*ngoho*) her with the £8. (The word here translated 'marry' means that he acquired certain rights in her—it does not necessarily mean that he acquired them for himself. The word is used by a woman when she acquires a new daughter-in-law, and by a guardian when he acquires a new ward, as well as by a husband when he acquires a new wife. Wannongo had neglected to tell the girl that he was courting and 'marrying' her for his father.)

Having made the initial payments, and said that they would be off next morning, Wannongo was expected to spend the night in the same hut with his new wife. The girl thought, of course, that he was her husband. The 'marriage' was consummated.

They left the next day and, on reaching home, Wannongo explained to Ornyiman, in the 'wife's' presence, that the original girl he had been sent to bring had married someone else, so he had brought this girl instead. I never could discover what she thought of this ruse; it is almost impossible to talk alone with women—or anyone else—in a household like Ornyiman's.

Subsequently Ornyiman asked his new wife how it happened that she was not a virgin. She told him that Wannongo had slept with her. This made Ornyiman angry—probably because he had Wannongo on his conscience, for the boy was over 20 and it was time his father got him a wife. He called Wannongo and confronted him with the girl's statement. Wannongo said it was not true. The girl repeated that it was.

Thereupon, Ornyiman 'invited' (*lôhô*) the moot. In this particular instance, he called only his father's half-brothers and his own elder brother, all of whom lived nearby. It was into this moot that I had walked. The girl repeated her story to the moot—in this instance, it might almost be called the 'family council'. Wannongo again denied the charge, but convinced no one.

The consensus was that Ornyiman could expect nothing else—a father should get his eldest son a wife, not vice versa. Tentative suggestions were made by the elders that Ornyiman should give Wannongo this wife—after all, he already had seventeen wives and his son had none, which they said was not a satisfactory state of affairs. One elder noted that unmarried sons of much-married fathers resent their bachelorhood. Ornyiman, however, was adamant. He was much the strongest character present and easily persuaded the others to agree with him.

A ceremony was performed which ritually separated Wannongo from the girl, and she was declared to be Ornyiman's wife. This ceremony was necessary if both father and son were not to suffer the effects of having transgressed the *akombo megh*—the fetish concerned in adultery. It is also important in that the eldest living brother of Ornyiman's father was the only person there who had purchased the right to perform the ceremony. His doing so, and the fact that he was the oldest kinsman, indicated that the entire group of elders concerned had concurred in the settlement which Ornyiman had forced upon them.

The ritual which ended this moot is of great importance. Were it not that the ritual must be performed in a case of this sort, the moot might possibly never have been called. A man cannot perform ritual alone—if he does, it is said to be *ipso facto* evil ritual which he is ashamed to show to his agnates and neighbours.

The dispute was between father and son, and Tiv say that it is in the worst possible taste for a man to bring his close kinsman before the *jir mbatarev*. However, kinsmen often have arguments and disagreements. In such a case, it is the neighbours and agnates (for most are both) who must be called in to settle the matter; it must be done peaceably by one's own community.

Moots settle disputes between persons in relationships that can never be broken or ignored. The function of a moot is only incidentally the settlement of particular grievances: its main function is to make it possible for people who must live together to do so harmoniously. Marriage ties can be broken; marriage disputes can be heard in the court. But ties of agnation are unchangeable, and are the basis of all citizenship rights of adult males. One must either get along with one's agnates or become an expatriate. The moot is one device for getting along with them.

Tiv recognize that moots do settle disputes. But they also insist that the real purpose of the moot is not to settle the dispute itself but to allay the mystical factors which are behind it, which caused it, or which it caused. The moot deals with repairing the *tar* in both the mystical and the political senses.

The next moot occurred in MbaGôr of MbaDuku, and also concerns near kinsmen.

MOOT NO. II. *Taka convenes his lineage (MbaGôr)*

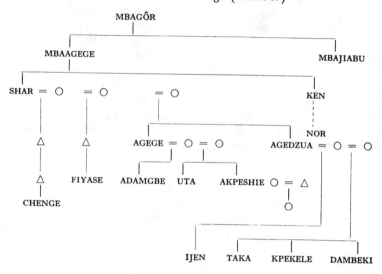

Taka went himself, or sent his eldest son, to invite all the elders of MbaGôr to his compound to discuss a matter. The *jir* began about noon, as the various elders came drifting in, by twos and threes.

Taka's three wives had prepared food for them. After eating—and only the elders ate, none of the numerous young men were fed—all settled down to begin the *jir*. Most of the elders sat under a drying platform in the middle of the compound yard. A few feet away was a small fig-tree in the shade of which I sat beside Uta, the elder most nearly related to Taka. The elders were called 'the agnatic lineage' (*ityó*) and were to act both as judges of the dispute and, in some sense, as we shall see, also to stand as accused. Opposite, under the eaves of a hut—Taka's is a small compound, so the distance was less than fifteen yards—sat the age-set of which Taka was a member. Under the eaves of the adjacent hut sat the age-set of his next younger full brother, Kpekele. There were few of each, for they comprised only those members of the age-sets actually resident in MbaGôr. It is unusual to see two age-sets: this

Taka's compound

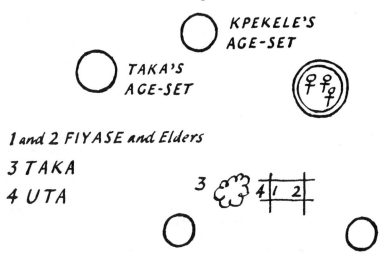

could have meant either that the brothers had had a serious fight, or that they were joining together to 'ask' the elders of their *ityô*.

Fiyase opened the proceedings. He was actually the second oldest man in MbaGôr. The oldest, Nor, was doddery and foolish with age, and his activity at *jir* was limited by the more efficient elders to repeating, chorus-like, the platitudes uttered by the speaker of the moment. The third oldest man was Uta. He was perhaps more intelligent than any of the others, but also more impatient and hot-tempered, traits deplored by Tiv, and hence he was less influential than Fiyase.

Fiyase began in the customary way by calling to the man who had invited them together: 'Taka! Taka!' He had to call two or three times before getting an answer. When it came it was the high-tone, long-drawn 'NNNNNN' which sometimes means 'yes', but is more accurately rendered, 'I acknowledge that I heard you.'

Fiyase, again following prescribed etiquette, said, 'What is it? Why have you called us together?' And again Taka answered with the conventional reply, 'My mind is not at rest. I have seen omens.'

Fiyase then asked: 'Have you consulted the divination apparatus?' Whereupon a representative from each of the age-sets came forward. The first to speak was the spokesman for Kpekele's age-set. He looked at the bundle of five tallies in his hand and asked, 'Where is the fetish?' Fiyase roared, 'Bring the fetish!' and the cry was taken up by all. Taka picked up his matchet and left the compound. He was soon back, having cut a palm-branch, symbol of the *akombo igbe*. The representative of

Kpekele's age-set took the branch and held it in his left hand (this is a *tindi* or law of this fetish—most would be held in the right), and one by one named his five tallies, which represented the five points that the diviner had told him were at issue. The first tally was for the fetish known as *akombo chigh*, the second for the *akombo iwa* (blacksmith and lightning), the third the *akombo dam* which causes sores and cough, the fourth concerned the marriage ward, and the fifth a curse. Fiyase repeated them one by one as he spread the tallies on the ground before his chair.

Then the spokesman from Taka's own age-set came forward. He held only four sticks as tallies. He too grasped the fetish in his left hand and informed the elders of his four points. The diviner consulted by this age-set had diagnosed (1) the *akombodam*, (2) the *akombo chigh*, (3) the marriage ward, and (4) the *ifan* or curse. He had not mentioned the blacksmith fetish—a very minor point, which played no further part in the discussion. The two fetishes were discussed briefly as a single situation. Taka's father, Agedzua, had died of a disease—probably tuberculosis—which involved them both. He had never performed any of the proper ceremonies that would bring the two fetishes under control, and it was decided that several rites should be performed when the money could be raised to provide the sacrificial animals. This decision was reached very soon, because Fiyase insisted that the matter had come up twice before, they had already agreed what to do, and he wanted to hear no more about it.

The marriage ward and the matter of the curse, on which the two diviners had agreed, were now discussed in turn.

Fiyase began this part of the moot by asking, 'What is the business of the marriage ward, now?' Only a few terse sentences of explanation followed, for the position was known to most of those present; I had, by careful questioning afterwards, to reconstruct most of the situation concerning the allocation amongst agnates of sisters and daughters to be marriage wards. Long ago Agege, Agedzua (Taka's father), and all their brothers were living in a single compound. Agege, being the eldest, was compound head. When he died, Agedzua replaced him. Agege had many daughters, Agedzua none. When Agedzua died, the oldest man in the compound was Agege's senior son Adamgbe. Adamgbe took his father's daughters, these marriage wards, and exchanged them for women whom he presented as wives to the youngsters in his compound, including the sons of Agedzua. He did not call the *ingôl* group together before taking these steps and, so far as I could gather, the women were never really assigned as wards to any particular men. So long as Adamgbe was alive, he took care of everything needed by the wards and got wives for all his youngsters. When he died, still fairly young, Uta became compound head. Uta's irascibility made it difficult to keep this large compound together. First, all Adamgbe's wives, children, and full brothers left the area—they are described today as having 'gone to the bush'. Secondly, the children of Agedzua split off and built their own compound. A little later, Uta's own brothers built separate compounds.

Uta claimed that all these women had been Adamgbe's wards and, since he had taken over the compound from Adamgbe, they were his wards. The others assumed that each man was the guardian of his wife's exchange partner (or the woman whose bridewealth was said to have furnished bridewealth for his own wife).

Uta had a younger full sister named Akpeshie who had married into a nearby lineage, and for whom no exchange or bridewealth payment had ever been made. This being the case, when Akpeshie's eldest daughter married recently, it was arranged that she was to become a ward in her mother's marriage ward group, thereby replacing her mother in the group and cancelling the debt. Taka and Uta each felt that he had over-riding claims to this girl as his marriage ward.

Some months before the present moot occurred, Taka (acting as guardian) went to the girl's husband and got £3 in bridewealth. He 'ate' this money—that is to say, he kept it and used it. Uta felt that the £3 should have been turned over to him. It was this dispute which was brought to the mind of the elders when the divination apparatus indicated trouble over a marriage ward.

Taka said that he had used the £3 paid as bridewealth for this girl to get his brother Kpekele a wife. Kpekele interrupted, saying that Taka had given him only £1. 10s.

When he had been silenced, Uta said that Taka had also got another £2 from MbaAji lineage which should have come to him—this concerned the marriage of yet another ward. Taka explained that it was his own money, and that he had got his youngest brother Dambeki a wife with it. He added that the matter had already been discussed. Taka now summed up and said that he gave £2. 10s. to Kpekele and £2 to Dambeki, his brothers, towards wives for them.

Without discussion, Fiyase thereupon told Taka to 'bring the money'. Taka handed 2d. to Uta, to indicate that he would repay the £2 which he had given to his youngest brother Dambeki.

The elders then decided that Akpeshie's daughter should become Kpekele's ward, since money for her bridewealth had provided Kpekele with a wife. Hence, they said, Taka must pay Kpekele that portion of the money which he got for this girl, but had not already passed on to him. The matter of marriage wards was declared settled.

Fiyase took up the next point. He turned to Taka and asked, 'What do you know about this curse?'

Taka said slowly that Kpekele had entered the hut of Ijen's wife. At the time, I had never heard of Ijen and was somewhat baffled, though

Uta (a good informant for all his temper) gave me details after the *jir*. When Taka's father, Agedzua, was a very old man, he married a young wife named Aveve. She was a virgin on entering his household, and remained so until his death. She was then inherited by his eldest son, Ijen, but refused to have anything to do with him because he was a leper. Ijen thereupon told Kpekele—also very young—that he might enter her hut in his stead. It is fairly common for an old man or a sick man to assign sexual rights in his wife to a brother, son, or even grandson. In this case, Aveve was originally Agedzua's wife ; however, she had not borne him a son. Had she done so, she would have remained his wife and Ijen or Kpekele would have become her levir. Since she had not, she would become the wife of her inheritor, Ijen, if she bore a son before his death. She did not, in fact, bear a son until later.

When Ijen died, the elders met and arranged for the inheritance of his women, both wards and wives. They gave Aveve to Taka instead of to Kpekele. All agreed that this was a very bad move. If Aveve had been given to Kpekele, there would have been no trouble. A woman should always, if possible, be inherited by the man who has already been given sexual rights in her.

When Taka told the elders that Kpekele had entered the hut of Ijen's wife, he referred to Aveve. 'To enter the hut' is a euphemism for sexual relations.

Fiyase looked at Uta and asked Taka, 'When Ijen died, did Uta give Taka Ijen's wife?': the enmity between Fiyase and Uta was apparent.

Uta said that Taka had been given the girl, but at first she had refused to have anything to do with him.

Fiyase interrupted: 'The elders gave that girl to Taka when she *should* have been given to Kpekele. I know what happened. I was there!'

Fiyase turned to Kpekele and asked him to say what he was doing in Aveve's hut. Kpekele came and sat before them in the sun. He said that it had happened many years ago. As a young man he had thought of Aveve as his wife—as his first wife (before Ijen's death, he was indeed the only man who had sexual rights in her). One day, after she had been inherited by Taka, he was sitting in the doorway of her hut spinning in the heat of the day. 'We were talking,' Kpekele said, 'and suddenly we were bound in sexual intercourse.'

When Taka discovered what had happened—and, so far as I could determine, no attempt was made to keep it from him—he and Kpekele fought, and Kpekele was wounded.

Fiyase called Aveve to give her version of the incidents and dispute. She was a woman of 35 or so, but looked older. All her husband's lineage were there—including her three sons, the eldest aged about 12. With complete selflessness, she told her story, in an attempt to bring the brothers together.

She said that originally she had been a wife of Agedzua. At his death, she had been inherited by his oldest son, Ijen, but had refused him because he was a leper. Ijen had expected nothing else, she said, and had asked her which man she wanted him to send into her hut: Taka or Kpekele. She had replied (as a good woman should, under the circumstances) that she was his wife, therefore he was to decide who should beget his children. Ijen sent Kpekele into her hut, because at that time Taka had a wife and Kpekele hadn't. She was, she said, happy with this arrangement. Kpekele was a good husband to her.

Then Ijen died. For a year following the death, before the widows are inherited, she continued to live with Kpekele. Then, knowing that when a husband dies his wife should be given to that one of his sons or brothers who has been given sexual rights in her, she left the decision of her inheritance in the hands of the elders. This, she now insisted—and all present agreed—was what a good woman should do.

She said that it came as a considerable shock to her that, without being consulted, she was given to Taka. At first she shut herself in her hut, and refused to have anything to do with either brother. But, she insisted, you can't do that indefinitely. She kept expecting Taka to give her back to Kpekele. He didn't. Finally she yielded to him.

At this point a giggle came from one of the women in the reception hut. With an explosion of anger, she shouted in that direction, 'Don't you bitches laugh at me!'—the word *ngoiwav* was hers, not mine—'It should not have been up to me to make this choice.' She turned back to the elders. 'Kpekele came into my hut well,' she said. With a wave of the hand she indicated Uta and Fiyase: 'Then the elders gave me to Taka. Taka isn't repulsive or ugly; he never mistreated anyone! Taka is a good and handsome man; Kpekele is a good and handsome man!' And for a while, both came into her hut.

'Then,' Aveve said, 'a child came to sleep in my womb.' It was at this time that Taka and Kpekele had their biggest fight and 'split their fields'. Each began to farm separately, and ceased to co-operate in agricultural labour: a serious breach for Tiv. They did not, however, split the compound and live in two separate places, because Aveve said she wouldn't live with either of them if they did so—they were full brothers and were behaving very badly. The younger brother, Dambeki, also began to farm on his own at this time because he refused to take sides with either of his brothers.

Aveve told at some length the pains to which she had gone to make them settle their dispute. She even managed to get them to eat together, and impressed on them, 'You are brothers; you have eaten together. Since you have eaten together, you cannot be at enmity!'

Then she looked at the ground, 'But they didn't do right,' she added softly. 'They ate together, but their anger wasn't finished.' After a pause, she again flared up: 'It shouldn't have mattered. The child is certainly MbaGôr. It is certainly the child of Agedzua. What difference does it make which of full brothers begets a child?'

When she had finished, Fiyase turned to Taka and said, 'Taka, you have done something awful (dang). She is your wife. She was your brother's wife. You don't split your fields just because your brother enters the hut of your wife—especially not when she was also his wife! You and your brother Kpekele ate yam-porridge together, but still you did not finish your quarrel. You have behaved very badly indeed.'

Taka started to object. Fiyase shouted sternly, 'Taka, it wasn't a matter of half-brothers!' And Nor, the elder with the platitudes, came into his own and muttered over and over, 'It's the mother; it is a matter of one mother.'

Fiyase told Taka that this sort of dispute might have been understandable, but no more justifiable, over a wife whom he had married for himself. But Aveve was an inherited wife—brothers must never quarrel over an inherited wife!

Fiyase now said that Taka and Kpekele must both be fined in this matter, that they must 'kill a tia'.

Taka handed 1s. to Uta, saying that he had no animal and must pay a 'dry goat'. Fiyase demanded that he bring another shilling; Taka stared stubbornly at Fiyase who told him, 'It isn't we who have done this; it is yourself!' Taka said nothing, but went and got another shilling.

As they were turning to settle Kpekele's share in this fine, the spokesman of Taka's age-set jumped up with the statement that something must be done about the time that Kpekele beat Taka so seriously. A furore followed. The entire story never emerged in this session—because the elders all knew about the situation, they talked in a very cryptic manner. I never came to know it all, but it was a dispute about another marriage ward between Taka and Kpekele, which had already been settled and had nothing to do with the case in hand. Fiyase, however, took this opportunity for moral exhortations, and lectured Kpekele saying, 'The younger brother is like a woman! He dare not beat his elder brother. Kpekele was at fault in this matter, that's all.'

During the shouting that again ensued, Uta went over to Fiyase and said that it was quite obvious that there wasn't any witchcraft involved in this matter; therefore they should simply settle the matter of the wards and the curses without further ado.

When the shouting died down, Kpekele came forward with 2s. and was sent back for two more: two for each offence. When he brought them, Uta offered the 2s. to Taka. This was in the nature of a present from Kpekele, an admission that he had been in the wrong. If Taka accepted the 2s. it would be a sign that Kpekele was forgiven.

Taka refused the money.

At this point one of the other elders in the crowd jumped to his feet shouting vociferously at Taka, over and over again, 'Isn't he your brother? Isn't he your brother?' Nor took his cue to chorus again, 'It's the mother; it is a matter of the children of one mother.'

Kpekele added a shilling. The elders finally achieved quiet and Taka, with some show of reluctance (and the reluctance was, I believe, mainly show) accepted the 3s., and with it the implication that the argument was over and forgotten.

Fiyase now made a long speech to the effect that they had tried to settle this matter and keep the compound of Agedzua from falling down around the heads of his children. Taka brought a further 5s. at this point, to pay the elders who had come to hear his *jir*. They told him to bring three more and a hen. He said he didn't have a hen. Fiyase lost his temper. 'You have baby chicks,' he shouted, 'I saw them as I walked in! All we need is a female chicken!' Taka took quite a long time getting this 3s. and the baby chick, but finally came back with both. He handed Nor, the oldest man present, the chick and a penny, the latter being Nor's fee for performing the rite that now followed. Taka brought a small gourd full of water and called his two brothers, Kpekele and Dambeki. The three of them squatted in a semi-circle before Fiyase and Nor. Fiyase again reminded them they were all full brothers and ended his exhortation: 'And also in the matter of your food—eat it together.' Commensality is the symbol of unity.

Even at this late date, someone tried to introduce another issue— Agedzua had one more son who was 'sitting in the bush'. Fiyase refused to be swayed, so something was left still unsettled which would come up some day. Fiyase turned to the three brothers sitting around the gourd of water and said, 'Drink, you, drink!' One at a time, in order of age, each took some water in his mouth and sprayed it out on to the ground. This is a rite known as 'cutting the curse' (*gber ifan*) or 'blowing out the curse' (*hamber ifan*). Fiyase, Nor, and Uta—the elders most directly concerned in the settlement—also performed it to show that they had no reservations in the matter.

With the help of Fiyase (since his own hand was unsteady) Nor then cut the chicken's throat. The bird was allowed to fall to the ground and kick until it died. Nor then threw it into the bush. This rite includes the dead—Agedzua and Ijen in this instance—in the ceremony of 'cutting the curse'.

All that remained was for the elders to divide the money of the *tia* among themselves. Had this been a traditional moot, with a live instead of a 'dry' animal as fine and fee, the animal would now have been killed and the meat divided among the elders, so that each could take home his share. As it was, they decided that, since nobody had change and all

these shillings would have to be changed into pennies before an equitable distribution could be made, they would make the division another
time. And, just as it had drifted in, so now the *jir* drifted out of being.
Age-mates and elders gradually left by twos and threes until finally all
were gone.

This moot, like the preceding one, ends with the performance
of a ritual. In this instance, the ritual was a simple one of 'cutting
the curse', which signified that all the persons involved in the
disputes leading up to the *jir* resolved not to cherish grudges about
past events and that they would carry out their obligations in
future.

The third moot concerned a situation brought to a head by the
widow of a lineage member. She could not convene the moot
herself; nevertheless she instigated the series of acts which led to
its meeting.

MOOT NO. III. *MbaAkanshi has her late husband's lineage convened*

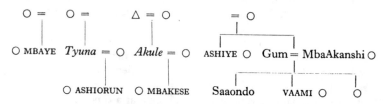

I first heard about this moot when Tyuna came to my hut and said
that something terrible had happened to his wife and that he was going
to MbaAji to see about it. He was in too much of a hurry to tell me what
the trouble was, but said that he was convening his *ityó* and, if I would
come to his compound the next day, I would find out. He himself hurried
off to MbaAji.

I asked a few questions and discovered that Tyuna's wife was one he
had inherited from his elder brother, Gum, who had died a few years
before. Her name was MbaAkanshi. She had run to the neighbouring
lineage of MbaAji because her secondary guardian was a man of that
lineage. He was, moreover, a member of her dead husband's age-set, and
he and the age-set were 'bringing her back' on the next day and intended
to 'ask' Tyuna and his younger brother Akule.

The next day, I found an interesting arrangement of people under the
mango trees of Tyuna's compound:

1. MbaAkanshi flanked by the members of Gum's age-set, drawn from all of Ikakwer lineage. Men of about 60
2. Tyuna
3. The elders of MbaGôr
4. The age-set (drawn from MbaGôr only) to which Gum, in his lifetime had been *igba*; these were men of about 45
5. Akule
6. Iyorkôsu (my clerk) and I

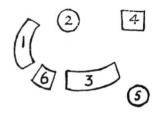

There are several interesting points here with reference to age-sets. First, a man's effective age-set increases in lineage span as he gets older. Gum, had he been still alive, would have been some 60 or 65 years old. His age-set, continuing to fulfil its duties towards his dependants, now convened members from a lineage containing four minimal *utar*.

Secondly, members of another age-set were present: younger men, about 45, with whom Gum had been connected as *igba*. Each age-set has within each minimal *tar*, three or four such older men for their *agba*. When the men of an age-set are still young, the *agba* accompany them to diviners and instruct and assist them in acting the age-set roles in moots. As the *igba* of an age-set gets older, or when he dies, the men of the younger age-set with whom he 'ate *igba*' act on his behalf or come to his assistance.

In the present case, the two age-sets had gone independently to diviners to determine the cause of MbaAkanshi's disquiet.

The actual meeting began when Nor, the oldest man, called out, 'Tyuna, Tyuna. Why have you invited us here?'

Tyuna replied, 'MbaAkanshi is in the hands of this age-set, and the age-set is bringing her today. I have invited my *ityô* to come and hear what the age-set will say.'

Nor said, 'The age-set will speak. I will listen.'

At this point a general cry broke out that someone must bring a fetish emblem on which the spokesmen for the age-sets could swear. Tyuna brought a branch of the palm known as *hulugh*, the symbol of the *akombo igbe*.

One by one, each man who had consulted a diviner grasped the frond in his left hand and laid his tallies before the elders. Three diviners had been consulted in this case: one by the age-set of MbaAkanshi's late husband—their spokesman presented two tallies; MbaAkanshi's secondary guardian had consulted a diviner in that capacity—he presented three tallies; the younger *igba* age-set had also consulted a diviner—their spokesman presented two tallies.

After the three men had been sworn, Uta took over from Nor. The men put down their tallies before the elders. Uta held up one and said,

'What is this?' It belonged to the guardian and he answered, 'It is the
akombo chigh.' Uta—an impatient man who tends to skip the formalities
—immediately turned to Tyuna and said, 'All right, tell us about that
akombo chigh of Gum's, Tyuna.'

Thereupon Chenge (who often could not come to moots because
he was engaged in official duties) said to Uta, 'Wait. Who else got the
akombo chigh from the diviner?' The spokesmen of both age-sets said
that they had been 'given' this fetish by the diviners. Each picked up
one of his tallies.

Uta then held up the guardian's second tally. 'What's this?' he asked.

'It is the matter of the inheritance (*dyako*),' the guardian replied. The
representative of Gum's age-set said, 'I too got inheritance,' and picked
up his second tally. The representative of the *igba* age-set said, 'I know
nothing of the inheritance.'

Uta held up the third tally. The guardian replied, 'It is the marriage
ward.' The spokesman of the *igba* age-set said that he too had got the
marriage ward, and added that there was some money concerned in the
matter.

As soon as the findings of the diviners had thus been reported, it was
necessary to decide in what order the matters were to be discussed.
Chenge stated categorically that the inheritance and the marriage ward
were the same thing. Thus, he said, all the statements by the three
diviners were brought into accord. There were two main items to be
discussed: the *akombo chigh* and the inheritance of marriage wards.
Chenge further said that they had better begin with the matter of the
marriage ward, because it was very complicated, and the matter of the
akombo chigh was not.

At the time of Gum's death, there were five marriage wards who had
been assigned to him. The relationship of these women to Gum and
to the other men concerned is shown in the diagram. After Gum's death,
one of them was assigned to Saaondo, MbaAkanshi's only living son,
another went to Tyuna, and another to Akule, Gum's half-brothers.
The disposal of the other two had not yet been decided—they were
what Tiv sometimes call 'on the ground' (*shin nya*), and what Chenge,
in the course of the moot, expressed by saying that 'Tyuna (who suc-
ceeded Gum as compound head) has two wards on his hands.'

Gum also had five wives when he died. It is more urgent for widows
to be inherited in good time than for decisions about the inheritance of
wards to be made. Inheritance of wards is seldom decided until some
circumstance arises to make it relevant. Wives, however, are inherited
at a ceremony, if one can call it such, usually held about a year after the
death of their husband. In the present case, two of Gum's wives were
inherited by his son Saaondo, two (including MbaAkanshi) by Tyuna,
and one by Akule.

In this situation, MbaAkanshi began to have bad dreams. She told me she dreamt that her hut broke in two and crumbled to the ground. Sometimes she dreamt that a crack appeared in the floor of her hut, and a night worm, which she indicated to be about eighteen inches long, came out of the crack. This last, she said, was a sure omen that someone would die unless the matter were 'discussed thoroughly' (ór dedo). Since she could not herself convene a *jir*,[1] she ran away to the compound of her secondary guardian in MbaAji and bullied him into sending word to Tyuna that she was unhappy and afraid in his compound. Her guardian notified the members of 'her' age-set.

Although the *jir* was ostensibly concerned with the two wards whose inheritance was in question, the discussion soon turned to wives. Wards and wives imply one another in the Tiv way of thinking. This *jir* gave much more time to Gum's widows than to his wards. To Tiv the subject had not been changed: questions concerning bridewealth payments or exchange for the wards led to the question of the bridewealth or exchange given for MbaAkanshi. This was the heart of the matter, and it seems to have been her fancied lack of security that brought on her dreams and omens in the first place. Tiv would agree with that statement, but would cite a magical cause as well.

The touchstone of the difficulty in MbaAkanshi's position appeared when her secondary guardian asked, 'What about the cow?' Furore followed the question.

I could only reconstruct the background of the story after the event. Zegejir, a man from Shangev, had come to marry one of Gum's wards, Vaami, who was his daughter by MbaAkanshi. Zegejir took Vaami without making any bridewealth payment at all and, in addition, borrowed £1 from Gum's younger brother, Akule. Everyone thought it foolish of Akule to have lent the money, nevertheless he did.

Some years later, Zegejir brought a cow as part payment of his debts. Gum refused the cow as inadequate for bridewealth, leaving the matter of bridewealth for his ward unsettled. However, Akule advised him to take the cow in payment of the £1 debt. So Gum (not Akule) took the cow, butchered it and sold the meat. The situation could now be interpreted in two ways: either Gum had after all taken the cow as bridewealth, or else Gum owed Akule £1. If Gum had accepted the cow as payment of bridewealth for his ward, he should have applied it to bridewealth payment for one of his wives—notably MbaAkanshi, for whom he had paid only a very small amount of bridewealth. Since he did not apply it thus, and since it was at Akule's request that he had accepted the cow, it was generally assumed that Gum had taken over Zegejir's

---

[1] *Swem ikul*, which enables a woman to convene a moot, is not used in Kparev lineages, but only in Utisha.

debt to Akule—that is, instead of Zegejir's owing Akule £1, Gum now owed him a cow.

In response to the guardian's question, 'What about the cow?' Tyuna replied, 'I paid that £1 once, but Gum ate it at his funeral again. I am willing to pay it, but Akule will not accept.'

Again it took a good deal of questioning to discover the meaning. Gum died owing his brother Akule the cow (or the £1). Then, when Tyuna became compound head after Gum's death, he paid the £1 to Akule. This was very shortly before Gum's second funeral, and Akule spent the money on gunpowder which he fired at that funeral. Some time later this was interpreted by a diviner, whom they had consulted on another matter, as 'Gum returned and ate the pound again'. Hence Tyuna, as Gum's heir, had to give Akule another £1. He said now that he was ready to do so, but that Akule refused to take it.

This cow had also played a further part in Zegejir's life. He had once been told by a diviner that an illness of his child by this MbaGôr wife (MbaAkanshi's daughter) was due to the fact that he had never paid any bridewealth for her. When the matter came before a *jir* in Shangev, Zegejir cited the cow that he had paid to MbaGôr and said that it represented bridewealth; therefore the divination apparatus must be wrong, or else the Shangev moot had not found the right debt to discuss. MbaAkanshi agreed with Zegejir—the cow was bridewealth. She was acutely aware that Gum had never paid sufficient bridewealth for her (although her eldest daughter had indeed returned as ward to her natal lineage, Mbara).

Akule refused to accept the £1 a second time, for had he done so it could have been interpreted as a tacit admission that it was he who was sending the omens or dreams to MbaAkanshi. Tyuna also had an illness that left him temporarily impotent, and one of the points made by the divining apparatus which he consulted in that matter was that he had unpaid debts. He interpreted this as an instruction to pay the pound to Akule. The confusion was complete: MbaAkanshi wanted the pound to go to her guardian in Mbara to secure her position; Tyuna wanted to pay the pound to Akule to cancel the debt begun with Zegejir's cow so that he could perform *akombo* ceremonies to cure his illness; Akule refused the pound because accepting it would brand him a witch (*ormbatsav*).

MbaAkanshi herself now told the *jir* that she wanted the matter settled so that she could sleep at night without being disturbed by omens. I have seldom heard a Tiv woman speak with so much passion or use so many platitudes. The tenor of her words was that she had been a good wife to them and produced sons and daughters for them, and they had not responded with bridewealth sufficient to give her a secure position in MbaGôr.

She was allowed to finish, but then Chenge said that everything she had said was beside the point (*gbilin kwagh*) and that she was a senseless interfering woman. Fiyase (Chenge's elder in context of moot) rose and said that MbaAkanshi had done a very serious thing—she had brought about a charge of bewitching among brothers, and the most serious fault a wife can commit is to turn brother against brother.

MbaAkanshi wanted to answer back, but was restrained by her guardian. Fiyase went on to say that the divination apparatus was quite right—there was unsettled business about two marriage wards. But, he continued, it was not this business which had caused the dreams and omens in the present case—it was merely the imagination of a silly woman. None of the wards was ill; it was merely a wife who was disgruntled.

A member of the *igba* age-set, obviously interpreting these statements as an attempt on the part of the agnatic lineage to elude further questioning and to evade blame for causing the omens, said that obviously the matter of the *ichaver*-cloth should be discussed. The elders, and Tyuna and Akule, all agreed that there was no need. This matter, I discovered later, concerned the original marriage of MbaAkanshi: when Gum had eloped with her, he brought her to Kyagba (Chenge's father, who had died about a year before this *jir* was heard), and Kyagba had given Gum an *ichaver*-cloth to pawn in order to give the money he got for it to MbaAkanshi's guardian so that the latter could not rightly take her away. Later Gum had redeemed the pawned cloth and returned it to Kyagba. There was nothing unsettled here.

It looked as if the *jir* had dwindled for lack of subject-matter. Someone suggested that perhaps the 'inheritance' which had been given by the diviner wasn't merely marriage wards—perhaps there was livestock in it as well. Tyuna and Akule said that Gum had only three goats when he died, and all these had been 'eaten' without dispute.

After an awkward pause, Fiyase turned to Tyuna and said, 'Tyuna, have you been bothered by omens?' This was obviously the right question. The implications were that if Tyuna, as well as MbaAkanshi, had suffered evil omens, it was almost surely Akule who had, by means of *tsav*, sent them. Everyone was quiet as Tyuna said softly, 'Chickens in my hut which I had placed under baskets for safety at night have twice got loose and fought in the hut. On one occasion a cock woke up and went outside at night. A little later that same cock was found paralysed in the morning, but I ate him all the same and dared my jaw to become paralysed too!'[1]

Fiyase would not, however, allow the implication to be discussed. He

---

[1] *Sombu* means to be broken, as of a bone, and also to be paralysed or useless or misshapen. The meaning, when applied to the jaw, means permanent dislocation. Tiv cannot reset the mandible when it disengages from its articulations with the other head bones, as they can most other bone injuries.

O

said immediately that the ward-sharing group to which the two brothers belonged must meet and complete the business of the inheritance of Gum's wards. He said further that no bridewealth was owing on Mba-Akanshi because the initial payment had been made from the proceeds of Kyagba's pawned *ichaver*-cloth, and completed when one of Mba-Akanshi's daughters had been sent to be a ward in her mother's ward-sharing group. He assured MbaAkanshi that she could live here well and with security, and he told Nor to set up a small *swem* beside Mba-Akanshi's door so that no more dreams and omens could reach her, even though they might be sent.

While Nor was attending to the *swem* Fiyase turned to the *akombo chigh* which the divination apparatus had indicated. 'Did Gum have an *akombo chigh*?' he asked, knowing the answer already.

Tyuna answered, 'Gum had finished the *akombo hindan*.' The *hindan* is a fetish that includes both the *chigh* and the *twer*, and is one of the most powerful and important fetishes the Tiv know.

'Where is it now?' Fiyase asked.

'In the kitchen gardens,' Tyuna replied. 'None of us has brought it back into the compound' (i.e. no one had reactivated it since Gum's death).

'That is the trouble,' Fiyase pronounced, and Chenge and the other elders agreed. 'You must seek the sacrificial animals and call us all together and re-establish the *akombo hindan* in your compound.'

With this matter thus summarily settled, the *jir* was finished. Tyuna's wives produced porridge, and Tyuna gave a chicken to each age-set and another to the elders of MbaGôr. They were all killed and cooked there.

My clerk and I were both dissatisfied with the course which this *jir* had taken. It seemed to me that the whole thing had bogged down, and when no further matters of possible dispute between the members of the compound could be found, the 'blame' was put on a fetish. I began to agree with Chenge's statement that there was no need for a *jir*: it had been called because of a silly woman's discontent. Iyorkôsu, however, interpreted it differently: the *akombo chigh*, disorder of which was associated with the omens, cannot act by itself; someone has to use it for it to become active. Obviously it was the *mbatsav*—the elders who had rushed the meeting through its last stages. I asked Iyorkôsu why the *mbatsav* would be interested in such a matter. He replied that probably they weren't, but that they were hungry for meat and wanted Tyuna to repair the *akombo hindan* because a great many animals would be killed in the course of so doing. Only those elders who had finished the *hindan* —those same men who, in another sphere, were members of the *mbatsav*—would be eligible to eat the meat. There would be a great deal of meat which could be eaten by only a few people.

The issues in this moot were never as clear to me as were those in the moots described earlier. I believe they were also less clear to Tiv, though it may be that there are values and categories of thought in my own culture which made it difficult for me to understand the matters they were explaining.

The moot does, however, conform to the others we have already noted. It ended with the performance of a ceremony: in this case, the erection of *swem* outside the door of MbaAkanshi's hut. It also illustrates how antagonisms which occur among agnates and other close kinsmen who must live together are brought, in mystical terms, before the moot. MbaAkanshi fancied that her position—and *ipso facto* that of her son—was insecure both because insufficient bridewealth had been paid for her and because there were hidden animosities among the brothers in the compound. She linked these two factors in her interpretation of her dreams as evil omens. She considered—perhaps not quite explicitly—that her position would be improved if the compound members were made to agree on certain points of their dispute and if the elders of the lineage were to make a statement about her position. It is the task of the elders of the community to smooth social relationships by resolving difficulties, and they do so by means of the moot.

I should point out that, although the implications of witchcraft which I have assigned to various utterances recorded here were all present, nevertheless I have unavoidably given them undue emphasis in the translation. I can only warn the reader that the implications are there, but that Tiv would be shocked at the baldness and lack of finesse with which I have expressed them.

It is when the moots touch on death, its causes, and the source of the volition which brought it about that they become most tense. They are also often dreaded by elders who must participate. Illness, omens, and death must be willed by the *mbatsav* in some way mysterious to Tiv. Serious illness usually brings a moot. Death of an adult always brings a moot, in no matter how curtailed a form. The source of the volition for the death must be made 'known'; it is in the moot that it is made known.

Death is caused by *tsav*. Death of persons who have no *tsav*, or of those who have not misused their *tsav* for selfish and personal ends, is always attributable to the *tsav* of other persons. A man who has *tsav* of an enlarged and evil sort on his heart has, by eating human flesh, willed his own death. Evil *tsav* of this sort attacks its own host when it is in the presence of *swem* or sass-wood.

Much of the imagery in which Tiv discuss and think about matters of death, and its volition by men of *tsav*, sounds, when translated into English, like cannibalism. The imagery is not so obvious in the Tiv language, although it is still there. The 'actual' existence, whether present or past, of cannibalism among Tiv is beside the point here. I do not know whether it existed or not. I do know, however, that the idiom is logical if one accepts the postulate that some persons must be sacrificed on those fetishes which benefit the entire community, and the accompanying postu-late that the meat of a sacrifice must be eaten in concert by those members of the community who have already mastered the fetish concerned. Tiv metaphor and imagery, however, are rich, and there are many ways in which all this can be said to have taken place without having 'actually' occurred, to put it our way.

The following two moots concern illness and death, which are ultimately of the same nature as evil omens: they are willed by the *mbatsav* and caused either mystically by 'bewitching' (*tamben*) or through the medium of fetishes.

MOOT NO. IV. *Akusa calls his* ityô *to discuss his mother's illness*

My clerk's notes on this *jir* put the situation clearly and bluntly: 'Akusa collected his *ityô* for a moot because his mother is not well, and if he didn't tell the lineage she was ill, and if his mother then died, the lineage would say that it was he who had killed his mother.'

Akusa's mother, MbaCie, was a woman of about 70. She had been ill for over a year, and it seemed probable that she would never recover. Gossip—especially among the women—blamed Akusa rather severely because he had not already gone to a diviner and then collected his lineage to inquire into the nature of her illness.

When he finally did so, he sent one of his young sons around to ask the elders to come. They debated doing so when they had been sum-moned in such an inauspicious way,[1] but decided in the end that they would go for the sake of MbaCie, and that they would call Akusa to task for not having behaved properly by inviting them himself.

MbaCie was, I knew, the daughter of an uncompleted exchange marriage. Therefore she had returned from her agnatic lineage, Shangev

---

[1] Had they wanted to attend, this method of summoning them would not have been questioned, for it is often used.

Tiev, to become part of the ward-sharing group of her mother's agnatic lineage (her own *igba*), which was MbaDigam of MbaDuku. Her guardian in MbaDigam had then given her in exchange to Akusa's father, and this exchange had been completed.

It is part of Tiv belief that the *mbatsav* of a lineage can kill a woman married into that lineage only if they have the permission of the *mbatsav* of the woman's agnatic lineage or if she has eaten human flesh (that is, in some way shown herself a person of the *mbatsav*) in her husband's lineage. A woman such as MbaCie, whose guardian and agnatic lineage are separated, is in an unfortunate position, for the people immediately concerned in her exchange are not the people who must come to discuss

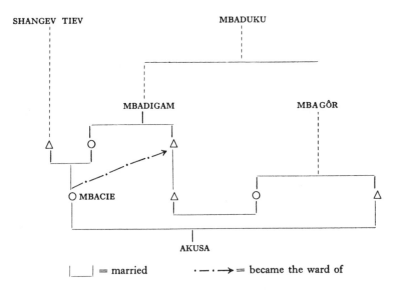

| | = married   · — · —➤ = became the ward of

the mystical aspect of her illness. In MbaCie's case, it was Shangev Tiev, her agnatic lineage, whose representatives should discuss her illness, although they were not and had never been concerned in her marriage. Secondly, a very old woman tends to lose touch with her natal lineage. The people among whom she grew up are no longer living and managing the affairs of the lineage. Their heirs have never known her, and take little interest in her. It is for such reasons that Tiv say of an old woman, particularly if she has adult sons, that she 'becomes your agnate' (*kwase u vesen hingir ityô*).

This moot was unique in my experience for one other factor. The women—the 'wives of MbaGôr'—turned out in mass and took on the role of inquisitor. They 'asked', a part which usually falls to the age-set or to the representatives of the victim's mother's lineage. This was the seating arrangement under the trees in Akusa's compound:

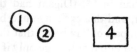

1. The hut in which MbaCie lay
2. Akusa
3. The *ityô* or elders (among whom my clerk and I sat)
4. The 'wives of MbaGôr'
5. The other members of Akusa's compound—none of whom were related to MbaCie.

This moot, like most others, began about noon. The elders sat about chatting and joking. The women, much more quietly, also talked among themselves, and allocated the work which they would do during the course of the moot—picking the seeds from cotton, spinning, removing the husks from gourd seeds.

Uta, who was impatient, began the *jir* by shouting at Akusa, 'Akusa, why have you called us together?'

The crowd became still as Akusa answered, 'Sleep is not good to me' (*Myav doom ga*).

Fiyase took up the questioning, 'What is it?'

Akusa replied, 'Something is hurting my mother and I have called my lineage together to tell them that she is ill. I will not eat her alone.' The last was a reference to the fact that if he did not invite his agnatic lineage together to discuss her fate, he would be held responsible for her death.

Fiyase asked, 'What did the diviner say?'

Akusa replied, 'I have not consulted a diviner.' This reply could have meant either that he did not do it himself, or that no one had done it.

Fiyase turned to Anyam, Akusa's half-brother and asked, 'Who went to the diviner?'

Anyam replied that he did not know—he had not been asked to go and, since it was neither his mother nor his ward, he was not concerned. [Had he gone to a diviner without being requested, he would have been guilty of interfering and would probably have been charged with being over-solicitous and therefore in some way implicated.]

Fiyase made a show of anger. 'What do you mean,' he railed at Akusa, 'calling us together to discuss the matter of your mother when you have not been to a diviner so that we shall know what needs discussing?'

Fiyase threatened to leave immediately, but the women raised such a shout that he made no move to go. The elders began to ask questions about the exchange marriage. MbaCie's exchange partner had died in MbaDigam, and at that time MbaDigam had come to 'ask',[1] and soon thereafter sores broke out on MbaCie's legs. But this matter was taken care of by her husband and it was finished. The number of children born to each of the two marriages was approximately equal, and the exchange was finished.

The elders had explored one possible cause of MbaCie's illness and had found nothing. Again Fiyase complained that the divination apparatus had not been consulted. 'When starting a moot,' he said, 'you begin with the divination reports. If nobody has been to a diviner, where can we start?' A member of the moot who was himself a diviner answered this rhetorical question: 'Unless you know what the divination apparatus says, you cannot start.' It became apparent that anyone who spoke, anyone who 'knew' anything about MbaCie's illness would, if he revealed his knowledge, stand self-accused of witchcraft because he 'knew' without revelation from the divining apparatus. There was an awkward silence.

'Akusa, speak,' Fiyase said.

'My mother is ill, and I've called my lineage together to discuss her illness.'

'When did it begin?' Fiyase insisted.

'It began last dry season. You came and said to repair the *akombo kwambe*.'

'And you didn't do it,' Fiyase said. 'Her illness began with the *kwambe*.'

'You must ask Uta,' Akusa said. Uta was the oldest man in Akusa's ward-sharing group. 'I told Uta.'

'Akusa,' Uta exploded, 'you did not! You told Anyôgo and told him to tell me, but he said it was not important and did not do so.'

Fiyase commented, 'It is not for me to ask Uta. You must ask Uta.' Akusa refused to 'ask' Uta—that is, to 'ask' Uta why MbaCie was ill, the implication being that if Uta knew, he had something to do with making her ill.

Uta (partly to take a side-swipe at Fiyase) said that since Akusa had not consulted the divination apparatus and since Fiyase had originally cited the *kwambe*, Fiyase had better 'tell' them. That is, Fiyase as head of the *mbatsav* of MbaGôr would therefore 'know'. Fiyase replied that since Akusa had not gone to the divination apparatus, he had nothing to say. That is, he had not been accused and would not admit that he 'knew' anything about the reason for MbaCie's illness and probable death. 'Let whosoever knows do the talking,' Fiyase summed up.

---

[1] i.e. to 'ask' the girl's agnatic lineage why they had 'killed our wife'.

My clerk's summary of this section of the moot says simply, 'Nobody knew what to say.'

After a silence, Fiyase asked the women whether they had anything to say. They replied that they had. Their spokesman was Samaakpe, senior wife of Chenge. 'Many years ago,' she said, 'MbaCie was ill. None of her husbands [men of her husband's lineage, MbaGôr] did anything about it, and MbaCie ran away to the home of her guardian in MbaDigam. She stayed there for many months. Her husband went for her, but the guardian refused to give her back to him.' Finally Kyagba had sent the women of MbaGôr to fetch her back. 'When the wives of MbaGôr arrived at the compound of MbaCie's guardian in MbaDigam, the entire ward-sharing group was called. I was younger then, but I was there.' Several other old women nodded or muttered that they also had been there.

'MbaDigam asked us,' Samaakpe continued, 'what we had come for and we told them that Kyagba had sent us to fetch MbaCie. MbaDigam consulted among themselves and told us that had it been we women alone they would not hand MbaCie back to us, for MbaCie had been taken ill in MbaGôr and MbaGôr had done nothing. But since it was Kyagba who sent us, they would send her back, for Kyagba was their child [his mother was an MbaDigam woman], and he would not let her die [Kyagba as head of the *mbatsav* would not select his maternal kinswoman, MbaCie, as one of his necessary victims for sacrifice, and would not allow any other of the *mbatsav* to harm her] if he sent all his wives to plead for her. But MbaDigam also told us that if anything ever happened to MbaCie, they would hold us responsible. They said that they would never let us alone again if anything happened to MbaCie.'

The whole position of the women became clear: they were not only concerned because MbaCie was dying, but because the responsibility for her death might be put at their door, as a result of the statement made by the elders of MbaDigam long ago.

When Samaakpe had finished Fiyase said, 'The women have spoken well. But it is for the elders (*mbatamen*) to decide.' [That is, women can't decide which persons are to die next; only the elders, in their role of *mbatsav*, can make such a decision.] He went on, 'We *mbatsav* of MbaGôr have nothing to do with this.'

Uta broke in here and said, 'It is God (*Aôndo*). The wives of MbaGôr are in no way at fault.'

Fiyase again spoke, 'The wives have the right (*isho*) in this matter. It is for the elders of MbaGôr and the elders of MbaDigam.'

Samaakpe said that she was glad the women were free from suspicion, and that they wanted the elders of MbaGôr to 'refuse' [to let MbaCie die]. 'If anything happens to MbaCie,' she finished, 'it will not be the wives of MbaGôr, and we want it not to be the elders of MbaGôr.'

Uta added, 'If anything happens to MbaCie it will be the affair of MbaDigam. We refuse.'

Fiyase said, 'I refuse.'

Nor, who had said nothing so far, also added, 'I refuse.'

The elders and the women had made sure that none of them were implicated in the death of MbaCie, which they expected would occur soon.

Fiyase now ordered Akusa to bring water in a small gourd-cup so that they could perform the rite of 'blowing out the curse' (*hamber ifan*). One old woman, about the same age as MbaCie, shouted out that she would not perform the rite with Akusa, that Akusa had neglected his mother for years and now had not gone to a diviner and the elders were asking her to drink water with such a man!

Fiyase told her she was speaking wrongly. She said that she was speaking correctly: several years ago MbaCie had called the wives of MbaGôr together and told them that Akusa was not giving her food or cloth and was not treating her properly. The women had given Akusa a great deal of trouble at that time, but still MbaCie complained.

Fiyase, again with a display of anger, told this old woman that she was merely causing trouble, and that she had better blow out the curse with Akusa or all of them would know what to think. [If you don't, you are the witch who is causing MbaCie's trouble.] Grudgingly she complied.

Akusa and his half-brother Anyam, Fiyase, Uta, Nor, and a few of the younger elders, and the four or five oldest and most important of the women, performed the rite. Fiyase said, 'We all *hamber ifan* so that MbaCie will not die.'

Akusa was also remiss about feeding the elders—no food was offered, and the elders left grudgingly. Akusa, they concluded, was not a man who knew things.

MbaCie died three days later. I was in Iyon and thus could not attend her funeral, but Iyorkôsu, my clerk, did attend. He wrote a text on it and several of the elders described it to me in detail. It was a short ceremony because they had decided, at the moot held three days before, everything that ordinarily would have been 'asked' at the funeral; matters were therefore easily settled. I have selected a few passages from my clerk's text:

'Akusa called MbaCie's people to bury her. When her husband's people had all gathered, Fiyase asked Akusa, "What kind of death have they killed MbaCie with?" Akusa replied that he did not know. Fiyase told Akusa to stop joking and tell him what kind of death they had killed MbaCie with. Akusa again said he didn't know, and told Fiyase to ask Uta.

'So Fiyase asked Uta, "Uta, do you know which death they brought to kill MbaCie?" Uta did not answer immediately, and Usaka [a member of MbaJiabu lineage of MbaGôr, and in no way concerned with the affair] asked, "Where was MbaCie's guardian?"

'Fiyase told Usaka, "You ask well. That is the reason for asking Akusa what sort of death killed MbaCie. . . ."'

'Fiyase said that for the present they had better bury her and afterwards they would search out the cause of her death. MbaCie's time had come. They would not give MbaDigam [her guardian's lineage] the whole death, neither would they give the whole death to Shangev Tiev [her agnates], nor would they give the death to MbaGôr. . . . Old Nor indicated the place where they should dig MbaCie's grave. While they were digging the grave, Fiyase asked the women if they had anything to say. The women said that they had nothing to discuss. Fiyase asked the women, "But the other day you had something to say." The women admitted that they had. Fiyase asked the women, "What do you make of MbaCie's death?" The women [actually Samaakpe, their spokesman] replied that they had seen the elders "refuse" MbaCie's death, and when MbaCie was dying they asked her what sort of death she had met, and she replied that she had never eaten anything belonging to anyone [this meant that she was not herself a person with *tsav*, and therefore her death could not be charged to herself].

'Nor told the women to go inside the huts. . . . The women went into the huts; the kinsmen took MbaCie and buried her.

'When they had finished burying her, Nor "dressed" *swem*. Nor then began to chant a spell (*ta acia*) saying, "The man who knows about the death of MbaCie, he may come and remove her, but he must not frighten anyone. If he frightens anyone, *swem* will go for him." Then Nor broke *swem*.'

This *swem* was actually made by mixing the ingredients together in a large potsherd. Nor held the sherd over his head while he chanted the spell, and then dashed it to the ground. The sherd broke, scattering the ingredients of *swem*.

When I discussed this case with Fiyase later, he told me that the damage to MbaCie had already been done when he and the other elders 'refused'—the *mbatsav* [of MbaDigam is implied] had already killed her, though she had not died yet. *Swem*, he said, would 'seize' (*kôr*) whoever was responsible for killing her. Thus Fiyase's statement to me differed somewhat from Iyorkôsu's interpretation. Fiyase said that the *swem* would seize whoever killed her. Iyorkôsu's statement implies—and in our discussions he confirmed—that *swem* will seize the killers of MbaCie only if she was killed for anti-social reasons. That is to say, if the *mbatsav* killed her for a necessary sacrifice in repairing the *tar*, then the *swem* will not take effect.

This moot, like all the others we have considered, ended with a rite: the 'dressing' and smashing of *swem*.

It also illustrates the fact that when the moot discusses matters of illness and death, and the witchcraft, fetishes, and curses that are deemed to accompany them, it delves not only into past social relationships, but also into the readjustment of social relationships which must take place at the time of death. MbaCie was an old woman; her death occasioned little surprise and little grief. But, given the Tiv doctrine that death must be not merely caused—as MbaCie's was caused by the infirmities and diseases of old age—but also willed, then it is necessary to determine the source of volition. Perhaps it would be more accurate to say that when death is believed to have an agent as well as a cause, the moot either establishes the innocence of those persons who might conceivably have a motive and leaves final 'settlement' to *swem*, or else very occasionally it makes honourable the motive of the elders *qua mbatsav*.

To put it in another way, in Akusa's *jir* the members of the moot directed the blame or volition for MbaCie's death into a foreign lineage. They removed the suspicion of evil from themselves and restored smooth relationships to the entire lineage. The evil was made into an outside evil; all were assured that it was not an evil within the lineage and the *tar*. There is an elaborate doctrine among Tiv, connected with this point, that the *mbatsav* of various lineages carry on feuds with one another in terms of killing 'by night'. All the deaths which occur are, they say, part of such a contest. Tiv have no feud 'by day'; but they have a belief about vast feuds between lineages that rage 'by night'.

The *jir*, in the context of illness and death, smooths over the social relationships of the living and tells them how to behave in order to gain and keep their community's support and approbation, just as the moot does in the context of bad dreams and omens. Bad dreams, omens, illness, and death—all are related in Tivland, for all imply the machinations of the *mbatsav*.

When the field-worker in Tivland first attends funerals, he is struck by the fact that they are noisy, that little respect is shown for the dead (or anyone else), and that there is a wild orgy of accusation. Only later does he come to realize that, in the social upheaval and incertitude that accompany death and funerals, the moot settles most problems of status and wealth and channels the grief and distress into recognized activity and against recognized targets.

The first Tiv funeral that I understood was Gesa's. I had been in Tivland about nine months and was yet without clerks; but I understood the language sufficiently well to follow some of the action and debate and to make exhaustive inquiries afterwards.

MOOT NO. V. *The death of Gesa*

Gesa was not an MbaDuku man and his compound was several miles from mine, but I visited it occasionally. I went there one afternoon in March 1950, and found a moot ending: several of the principals were just finishing the rite of 'blowing out the curse'. I was told that they had been discussing the matter of MbaWuam, a young girl who had been brought back to the compound of her mother's brothers for treatment. Orya, the compound head, then asked me to come along to Gesa's reception hut and have a look at him.

Gesa was lying on a mat, breathing with difficulty. His senior wife told me, when I asked, that he hadn't eaten or drunk or been awake for over two days. He could still hear conversation, however, and when I, wondering if he had some sort of paralysis, asked his wife if he could still move his legs, he did so. I turned to him, and told him to move his fingers if he could hear me. He did so. Outside again, the compound head told me that about two or three months ago Gesa had been working together with his age-set in a communal task of road-building. Not feeling well, he had come home. He had got steadily worse and in the last three days his feet and his belly swelled up.

Orya described the symptoms in the words always used in describing the action of *swem*—'your feet and your belly and your head swell, and you die'. I went back to look more closely at Gesa. He was a man in good physical condition, in spite of his illness, and there was no sign that any part of his body had swelled.

On my walk home, I was accompanied part of the way by the oldest man of Gesa's lineage, whose compound lay in my general direction. Once we were on the path, he turned to me and said simply, 'He will die.' I asked him what the trouble was. He said he didn't know. I asked if the divination apparatus had been consulted. He said that it had not, and added that it was unnecessary—this was a matter of the *mbatsav.*[1] I asked what I knew to be a rude question containing a serious charge: 'How do you know it is a matter of the *mbatsav?*' He forgave my 'ignorance' and replied evasively, but probably truthfully, that everyone in Orya's compound 'knew' it and that they had told him.

I thought that the old man was probably right—that Gesa would die. The next morning at dawn I started in that general direction soon after waking. On the way I encountered two youths bathing in a stream. One of them, whom I knew slightly, asked if I was going to the funeral. I asked who had died. He replied that it was Gesa; he had heard this from a woman who had come to the stream for water some time after having seen people from Gesa's compound. I walked on to the home of Orya and Gesa.

When I entered the compound, Gesa's corpse was outside the reception hut where he had been lying the day before. A small piece of hand-woven cloth was tied over the face. His half-brother, a few months his senior and a member of the same age-set, whom I knew fairly well, greeted me only with, 'It defeated him', using for 'it' the pronoun of the noun-class to which death belongs. Gesa's younger full brother, one of his MbaDuku affines, began to wash the body. When they had finished, they put Gesa's best cloth on it, wrapped the whole in a large white cloth of the sort that Tiv call *pupu*, wrapped a mat about that, and tied it. This process took almost an hour.

About 9 o'clock the members of Gesa's age-set began to arrive in numbers. The women, who had been in the kitchen gardens wailing, filed back into the compound, still wailing. They went into Gesa's reception hut, where the corpse had been placed. By about 10 o'clock, almost fifty members of Gesa's age-set had arrived. The largest collection of age-mates I have ever seen, they were drawn from a lineage containing some 8,000 people. They soon began to be restive, and shouted at Orya, the compound head, asking if he had not notified the elders. He insisted that he had done so, and that they would be coming. Half an hour later, when none of the elders had arrived, the age-mates began to complain that the elders were refusing to come to hear this *jir* and bury their dead. Orya, nervous and distrait, tried to reassure them. One of the age-mates said that, since the elders of his *ityó* wouldn't bury him, the age-set must bury Gesa's body in the bush. Orya answered patiently that he was himself the oldest man in his segment within the hut; therefore they could not say that the elders had not come. The eldest of the minimal *tar*—with whom I had walked the day before— would be along soon. He named several other elders whom he had notified.

[1] The implication here, that the divination apparatus cannot cope with matters of the *mbatsav*, is not true. There are, however, few diviners who have the courage to tackle this sort of problem. Most find it safer to profess ignorance.

The seating arrangement was becoming apparent:

1. Gesa's lineage—the elders
   —were sitting under and
   near a drying platform,
   set more or less in the
   centre of the compound
2. The age-set, who far out-
   numbered the lineage, sat
   in the shade of mango trees
3. Gesa's reception hut
4. The women of the com-
   pound, and women rep-
   resenting the wives of
   most of the compounds of
   the lineage
5. I sat with, but a little to
   the side of the age-set.

After another pause, when the most important elders of Gesa's lineage had still not arrived, Kwaghwam, the most respected member in
the age-set, rose and said firmly, 'Gesa has no agnates (*ityô*). But he
has an age-set. If all his agnates refuse to do anything for him, his age-
set will do something.' They made a move to prepare the body for
carrying.

The oldest member of Gesa's minimal *tar* present said tentatively
that what they said wasn't a bad thing, but that they were very impatient and must want to keep something from the agnates, who were
indeed coming.

Somebody in the age-set noted that this action, or lack of action, on
the part of the elders spoiled the *tar*. Another added that the age-set
had turned out early and in force, it was not the age-set who were
spoiling the *tar*.

A few moments later, a few of the age-mates rose, and got a pole
and some fibre rope. Others went into the hut where the body lay and
bore it out; the wailing increased as the body emerged and was put down
among the age-set. The few elders present tried to make them be
patient; the age-set remonstrated. They were just beginning to fear that
they might really have to make good their threat when the three most
important elders of the lineage arrived together. They joined the other
elders. The women came out of the reception hut and sat down
silently. Now that all were present, they seemed reluctant to begin.

Finally Kwaghwam, easily the most commanding figure of the full
age-set, rose and said to the elders, 'Did you ask Gesa before he died?'

The compound head also rose. 'We did not ask Gesa, but Gesa
told us.'

Kwaghwam asked the elders, 'Does that satisfy you?'

One elder replied that it depended on what the age-set said. Another suddenly exploded and said that it did not depend on the age-set; they all knew that Gesa was their child and therefore he had done nothing wrong.

The age-set replied, 'We must know.' 'We want to see,' they chorused. Kwaghwam shouted above them all, 'If our age-mate was evil, we shall desist. If his agnates killed him, we shall never desist!'

The implications of this exchange became clear after detailed questioning later. A full sister of Gesa had died some three or four months earlier. The divination apparatus indicated that she had been killed by *tsav*, but nobody had asked the apparatus whose *tsav* had been responsible. At the funeral, her body was examined and it was found that she herself did not have *tsav* on her heart; therefore she did not die from her own evil, but was killed by someone else—either the elders *qua mbatsav* or by an evil man of *tsav*. Loud and bitter accusations had taken place among her close male kinsmen though only a small moot had been convened. At the end of this moot, *swem* had been dressed and broken, so that whosoever might have caused this death would be caught by *swem*.

Within a month, Gesa had fallen ill. By the time his death was imminent, most of the people nearby were describing his suffering in terms of the symptoms of *swem* [although I could not see them]. Therefore, the exchange among the agnates and the age-set amounted to: 'Did Gesa die by means of his own *tsav* and the force of *swem* that was, of course, stronger, or was he bewitched and killed as a sacrifice by his agnates or by one of them acting individually and *ipso facto* evilly?' There is only one sure way to determine this fact; the divination apparatus—except the sasswood ordeal—is fallible. That one sure way was to hold a post-mortem examination of Gesa's heart. If it were found to have *tsav* growing on it, then Gesa would be buried and it would be said that his own evil had killed him. If his heart was found to be sound and healthy, without *tsav*—if, as Tiv would put it, his chest was found to be empty,[1] the age-set would know that he had been killed by his agnates: probably the same persons who had killed his sister and were trying to kill his second sister's daughter.

There were loud arguments, shouts, and accusations. The agnates constantly contradicted themselves, for it was necessary for them both

---

[1] The translation which East, following others, has given of this phrase—'empty-chested'—is indeed correct, but the flavour is not conveyed. *Vanger gbilin* means two things: a man of no talent or consequence, if he is alive and healthy. Applied to a dead man, it means a person who died for some reason other than his own evil propensity. It resembles our word 'innocent' in that it has connotations of good, but in other usages the derogatory connotations of lack of experience are dominant.

to protest their own innocence and to uphold the innocence of their 'child'. The age-set, on the other hand, said repeatedly, 'We must know. Our duty is to protect and revenge our age-mate if he be innocent. But we must know if he is innocent before we dare to raise our hands for him. You are his agnates, but you are also our agnates.'

Had Gesa been found innocent, the age-set might—in the days before the effective government of the British Administration—have attacked, punished, and perhaps even killed those members of Gesa's lineage who were deemed to have caused his death. This institution, known as *hoyo*, is no longer practised. Today the age-set, if it were to do anything in such a situation, must either resort to magical means or hire someone else to do so.

By about half-past twelve the grave had been dug by the same men who had washed the corpse. The body was, after a series of moves requiring some twenty minutes, transported to its side. All sorts of delaying tactics were employed. The age-set was reluctant to perform the post-mortem operation; they would have been saved from doing so by a tacit admission from the elders that Gesa's death was 'natural'— that is, that they had needed his body for sacrificial purposes. But the elders, each knowing that such was not the case and that no decision had ever been reached about Gesa, would not make the admission.

The age-set and the elders faced one another grimly over the grave. Finally Kwaghwam said to the elders and Orya, 'Shall we look and leave?' The eldest replied, 'This is Orya's child. You must ask him. It is your matter and Orya's—but I should say, don't do it.' Orya said nothing. Kwaghwam decided to force the issue. 'We, his age-set, must know why he died. We will look.' One of the elders brought up the case of Gbannor, who, I discovered later, had been examined, and the examination didn't help him, his age-set, or his agnates; his chest had been empty, and Gesa's chest, this elder had implied, would also be empty.

Another elder, feeling himself supported, said, 'We know that our child is all right. We would bury him and break *swem*. But his age-set will not believe.'

Kwaghwam said, 'His age-set must know.' He thereupon dispatched some of his age-mates to find a suitable knife. 'Bring Gesa's own knife,' he told one of them.

Orya said sadly, 'Who will do it?'

Kwaghwam said, 'His agnates should do it, but they fear. His innocence must be proved by his age-mates, for his agnates have nothing but fear.'

A few of the elders and age-mates stood and watched; most of them withdrew. Kwaghwam appointed one of his age-mates to perform the operation. The operator unwrapped the corpse from its cloths and mats.

It lay on its back in the sun on the pile of dirt beside its grave. Standing above the body, straddling it, the operator made a neat initial incision horizontally on the chest about two inches below the top of the sternum. Each corner, then, he turned down along the lower ribs so as to make the arc of an oval. The incision was deepened until he struck the bone of the ribs. He then drove the knife between two ribs, tapped its sides with an axe-handle, neatly cutting through each rib, one at a time, and finally through the top portion of the sternum. The knife was sharp and worked quickly. There was no sound except his tapping. When he had finished cutting, he took a hook (made from a forked branch which had been cut by another age-mate) and pried upwards the flap of flesh and bone. It rose with the slight sound of tearing perichondrium. It opened like a trap door and was laid down on the corpse's belly. Another layer of perichondrium was visible. The operator cut through it; the organs were exposed. He placed his knife and hook carefully below the trap-door of flesh and bone and reached in, slowly, with his right hand. Again, there were a few sounds of tearing ligament and pericardium. He lifted the heart out of the opening, turned it slowly and said, 'You see?'

They all looked. A few said 'Mmmmmm.'

Kwaghwam turned to me and said, 'Jim, do you see the *tsav*?'

I asked him to point it out precisely. He and the operator used their explanation to me as an excuse to describe it aloud so that all could hear, including those who would not come to look. *Tsav* is a growth on the heart. It looked to me as if blood had been forced into sacks in the pericardium. There were two such sacks on Gesa's heart. The larger, dull blue in colour, was about three inches long and half as wide. The smaller, about half that size, was bright red. I do not know what they were. If they were sacks of blood, one must have been arterial blood, the other venous.

'Do you see?' Kwaghwam repeated.

'Yes, I see,' I answered. 'And that is *tsav*?'

'You have seen *tsav*,' the operator said. 'You yourself have *tsav* to look on *tsav*.'

'But *tsav* need not be evil,' Kwaghwam added a moment later. 'But this *tsav* is evil. It is large and it is of two colours.'

The operator replaced the heart in Gesa's chest, closed the trap door and wrapped the chest about with a strip of cloth torn from that about Gesa's loins. The body was again wrapped in the mat, lowered into the grave, and moved with some difficulty on to the shelf that had been prepared for it. The white cloth was spread over it, and everybody present helped to cover the grave.

The operator took the knife he had used for the operation and, with the aid of a small stone, drove it point first up to its hilt into a tree.

P

Such a knife must never be used again—if brought back into the compound, it might accidentally be used to cut food, in which case anyone who ate such food would have eaten the human flesh that had contaminated the knife. The wooden hook was buried with the corpse.

The tension was over. The moot could be finished quickly: Gesa had brought about his own death. Someone tried to joke about the elders and their knowledge that the situation would be as it was (i.e. one witch knows another); someone else tried to laugh. Then Orya began a dirge. He walked heavily back into the compound, singing as he came, those peculiarly Tiv dirges which start high and come down a minor scale for two octaves or more and end in formalized sobs. He sat down slowly and silently. The other agnates and the age-set also resumed their positions. The women, who had all gone down to the stream, did not return for another half-hour.

One of the elders said, 'It was the age-set. It was they who wanted him opened.'

Kwaghwam replied, 'I don't like it. But was it a lie (*yie*) which we did?'

One of the junior elders, a man very little older than the age-set, said that the whole thing was a matter of *swem*. '*Swem* killed him,' he noted through the other platitudes.

Slowly, over about fifteen minutes, they all admitted that this was indeed the case: *swem* had killed Gesa. Meanwhile, the women began to come back, a few at a time, into the compound.

There was nothing more to say. Someone in the age-set said, 'We have looked. We know. Let us go.' (*Se nenge mfe. Mough sha.*)

Then Kwaghwam rose and went before the elders. 'We must have his people,' he said.

This statement raised a turmoil again. Finally, however, Orya formally took each of Gesa's widows by the wrist and handed them to Kwaghwam, who grasped their wrists, thus signifying that he, for the age-set, was offering them protection. Gesa had a third wife, who had been absent for three months. The age-set asked several questions about her. Orya said he knew nothing about her, but would ask and be responsible for her well-being.

Kwaghwam said, 'What about Gesa's other people?' He referred to Gesa's younger full brother. The agnates shouted in anger, 'We did not kill Gesa. *Swem* killed Gesa. Why should Gesa's age-set seek to protect his brother, as if it had been we who killed Gesa?'

Kwaghwam was firm. Finally the agnates concurred, and the younger brother was handed to Kwaghwam, who grasped his wrist also, thus putting him under the protection of the age-set.

Kwaghwam then asked, 'What about the sick daughter of Gesa's sister?'

This time the agnates were more firm. 'She is here,' one elder said. 'She is safe with her mother's agnates. No one can harm her here, for we have refused to let them.' This point took almost ten minutes to settle. But the agnates were adamant—this child was not one of 'Gesa's people'. Had the elders let her go, it might some day be interpreted as an admission that they were bewitching her. If she remained 'in the palm' of her mother's agnates, then the assumption would be that it was Gesa who had bewitched her. The age-set eventually conceded the point.

The oldest man of the lineage then dressed a new *swem* in a large pot-sherd. He stood in the clear space, surrounded by all the participants, and held it high above his head. 'If we have not discussed this *jir* properly,' he said in a loud voice, 'and if we are wrong, then *swem* will catch anyone who has done evil deeds (*ishor i bo*) in this matter.' He dashed *swem* to the ground; the ashes in it raised a small cloud of dust which was carried away in the breeze.

The funeral—or moot, for it was both and could be called either *ku* or *jir*—was ended. It was a little after 4 o'clock in the afternoon. The whole procedure had taken about eight hours.

The first thing to note about this moot, as with the others, is that it was ended with a ritual: the dressing and smashing of *swem*. All the moots we have considered—and this applies, I believe, to all moots that are successfully concluded—ended with ceremonies of repairing fetishes, ceremonies of 'blowing out the curse', or cere-monies involving *swem*.

The second point of importance is that the moot settled a multitude of quarrels and fears among the people of the com-munity: the volition for several past deaths was now 'known', and the atmosphere was cleared of suspicion. All the dependants of Gesa had been assured that they and their interests were being mystically protected by his age-set, for his wrongdoing did not relieve them of their responsibilities to his dependants: he was still their age-mate; his wives were still their *mtene*, and his sons were still their sons. The first steps toward re-establishing social relation-ships on a new footing, in the absence of the dead man, had been achieved. They grieved for Gesa and about Gesa, but now they 'knew'.

Again, the moot had 'repaired the *tar*'—the *tar* of the lineage which in Maine's terms can be called 'the entire little society'.[1]

---

[1] Henry Summer Maine, *Village Communities of East and West.*

IV. RITUAL IN THE MOOT

We have noted that, following on the successful completion of a moot, ritual is performed, and in the moots discussed above we have noted three different sorts of ritual: the rite known as 'cutting the curse', a rite for 'repairing a fetish', and several rituals involving *swem*. We shall discuss them briefly in that order.

Blowing out the curse is a simple rite, performed by taking water into the mouth and blowing it out in as fine a spray as possible. Usually all who perform it gather in a group or in a ring, and one of the elders of the moot calls for a gourd-cup of water. This cup is passed round the ring and everyone takes his sip.

The rite is performed, I believe, whenever any dispute between close kinsmen or near neighbours is settled. It is also performed on many other occasions, particularly at those ceremonies in which fetish emblems are erected in a man's compound, when it is also a sign of good-will. 'Blowing out the curse' means that one has no reservations in the settlement or ceremony. If any one has reservations and performs the ceremony, the 'curse' will rebound on him.

'Blowing out the curse' means that the affair is settled. It is usually, but not always, omitted if fetishes are repaired. In Ornyiman's moot, the rite of blowing out the curse was not performed; in a more complex case it might have been.

If a fetish rite is performed after the *jir*, as it was after Ornyiman's *jir*, the rite is that variant of 'washing the fetish' which is suitable.[1] The rite must be performed by a person who has mastered the fetish sufficiently to be able to do so. There may be several such masters of any particular fetish within the minimal *tar*, or it may be necessary to go outside to find one. One would normally go to one's agnates of the segment equivalent to one's own minimal segment rather than to one's mother's lineage, which would mean that the rite was performed by the mother's lineage (the *igba*) and would have a different set of implications from a rite performed by agnates.

The fetish which is washed after a *jir* is usually one which has been mentioned by a diviner. In Ornyiman's case the *akombo megh* was repaired without advice from a diviner, for it is the standard

---

[1] For a preliminary statement about the types of fetish rituals see *The Tiv of Central Nigeria*, pp. 87–88. I shall examine all the rites in detail in my forthcoming book on Tiv religion.

rite for cancelling relations, including but not limited to sexual relationships between men and women.

Finally, there is *swem*. We have noted in the *jir* which involved MbaAkanshi's affairs that *swem* was planted outside the door of her hut. In the affairs of MbaCie and at Gesa's funeral, *swem* was 'dressed and smashed'. *Swem* is the force which sees to it that *tsav* is properly used.

Swem planted before the door of MbaAkanshi's hut ensured that no man of *tsav* came to her hut at night and caused her to dream evil omens. No person of *tsav*, Tiv say, can perform evil in the presence of *swem*. So long as *swem* was present, having been properly planted by the elders, MbaAkanshi was safe.

Breaking *swem* is more often encountered. *Swem* contains ashes, ground camwood, charcoal, and the leaves of several plants. It may be 'dressed' and kept, as with the *swem* used for oaths in the courts. In south-eastern Tivland it may be 'dressed' by any master'of *swem* and sold to any person who is an agnate or a wife of any lineage with whom the *swem*-master's lineage has an *ikul* treaty. Finally, *swem* may be dressed and broken.

When *swem* is broken (*hemba*) at the end of a moot, we can say that the principle of *swem* has been released. Tiv do not put it in this way, but I find it impossible to translate their ideas into English without adding to the imagery. Once *swem* has been smashed, and the principle of *swem* released, evil *tsav* will be 'caught' by the *swem*. Gesa's own evil *tsav*, it was said, caused him to be 'caught' by the *swem* broken at an earlier funeral of a member of his lineage. *Swem* was broken after the moot and again after the funeral of MbaCie. *Swem* was broken after Gesa's funeral and the moot which accompanied it. I asked exhaustively about why this had been done, since Gesa himself was to blame for his death and the deaths of others. I was told that it might be that he had not acted alone. Perhaps the matter was not really finished yet. Breaking *swem* was a safeguard. 'We break *swem* so that we can all go well and sit well in our compounds.'

Swem is said by Tiv to be the same thing as sasswood, which we encountered earlier in this book. Sasswood is *swem*, although *swem* is more than sasswood. Evil, of the sort Europeans would call guilt, kills its perpetrator in the presence of *swem* and *ipso facto* if sasswood is drunk. The innocent are safe in the presence of *swem*; they vomit sasswood.

Breaking *swem*, like swearing on it in the court, or like blowing out the curse, is a means by which human beings are relieved of responsibility for truth and for right action on the part of everyone save themselves. To break *swem* is to put everyone in the community in jeopardy if each fails to perform right action. In courts, individuals touch *swem*; the individual alone is in jeopardy. In moots the whole community is involved; the whole community shares the danger. The meaning is the same in both cases: in fact, in Shangev *swem* is often not broken, but every elder in turn must perform the individual act of jeopardizing himself if he fails to perform right actions, by dropping a pebble into the treaty *swem* owned by the person who convened the moot.

By taking an oath, by breaking *swem*, or dropping pebbles into it, man has passed the buck for the enforcement of the counter-action to any breach of norm and right action. Only so has he 'solved'—more accurately, perhaps, by-passed—the most difficult aspects of human relationships. '*Si Dieu n'existait pas, il faudrait l'inventer.*'

V. CONCLUSIONS

We found, in investigating those *jir* which Europeans in Tivland call 'courts', that the court could profitably be seen as a counter-action preceded by a breach of the norms of social relationships, and followed by any of several sorts of correction.

The social acts that precede and follow a moot are more complex and diffuse. Those following a moot, which comprise the correction, are ritual rather than secular. Although a great many secular corrections of social relationships have also been made in the course of the moot, these reparations are considered by Tiv to be incidental to the main fact that a ritual correction for the entire community, or a sizeable proportion of it, has been achieved. A new statement of the good-will which is the essence of peaceful community existence has been emphasized, and symbols of it have been exchanged ritually.

The social act that follows upon a moot is a ritual act: the 're-pairing' of a fetish, 'blowing out the curse', the planting or the breaking of *swem*. The ritual is made to stand for the many in-dividual corrections of social relationships: the individual corrections which are a necessary part of the community correction.

The individual and social acts and strained relationships which precede a *moot* are as diffuse as are the individual corrections which the successful moot brings about. The disputes, the wrongs, and the grudges which lead to moots tend to be those which occur among kinsmen and neighbours who cannot break off the relationships among themselves. Tiv bring all these difficulties in relationships among agnates and neighbours into a single concept: *tsav*. The events which precede a moot are: (1) death, (2) illness, and (3) evil omens. All are indications of a breach of norm on the mystical plane: *tsav* is active. Tiv convene the *jir* to determine the cause and the volition of the *tsav*. If the purposes are evil, they must be stopped; if they are not, they must be 'known'.

Moots occur when disorders in the social group, the lineage, occur. Moots, if successful, correct the individual difficulties and mark that correction with a ritual. The whole is carried on in the idiom of witchcraft and religion. I do not mean to imply that Tiv religion is no more than an idiom for correcting the community: it is much more. But it is that aspect which is of importance in this study.

In analysing moots, we are dealing with a complex set of interrelationships which is subject to difficulties, and, at the same time, with a mystical idiom for categorizing—for simplifying—that maze of relationships and its shortcomings. Moots deal with more complex issues than do courts: the case of Ornyiman is relevant. There, it will be remembered, the mystical idiom and imagery scarcely entered. The other four cases have been arranged in order of the increasing use of mystical imagery. The arrangement also shows an increasing complexity of the relationships involved in the moot. At funerals, and at times of epidemic or of great political stress, in which the community is distraught, the mystical idiom comes fully into use.

We must not allow the mystical idiom to cloud the fact that the *jir* remains a counteraction following upon breach of norm—usually many breaches of many norms. It is in turn followed by some sort of correction which is symbolized, and thus brought about, by the ritual. The moots are counteractions to complex disturbances in many social relationships, much as the courts are counteractions to simple disturbances in single personal relationships. Tiv say that courts deal with minor matters. Moots deal with big matters—nothing less than the whole social order.

CHAPTER X

CONCLUSION

THE purpose of this book has been twofold: to elicit the systemization of jural phenomena in the folk system of the Tiv, and to give a sociological explanation, in more general terms, which will serve as an analytical system for comparing Tiv jural institutions with those of other societies.

We found that two folk systems are operative in Tivland: one is the systemization of jural phenomena by the Tiv themselves in their own language; the other is the systemization in English of roughly the same phenomena by administrative officers. The English folk system occupies an unduly large place in the social field because the ultimate political power in the colonial society is thought by all to lie with the British. There is an interplay between the two systems, but the English has more influence upon the Tiv than vice versa. The folk system of the British covers two sorts of tribunals, which they term respectively native (or Native Authority) courts and magistrates' courts. The folk system of the Tiv also covers two sorts of tribunals, both of which they call *jir*. One type of *jir* is the same institution as the Native Authority courts, seen from a different angle. The other is what we have described in this book as the moot. We can, thus, say that there are three types of tribunal in Tivland, and that they are divided between two conceptual systems:

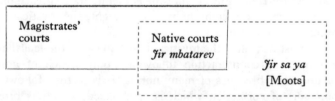

One of the first tasks which the Government set itself in Tivland was the establishment of courts. Records in the Provincial Office in Makurdi show that by 1914 charges were being made against groups of elders for administering the sasswood ordeal, and that statements could be made that 'law and order have been established for a sufficient time for the Munshi to know' that courts had replaced their own 'inadequate' methods of dealing with wrong-doers. By the middle 1920's, the court organization was more or less complete; only minor changes and reorganizations have been made since.

Tiv are, for the most part, grateful for courts. Courts and administration have greatly increased the safety of the countryside. It is, however, important to note that courts did not 'replace' moots, but were fundamentally a new idea. The Tiv concept *jir*, applied originally to meetings and functions somewhat similar to those of the present-day moot, provided a framework and a vocabulary by means of which Tiv built the court into their culture.

When the Administration came in and 'pacified' the Tiv, the indigenous methods for dealing with wrongs and disputes between members of distant lineages were denied them. They could no longer fight; they could no longer make armed 'raids' for the purpose of 'taking in a matter of debt'. Because self right-enforcement was outlawed, some new institution was required: the newly introduced courts served the purpose. The British Administration thus brought, not merely the courts, but the social system that made them necessary.

Courts did not 'replace' moots, but rather 'replaced' many of the recognized non-jural means of self right-enforcement. The moots, which dealt with relationships between groups and between individuals and their groups, and which did not include violence, were more or less unaffected by the new social situation.

In 1927, when the Government abolished exchange marriage, it struck its first and only blow against the moots. Traditionally, Tiv say, disputes concerning exchange marriages were heard by moots. The wife's lineage 'asked' the husband's lineage if any serious difficulties appeared in the marriage or if the wife died. With the introduction of courts, a device was created in which the naturally slow exchange—some took several generations to complete—could be speeded up. Money, furthermore, created a medium of exchange in which the return could be made. Tiv themselves, it seems, took exchange marriage into the courts because they saw a chance there either of getting something for nothing, or of getting their rights more quickly. The situation became so tense that (although it could not have been seen at the time) either exchange marriage had to go, or a new jural institution for dealing with it had to be developed. In view of the fact that the most prestigious cultural values were European, young Tiv were able, with European assistance but against the better judgment of their elders, to push this 'reform' through the Tiv Native Authority.

Moots, both traditionally and at present, are concerned primarily with disputes *within* a social group; even in cases about exchange marriage the two opposed social groups saw themselves as the moot of the lineage which included them both. Courts fundamentally are concerned with disputes *between* social groups or between individuals.

Tiv consider that moots are a traditional institution; courts are a governmental innovation which has today become more or less at home in Tiv culture. The courts first set out to settle those disputes that could no longer be settled by the traditional means of self-help, which might include violence; they then, gradually, came to be used as tribunals to hear marriage cases, because in that respect alone were they more rapid than moots. As Native Authority regulations were added, courts became busier. As policemen were trained and stationed with the new chiefs, they became busier. Tiv are litigious people, but their courts make them more so. The courts have created and are creating the situations upon which they feed: whereas there have always been disputes (*iyongo*), today there are *jir*.

One of the distinctions which the European folk system has effected in Grade-D Native Authority courts is that between civil and criminal cases. We have followed this distinction in presenting Tiv case material. The civil cases, we found, dealt mainly with marriage matters and with matters of debt; the criminal cases dealt mainly with stealing.

In our investigation of marriage *jir*, we set forth a series of 'legal norms' but admitted that this arrangement was only an analytical system and had no significance as a folk system. Tiv do not reorganize a portion of the norms of marriage (or any other institution) as subject matter of their jural institutions; rather, the folk system of the entire institution enters into consideration by the *jir*.

It does not occur to Tiv, who organize their jural notions round the idea of *jir* instead of round one resembling the English 'law', to list their rules (*tindi*). Some African peoples do, I believe, organize their conceptualizations of jural institutions around ideas resembling the notion of 'law': Professor Gluckman's analysis of the Lozi concept *mulao* is a case in point. Dr. Peristiany tells me that Kipsigis do indeed 'think like lawyers' and organize their whole system around the concept *pitet*, which closely resembles the English word 'law'. Tiv, however, do not organize their institutions and their 'rules' in this way.

In examining the ways in which the *jir* entered into the other institutions and hence into Tiv daily life, we found that the *jir* was a counteraction on the part of society following upon the occurrence of social acts which could be called 'breaches of norms'. The *jir* is followed by still other social acts which bring about a correction: either re-establishment of the norm or retribution for its breach.

We arrived at the series of social acts:

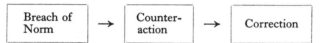

And we found that there were several variations of institutionalization of this series of acts within Tiv culture:

Courts:

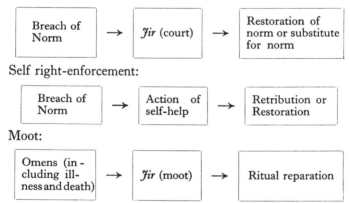

Self right-enforcement:

Moot:

There is one other variety, which we mentioned only briefly in connection with incest, and which is not really a jural institution:

We can see that Tiv organize their jural institutions around a notion which falls squarely into the column of 'counteraction'. If our own method were similar we should not speak of law, but of 'the court'. 'Law', if it be reducible to so simple an analytical scheme, would certainly demand a different one: law is primarily the rules and the body of rules which are broken; it falls in the first column, not the middle one. However, it overlaps into both other columns because it includes notions of procedure and, since the notion of 'sanction' is involved, it is concerned with a penal system and other systems of 'enforcement' of 'decisions'.

Again, when we turned to that other category of civil cases, debt, we found it would be possible to say that Tiv 'have' actions which resemble tort, contract, or the like. However, were we to do merely that, we should miss the organizing concept which contains several English categories. This categorizing concept is 'debt' (*injô*). Many torts have debt aspects; most contracts have debt aspects. Tiv 'classify' on the notion of debt, as it were, not on the notion of 'tort' and 'contract'. It is not for us to say that Tiv do not understand tort or contract; neither is it for Tiv to say that the English do not understand debt. We must realize that the same general type of material can be classified in several ways. It is, in the long run, the folk classifications that are important to social anthropology, not the 'presence' of torts or contracts which are both folk and analytical concepts in another society.

In investigating criminal cases, we changed our frame of reference. We found that *jir* was only one counteraction of several which could be brought into action following upon the commission of *ifer* or wrong. Such a wrong might also be followed by ritual or by self-help. We differentiated two sorts of self-help. The first is self right-enforcement, either within or without jural institutions. It is counteraction leading to correction. The other we found to be of a different nature: the nature of revenge, and ultimately of the feud. In this the counteraction does not lead to correction, but rather to repeated counteraction. Within this system, correction is never reached. Tiv have not institutionalized the feud; their system led to wars and to eventual correction in an idiom of witchcraft and magic.

Thus, it seems to me, the European folk system sees the Native Authority tribunal basically as a court which, within established limits, applies 'native law and custom'. Tiv, in their folk system,

see the same organization as a *jir* which arbitrates disputes brought
before it. 'Native law and custom' as a 'corpus' of 'law' which can
be 'sure', is simply not a Tiv idea. Neither is it a Tiv idea that a
'court' may have 'authority' to carry out its 'decisions'. Rather,
Tiv believe that a right answer exists to all disputes; they take
disputes before the *jir* in order to discover that answer, and the
principals to the dispute must concur in it when it is discovered.

Tiv see their tribunals, both courts and 'moots', with a single
set of concepts. The two have different internal structuring, but
in the long run both are *jir* and the purpose of both is to 'repair the
tar', to make the community run smoothly and peacefully. The
elders of the moot also repair the *tar* ceremonially. Tiv see the
ceremony and the *jir* as two aspects of the single task of repairing
the *tar*: what we might call the government aspect and the religious
aspect of social welfare.

Because of its tremendous field of assumption and undefined
premiss, 'law' probably has one of the most extensive foundations
of ethnocentric metaphysic of any discipline. The anthropologist
cannot let this field of assumption stand without recognition; he
must assume that it may not be valid for the material he has
gathered from exotic societies. 'Law' is not a science; to make it
such would be to destroy it as a basis for social action. The comparison of legal systems—comparative jurisprudence—may be a
science, for it and sociology, to which it is related, are devices for
understanding social action. Law itself is a basis for social action.

Law, no matter how complex its procedure becomes, over-
simplifies human relations. In settling disputes, we over-simplify
the actualities by fitting them into the procrustean beds of law and
precedent. Tiv *jir* and its attendant concepts do not over-simplify
to the same extent: they have no need to do so. When Tiv over-
simplify human relationships, they do it in terms of *tsav*, curses,
and fetishes, not in terms of law. Both sets of over-simplifications
bring the correction of the social order within bounds believed to
be accessible to human action. It is the idiom of the conceptualization which is different, and it is this idiom which gives us the key
to understanding the differences.

Seagle has said, 'Developed systems of law at least deal with
nothing less than the whole of life, and the law is the one art
which, unfortunately, has no subject matter of its own.'[1] To this

[1] William Seagle, *History of Law.*

Q

we must add that no two systems of social control envisage this 'whole of life' in the same way and in the same categories. It is the cultural picture—the folk system for seeing this 'whole of life'— in which we are interested.

Europeans and Americans use the concept of 'law' as one of the major organizing and regularizing precepts for social action; they see the whole of life by its means. Tiv use a different set of notions best covered by the English word 'counteraction' as we have defined it here; as their key concept they have their *jir*.

I have not, in this book, merely used the technique of showing 'differences' whereas another anthropologist, of a different cast of mind, might have shown 'similarities'. To think that there are similarities and differences between English and Tiv law, and that all one has to do is to compare them, is sociological over-simplification of the most blatant sort. Rather, there are two idioms and two sets of images in which peoples see their jural institutions and their institutions of social control. Two things can be done: both can be expressed in non-technical language, 'the technical side of law moved out of the central position', as Llewellyn and Hoebel have put it,[1] or else both sets of 'technical' concepts can be compared, each elucidating the other. I prefer the second alternative. Only so have I been able to explain Tiv ideas, retaining their fundamental sense and dignity. Only so have I been able to see 'law' not as something universal but as the tremendous cultural achievement that it is.

[1] *The Cheyenne Way*, pp. 41-2.

GLOSSARY OF TIV TERMS

THE following Tiv terms have all been translated except those marked
*. I have retained them in Tiv because translation is not the purpose of
this study, or else because they have never been translated in the literature on the Tiv, and are untranslatable.

Tiv vowels are pronounced as Italian vowels; *ó* is the open *o*, as in
English 'hot' or American 'ought'. Tiv consonants approximate to
English ones; *gh* is a velar fricative; *gb*, *kp* are pronounced by releasing
velar and labial stops simultaneously.

Tiv words are indexed by the first consonant; this method was introduced in Abraham's *Dictionary of the Tiv Language*, and is the only
satisfactory solution.

bende, to touch; to fall foul of a fetish (*akombo*) without actively trans-
    gressing it
ibo, fault
bum, to swear
bume, to play the fool, act unreasonably
ibumegh, a foolish or unreasonable act
bumenor, a fool, an 'unreasonable man'

ifan, curse
ifer, crime

igba, a reciprocal term between a man and his mother's agnates
gber ifan, to break a curse (a ritual)
igya, an act of jealousy

hamber ifan, to blow out the curse (the same ritual as *gber ifan*)
hule, to fold under; to outshout

i a ii, to steal

**jir*, court, moot, case

kem, to make bridewealth payments
akombo, fetish (an inadequate translation, to be used in this book only)
ikul, a type of treaty between lineages

kwaghbo, a dangerous, anti-social act

kwaghdang, an act which is morally wrong

kwase bunde, breakdown in a marriage when the difficulty is in any relationship save that between husband and wife

laha, to behave presumptuously, beyond one's age and influence

lôhô, to convene or invite

lumun, to concur, agree, reply

mbatarev, plural of *ortaregh*

mbatsav, an organization of those elders of the community who have *tsav*

imborivungu, 'owl pipe'; a magical instrument made from a human tibia

mimi, 'truth', right

mpav, 'splitting'; divorce; breakdown in marriage due to difficulty between husband and wife

mtene, a reciprocal term used between a man and his age-mate's wife

mtôv, 'investigation'; the task of the *mbatarev* in a *jir*

mtsaha,   penalty, punishment

ingôl, an agnatic kinswoman who has been given to one to exchange for a wife; a ward

inja, character, habit, custom, meaning

injô, debt

nôngo, line, lineage

ipaven, segment

pev, to pierce; to transgress a fetish (*akombo*)

pine, to ask

ôr, to talk, discuss

or-jir (*mbajiriv*), judge

*ortaregh (*mbatarev*), 'man of the *tar*'. Now a title given to the chief of a 'clan' and those of his assistants who act as judges

or u fan kwagh, 'a man who knows things'; a reasonable man

sa apela [this is a simple term to understand, but a difficult one to translate. I find I have used all the following in this book:] by force, wilfully contrary to custom, arbitrarily, with malice, on purpose, without due process of law, by despotic action, a decision in which litigants do not concur

shagba, prestige

shieda, witness

sughul, to 'lodge' a woman with a man who acts as pro-guardian

shima, heart

shima i môm, with one heart, wholeheartedly

asema a har, with two hearts, ambiguous

isho, right action

*swem, the name of the religious and political fetish which contains the idea of justice

ta acia, chant a spell

**tar (utar)*, the territory occupied by a lineage

tia, an animal killed by the person who calls the *jir*

tien, marriage guardian. Reciprocal of *ingôl*

tindi, a rule or law

tôv, to investigate

*tsav, a substance which grows on the hearts of some persons, indicating special talent

tyo-or, chief

ityô, an agnatic lineage from the point of view of one of its members

ityough ki ter, 'father's head', a magical instrument made from a skull

aveghem, 'odds and ends', miscellaneous marriage payments

vough, correct, straight, precise

wam, to make a compensatory gift

iwuhe, an act of jealousy

iyev, revenge

yie, lie, broken promise, anti-social act

INDEX

[Tiv words are indexed by the first consonant]
[Case numbers are in parentheses following page numbers]